T0115165

THE SECOND COMING AND THE END

Vigyan Mitra

abbott press

Abbott Press books may be ordered through booksellers or by contacting:

Abbott Press
1663 Liberty Drive
Bloomington, IN 47403
www.abbottpress.com
Phone: 1 (866) 697-5310

Because of the dynamic nature of the Internet, any web addresses or links contained in this book may have changed since publication and may no longer be valid. The views expressed in this work are solely those of the author and do not necessarily reflect the views of the publisher, and the publisher hereby disclaims any responsibility for them.

"New Revised Standard Version Bible, copyright 1989, Division of Christian Education of the National Council of the Churches of Christ in the United States of America. Used by permission. All rights reserved."

This book is a work of non-fiction. Unless otherwise noted, the author and the publisher make no explicit guarantees as to the accuracy of the information contained in this book and in some cases, names of people and places have been altered to protect their privacy.

Any people depicted in stock imagery provided by Getty Images are models, and such images are being used for illustrative purposes only. Certain stock imagery © Getty Images.

ISBN: 978-1-4582-2315-9 (sc)
ISBN: 978-1-4582-2316-6 (e)

Library of Congress Control Number: 2022913709

Print information available on the last page.

Abbott Press rev. date: 08/10/2022

Contents

Foreword.. vii

Author's Note... xi

Introduction.. xiii

Chapter 1   Jesus, The Christ... 1

Chapter 2   The Aquarian Gospel of Jesus the Christ........................ 27

Chapter 3   The Second Coming 53

Chapter 4   Beginning of the End... 97

Chapter 5   A Message Across Two Millenniums............................. 117

Chapter 6   Prophet Daniel and His Visions.................................... 159

Appendix 1   The Collapse of Wave Unction..................................... 187

Appendix 2   The Aquarian Gospel 191

About the Author.. 197

FOREWORD

This world of ours has been created by a God which is 'Without a Beginning', 'Eternal' and Infinite. He has created it as a part of himself through his *sankalpa* (resolution) through the faculty of his *Yogamaya* and he can also likewise reabsorb the same in a reverse order. As a person in dream can effortlessly create a dream world comprising of things, persons and places out of its own 'self', manifesting as a 'self', the Universal Soul is also able to create the world with all its beings. The whole world, as it is known to us, remains manifest and illumined by the same principle of consciousness which is referred to by us—the humans, as 'God'.

This God is known by its three attributes, *Sat, Chit, and Ananda*, or existence, awareness and bliss, and it is supremely independent. It is capable of creating anything and everything out of its own 'self'. The saints and philosophers who were conferred with the status of a 'wisdom holder' by the ancient tradition were called the Rishis. These ancient Rishis of India have described this eternal truth in a variety of ways in the holy writings that have been left behind by them for the benefit of the posterity. Nevertheless, the proponents of the doctrine of a material world and the many self-proclaimed intellectuals among them have continued to insist on physically verifiable proofs and to raise doubts about existence of an intelligent cause.

Matter, Life, and Spirit Demystified is an intelligent work created by a very knowledgeable person, which should be able to remove many of the doubts and misconceptions currently harboured by most of the present-day intellectuals. However, they need to keep their minds open and make a genuine effort to understand the discoveries made by the Vedic seers in the past. Then they can fathom the realizations about the ultimate truth gained by the ancient wise and lend a sincere thought to re-evaluate that knowledge in today's context—in the light of modern scientific discovery and research. Further, they need to bear in mind that any set objectives and preconceived notions could be an obstacle in perceiving the fine truths—both about the reality of the world and of our human existence.

There is little doubt that while the ways to perceive the truth may vary, the truth remains what it is and it does not change. In fact, there is a famous Vedic aphorism too—*Ekam Sad Vipra Bahudha Vadanti*. This means that while the truth is 'one', often it is spoken about differently by various knowledgeable persons. And this is eternally true as well, as a part of our human nature.

There has been extensive research and investigation in the West about cases of rebirth, the strange yet similar narratives provided by persons undergoing near death like situations, distant seeing, distant hearing and the psycho-kinetic powers exhibited by a number of persons over the last several decades, among others. Renowned scientists, particularly in the field of medicine and human behaviour, have extensively investigated such phenomena. They have written books that are highly informative and have expressed wonder too, but there may be little by way of gaining of a real understanding. I am in full agreement with this book's author that keeping within the self-imposed limitations of the modern science, it is not possible to understand or explain these subtle and finer realms of existence. Knowledge of yoga and the consciousness has to be gained first, to know the fine and the subtle. In fact, there are separate disciplines and sciences with their own procedures to come to such understanding. It is just not possible to access these realms through the action of gross physical instruments, placed by the Nature at our disposal.

The author appears to have taken great pains to study and contemplate upon the principles of modern physics, chemistry and biology to be able to draw parallels between these and the truth discovered by the ancient seers. Surprisingly, he has also been able to point out that the sciences of the gross and the subtle complement each other—make each other complete as the means and the end. His insights are both highly logical as well as relevant. Besides, in line with the context, the author has also provided precise quotations from authoritative sources. I believe, a balance between the ancient and current knowledge is very much the need of the hour.

Those who are genuinely curious, and those who have an investigative bend of mind, may find that really important clues have been provided in this book which, I am of the firm opinion, should be able to guide them in the right direction in their investigation and understanding of the truth.

Between an atheist and a believer, between theism and atheism, between spiritual and the physical and between Vedic knowledge and the knowledge of science—this book can work like a bridge that should be able to address the notion of duality of the modern science and make a dialogue possible between them and the notion of one-ness and non-differentiation of the ancient wise. Meanwhile, the modern science has to go a long way. It can get very useful clues from ancient scriptures and also to put them to test to find their veracity. Thus, modern science and ancient knowledge can complement each other.

The Indian nation has been able to continue with its unbroken tradition over many thousands of years, and being the most ancient culture of the humanity—this land has also been hallowed by the presence of enlightened masters in all ages and at all times. By way of examples and as a proof, the author has also included in this book the narratives concerning several such masters from the more recent times. All these people were able to display many divine powers and to transgress the laws of physical nature with impunity as a divine play, as and when it pleased them. It is difficult for us, the ordinary folks—to fathom the play of the Supreme God and of the Masters who have been blessed by Him. The strange but true narratives of how *Mahavatar Babaji* has been guiding the mankind for hundreds of years towards the present, how the supra-normal *Gyanganj* Ashram in Tibet is being operated, how the enlightened Masters are able to appear in their subtle bodies to rid the problems and ailments of their disciples and devotees and to advance them on the path of spirituality, etc. etc.—are a true eye opener, both for the curious and an aspirant after the truth, alike.

Before I conclude, I would like to draw the attention of the readers of this work that deserves a really high rating, that not only the great Indian saints and foreseers like Vivekananda, Maharishi Arvind and Devaraha Baba, but also the renowned wise in the West like Bertrand Russel, Bernard Shaw and Tolstoy, have prophesied in their own times that in the coming age the world will begin to understand the importance of the great Indian thought. Because of its relevance and usefulness, this eternal truth will show the path to the different nations of the world. In other words, I can say, India will regain its status as the Vishwa Guru or the Teacher of the World. Conditions conducive to this development have now begun to appear and are clearly visible, and this book can be a really important step in that direction.

I laud the author for this age transforming and pathbreaking work created by him that can lead the mankind to its destined goal and hope that this book will be translated in other Indian and foreign languages as well, with the passage of time, so that the words and revelations of the Rishis can reach the world at large. For sure, this is a thought provoking and readable work which is worth possessing and preserving for every household.

December 16, 2021
Dr Satish Chandra Agarwal, (IRS)
Former Commissioner of Income Tax
Kumaun, Uttarakhand

AUTHOR'S NOTE

Our principal book, *Matter, Life and Spirit Demystified*, had been written many months ago. However, it had to remain in a semi-finished state until recently on account of some exigencies that kept arising. The present book is only a postlude or an extension for the above book, and would be incomplete on its own. Therefore, we have maintained the same 'Foreword'. Besides, it was really difficult to find a judicious person well familiar with Old and New, both Testaments of the Holy Bible, on one hand, and who could also understand the deep philosophy of fine structures of the wisemen of ancient India, on the other. We have, as such, decided against adding a new Foreword.

It should also be pertinent to state, that while contributing a 'Foreword' to our book 'Jesus Christ and the Spirit of Truth', an additional paragraph was added by Dr Satish Chandra Agarwal, stating: "In the concluding chapter of the book, the author has quoted extensively from the Holy Bible and the New Testament. I must admit that I never had an occasion to study the Old and the New Testaments. Accordingly, my comment and remarks are restricted to that extent, though I have full confidence on the integrity of the author in citing these holy books as well."

INTRODUCTION

We welcome our readers to the concepts of Vigyan Aagaar. We wish to place before the world, that invaluable knowledge which was once brought to light by the ancient rishis of India, and which is of a universal nature. Our aim is to present this invaluable knowledge, that holds good universally, after rearranging the same into a composite package, to suit the current level of awareness, when scientific knowledge and reasoning are widely in vogue and are commonplace.

We live in a beautiful world which can be known and experienced by different entities in relative terms. The basic substance that converts into everything of this world remains the same, yet it is known differently by a grasshopper, a bull, and a slab of granite. This difference in perception, according to the rishis, arises because of Maya. And it would be same thing if we called it a 'Relative' observation, instead. Such differences in perception may arise on account of sizes, motion, masses and the extent and efficacy of the means of observation at the disposal of a 'being' or the 'thing'.

We enjoy a major advantage in comparison to any other living entity, as we can see and interact with this world through the means available to us as a human being. Being intelligent—besides enjoying this wonderful world—we also wish to understand how it works, how it is being regulated, and by what or whom? The primary objective of 'Vigyan Aagaar' (the Bank of Knowledge) is to bring together all the relevant knowledge, from all the disciplines first, and then to try to seek some really comprehensive answers to all those ultimate questions that still confound our human thought.

Our principal work *'Matter, Life and Spirit Demystified'*, to which this book in your hands has been added as a postlude, is a major step in this direction. Our books aim to once again bring to light the knowledge that, at one time, had earned the epithet 'the Wisdom of the East', and which had conferred on India the status of a World Teacher. Many seekers after the true knowledge in those days undertook long and assiduous journeys to visit these lands and all of them were able to go back home fully satisfied, carrying a rich haul of knowledge. Gold was aplenty on this land, even in those days, but what made these lands special was its knowledge about 'spirit', the real substance.

We may call the First Section of our principal book as the 'Science' Section. Albert Einstein, the most talked about scientist of the 20th century, who discovered Relativity—both General and Special—and his famous formulae for mass energy equivalence, held the view that in the absence of the knowledge of the spirit, 'science' would be like a lame person striving to do things while standing on a single leg. This, however, constituted only half of what he had said, since in the same breath, he was quick to point out that religion too may soon begin to act as a blind person, should it try to explain the world ignoring the knowledge about 'matter' that had been gathered by mankind over the generations, and that went under the name of 'science'. In the five chapters of the First Section of our main book, accordingly, we have tried to cover more or less entire knowledge related with the modern science as may concern and interest an ordinary intelligent person.

Likewise, in the Second Section of our main book we have tried to include all the investigations carried out by the adherents of the modern science in the realms of what the famed biologist Lyall Watson likes to call 'supernature', since it covers such common happenings concerning which the science fraternity itself does not have answers that can be considered as satisfactory enough, or adequate. We have selected for inclusion in this section, several out of the thousands of cases of rebirths, and several out of an even larger number of narratives of the wonderous yet similar looking experiences undergone by the people who returned to live after a near death situation. Besides, we have also included cases of distant hearing, distant sighting, movement of articles from a distance by use of psycho-kinesis and several other phenomena of a similar nature, like dowsing and the poltergeist activity. All that we cite in this section has been thoroughly investigated by the science fraternity itself. However, nothing out of this own investigation of the science fraternity can be explained by it, since it tries to do so keeping within the precincts of its own definition of the reality.

It was natural that most of such investigations concerned with 'supernature' would be carried out by the persons associated with medical profession, who regularly come in contact with the events involving life and death. However, science too, in a way, at present, is conducted like a religion and the people at the apex in the hierarchy do not attach much significance to such trans-scientific research by its own people and their findings. As such, whenever any such investigation or finding is brought to their notice, they have a stock answer, "It is not possible for such things to happen or such events to take place according to the known principles of science (and this can be an illusion, if not a fraud; and in any case, it does not fit with our definition of reality)". They place a big full stop after this outright unscientific and provocatively arrogant statement usually given by them, and do not want to take the discussion ahead or forward at all; they neither have any understanding of such subjects associated with human lives, nor any interest.

Lyall Watson, author of 'Supernature'—a famed biologist and a category in himself, had summed the situation up in a humble but tacit manner a couple of decades ago. "The fact is that unusual things do sometimes happen", writes Lyall Watson. "I have seen them happening often enough now to be certain of that. And, as a scientist myself, I admit that they present us with a problem. But it is not insoluble and it does not require any desperate mental gymnastics. I see it, in truth, as more of a paradox than a problem. An apparent contradiction is produced by poor definition rather than a faulty procedure.

"Science decides what is possible by reference to its definition of reality. Anything which fits the definition is acceptable. Anything that doesn't fit is impossible and must be rejected. And the fact is that the acts of dowsing or poltergeist phenomena stand in direct contradiction to the current definition. So, the issue is reduced to a choice between rival facts; the normal versus the paranormal. And, of course, the normal wins—even if it does have to stand on its head to do so. …What is being ignored is the point that our definition of reality is a theory, not a fact."

The Third Part of our above book can be called 'the Primary

Sciences' or 'the Great Sciences' section, when compared to its first and second sections, viz., the 'Science' and the 'Super-nature' sections. The book in the hands of our readers is actually a postlude to this third section, the 'great sciences' section only. This section of the book, which has also been published separately as *Jesus Christ and the Spirit of Truth*, narrates and explains the three great sciences discovered by the ancient rishis. These sciences are called 'Samvit Vigyan' (the science of consciousness), the 'Tantra Vigyan' (the science of the fine structures) and 'Yoga Vigyan' (the science of 'recombination' or 'reunification') respectively, and between them these constitute the essence of all fundamental knowledge about being and becoming of our Father, God. It is Him that has become the world, according to the rishis—besides everything into it, including ourselves. Our human journey too, in fact, may have begun some billions of years ago as a particle, and may have progressed as a prokaryote, a single-celled amoeba, a plant, an insect, a fish, and so on; And then, progressing as a mammal, a primate, an ape and a Homo-sapiens, it would find its full fructification only when we are able to realize our one-ness with the 'Father' principle (in a kind of ultimate reunification).

The books describe the manifestation of the universe after the Trika philosophy, which had come to originate in Kashmir before it was first invaded and then overwhelmed. Trika means three, and this philosophy relies on a trilogy similar to the Holy Trinity of the Christian belief. It proceeds to explain the world not as a creation by God, but as God itself manifesting into all the things that we see, including ourselves. It does so by dividing itself in a cyclic order into three eternal principles, representing three different attributes of God that can manifest, and each with a distinct nature of its own.

What we bring to you through the pages of our aforesaid book(s) is the ancient knowledge gained by the rishis of India, that has been lifted by us from authentic texts and has been rewritten to suit the comparatively more evolved understanding of the present times. No changes in the ancient knowledge have been made by the author, and all he has done is to make an effort to take on board the modern science as well.

For the first time, an Indian author has tried to serve science, yoga, and philosophy, on the same plate. And this can only be attributed to the grace of God that we should have managed to do so in a way, that physics, chemistry, and the biology, actually appear as mere predictions emerging on their own from this very ancient knowledge—gathered by the holy and wise people of this ancient civilization.

Likewise, through our above books, we have also tried to show that Krishna in the East, and Jesus in the West, actually seem to vouchsafe the truth of each other, as two witnesses separated in space and time. They were both able to transgress the same laws of the physical nature, and they both have tried to teach and to explain the same truths as well. A hint to this effect had, in fact, been provided by Jesus himself, and has been mentioned by his disciple John in his gospel.

Jesus had told his disciples (John 15:26-27), "When the advocate comes, whom I will send to you from the Father, (to reveal) the spirit of Truth who comes from the Father, he will testify on my behalf. You also are to testify, because you too have been with me from the beginning (seeing and hearing what I do and what I tell, and by preserving them into the Gospels)."

"I still have many things to say to you", he had also said (John 16:12-13), "but you cannot bear them now. When the spirit of the truth comes (however), he (the advocate) will guide you into all the truth, for he will not speak on his own but will speak whatever he hears (from Krishna and the other masters of the Orient), and he will declare to you the things that are to come."

ESSENCE OF FINDINGS OF THE RISHIS

The search initiated by the *rishis* of ancient India led them to understand that in the beginning there is just one eternal substance, unbounded by space or time, which is self-effulgent and conscious, and which stands on its own without the need of an address or any other means of support. They called it 'Sat (the Truth)', which was 'the essence'—the real substance, or 'the final and unlimited potency to be'. It is the property of just 'Being'. When nothing else exists, eternal awareness still exists in a state of total self-contentment, and is called Nishkal Brahma, since it has no other parts or attributes in this state.

When it is awake or manifest, the attributes of awareness (*Chit*) and contentment (*Ananda*) of the 'supreme consciousness' come into prominence as well. The rishis then call it *Sat-Chit-Ananda* Brahma. This *Brahma* of the Vedic people is an abstract entity and a non-substance in material terms. It has no other form or body except consciousness with awareness as its expression and a blissful feeling of contentment or joy as its experience; and it always exists.

What is called *Brahma* by the Vedanta is referred to as *Param Shiva* by the Agama scriptures of the ancient Indian people. The Agamas, inter-alia, are the source for all Tantra disciplines, including the Tantra branch of Buddhism as well. The world, according to the *Trika* philosophical system of the Agama, also known as Kashmir Shaivism, comes to manifest in cycles. When nothing else exists, this principle of existence is said to be in sleep mode, like a tortoise that has withdrawn its head and limbs into itself. During its sleep, the world with all its constituents including space and the time remains withdrawn—held and hidden by this principle, in a merged state—like the hidden potential of its hidden and unseen qualities.

Since ancient times, and until a few decades ago, Kashmir in North India was considered to be a very important learning centre and a seat of scholastic spiritualism based on Shaiva doctrine of the Agama. Although usually the Agama is considered to be a branch of the Vedic scriptures, it belongs to the Atharva section, the 4th Veda. While the other Vedas are generally ascribed to the priests of the ruling clans and dynasties, Atharva Veda belongs to rishis who stayed among the common people, guiding them Godward—towards '*Sat*' (the Ultimate '*Truth*'). Accordingly, these are much broader in scope, and their origin goes much deeper in time. That, perhaps, may be one reason why the *Trika* dispensation of Kashmir Shaivism should be held in such high esteem, in the higher echelons of the scholastic circles associated with the Yoga and Siddha traditions in India.

The period of 300 years from the 9th to the 11th centuries is, in particular, marked with an upheaval of activity in the scholastic circles in the Kashmir Valley. The concepts of the Agama were reinvented during this period in the form of a sub-branch known as Trika philosophy under the Shaivite School.

A New Cycle, a New World

After a long and refreshing sleep-like state, which may have lasted trillions of years of our human time, a little 'stir' or *spanda* into the being of *Param Shiva* wakes it up. Slowly and gradually, a potential was probably building up all this while. The *samskaras* (proclivities) of the last cycle, which had gone into seed state, were probably trying to come to the fore and to sprout once again. The rishis call this condition '*unmesh*', which means the beginning of 'expansion'. It is like the opening of the eyes for the principle of consciousness and it heralds the commencement of a new cycle of manifestation.

'*Unmesh*' and '*nimesh*', expansion and contraction, are a part of the nature of *Param Shiva* and are two fundamental properties at the back of the manifestation of the cosmos which is vibratory by its very nature. The vibrations can exist at three distinctly different levels, and the stuff of the cosmos keeps vibrating at each of its three levels of existence, all the time, according to the rishis.

The little shiver, like the soft touch of a silken feather—tickling, pulsating, raising the expectation of something nice and adorable about to happen—felt by *Param Shiva*, which is Love or God itself, into the tranquil depths of its being, even if it should be point-like in itself, is stirring of its nature, *Para* Shakti. Apart from waking *Param* Shiva up, the stirring of *Para Shakti* also alters its experience: It is no longer asleep—it is awake, and now it has a nature too to go by, or to be known by, as well.

Under conditions of *nimesh*, *Param* Shiva had a unitary experience, that was comprised of a timeless awareness and absolute contentment—inseparable from each other. The contraction (*nimesh*) was absolute: There was no difference between its head and heart, or between its awareness and experience at this stage, one could say. *Para Shakti*, as it sets in as a vibe or a wave, however, draws a thin wedge, or the notion of a gap between the knowing and experiencing aspects of *Param* Shiva—between its head and heart. It forms a core or an interior into the dimensionless sphere of existence of the eternal awareness. This core arises as a feeling, or as the heart of *Param* Shiva.

This inner activity, the *spanda* or the vibration, makes *Param* Shiva gain the awareness of a within. There is something into its interior now that can know, and there is one other thing as well into the interior that can be known or experienced by it. With its acquisition of the attributes of awareness and experience, it has now turned into *Sat-Chit-Ananda Brahma* or *'Sakal' Param Shiva*, according to the rishis. There is one difference, however, between *Sakal Param Shiva* of the *Shaiv* Agama and *Param Brahma* of Vedanta; in contrast with Vedanta—the principal Hindu philosophy, the nature of the Principal of the Agama is of a dynamic kind. It is also 'energy', that appears as a vibration to register itself into the awareness of *Param Shiva*, as an experience.

All experiences right from the *Para* or the 'beyond' perception level involve use of energy of one kind or the other. However, the density of energy at this level is so low that it cannot even be perceived as a manifestation, with absolutely no possibility of its being measured or quantified.

With 'experience' being added to awareness, what was just 'pure spirit' thus far, now turns into *'samvit'*, which is the Sanskrit word for consciousness, and it comes to be called *'Para Samvit'*, or the supreme consciousness. All the knowledge concerned with it, accordingly, is known as *'Samvit Vijnan'*, or the science of consciousness, in the philosophical system of the Indians.

It is *Para Shakti*, the nature of the Supreme Being, and the united supreme force at the apex, according to this science, which issues forth as a vibration—to become the world in a cyclic order. It turns the experience of *Param Shiva*, which was mere contentment until now, first into 'joy' and then into the irrepressible energy of 'hilarity', full of zeal, to find an expression for itself. A one-to-one polarization, thus, sets into the internal space of awareness, which is called *'chidakash'*; And an instinctive impulse now arises into *Param Shiva* to express itself—to multiply, and to commence a play. And this play, needless to say, must be befitting its status and means as the Supreme Sovereign. It must be a grand show: On the grandest of scales, in what we mortals call as space-time.

The Most Primary Among All the Force Fields

The polarization of the cosmic consciousness sets up a force-field and brings two mutually complementary and yet opposite and counterbalancing powers of God into play, together with the infinities of two kinds associated with both of them. Of these, Shiva, the Male principle, stands for love, attraction, contraction, and the positive aspect into everything; while

Shakti, the Female principle, stands for force, repulsion, expansion, and the other negative attributes. Shakti is also energy at the same time though, which constitutes the stuff or the body part into 'any' and every 'thing' that comes to manifest.

Positive is love, attraction, bonding, and contraction besides thousands of other such businesses. Negative is force, repulsion, separation, expansion, and thousands of other powers; but it is never zero, and it makes itself count as the other extremity in every manifestation.

As a new cycle is about to begin, suggest the Agamas, there is *aunmukhya*, or the Male principle turning its gaze inwards, towards the Female principle (the 'Mind' part in the Param Shiva, the God, focussing its attention on its *now separate* 'Heart' part). The word '*yaamal*', used in the texts for the step that follows indicates a state of contact in which both principles are present in equal strength, and from which they can diverge in their respective directions without affecting their mutual dependence. The word used by the rishis to define this inviolable relationship of interdependence is, '*yugpat*' relation. The state of equal strength represents the point where the two opposing powers join. It is from this point that either of the two allows the other one to evolve to any extent into its chosen direction of manifestation—the former acting as its holder or 'the support' for it.

In language of the rishis, the two have a reciprocal relationship of *dharma-dharmi*, where dharma is a property, power, or the nature of a thing, while the thing is *dharmi,* which is the holder in possession of such property, and which can display the same. The relationship between the two is such, that they are equal in strength and also in mutual inter-dependence, so that one can manifest only when the other, as its holder (or support), is also around. For example, 'red' is a property that needs a kite, a balloon, or some other base or a '*dharmi*' to express itself. Likewise, a balloon or a kite too needs a set of '*dharmas*' or properties, to be able to register its existence. This relationship between the two, as stated before, is called a '*yugpat*' relation. It allows the two to make a large number of inroads into each other's territory, and to be able to give rise to a very large kind of the 'thirds'.

While maintaining a balance through attraction and repulsion in every entity or phenomena of the world, both of these elements remain present in a way that the two are linked and yet distinctly separate so that each can also enjoy the freedom to evolve according to its scopes and functions.

They manifest in two different dimensions of a common reality so that a non-zero manifestation is possible, so that a thing with certain properties can come into existence. In modern physics, Werner Heisenberg was the first to discover this relation of mutual interdependence, and in time it has come to be known as the Uncertainty Principle. The author must apologise to its readers with little or no knowledge about physics; While we do need to discuss some of its findings to show how they derive themselves from the manifesting intelligence, the readers after the '*Truth*' do not really lose anything, if they skip such parts of the discussion in either of our books.

The rishis call the state of equivalence of the two principles as their *yaamal* state, where the two infinite powers are exactly equal, ready to lock horns with each other. It may seem to be the zero state from which properties of either of the two principles come to manifest, this state of equilibrium the two of them must, nevertheless, remain present as the root for either of the two principles in all its manifestations. It is from this common root into the manifestation of either principle, whether positive or negative, that the other principle also keeps rising to balance the expansion of the former to any extent, while keeping to its 'own' territory, its own side. And to be able to do so, both of the two infinite potentialities must rise in perpendicular to each other at every point, whatever the degree or dimension of either of the two faces of the manifesting reality—in each particular manifestation, and at every point of time.

What follows the *yaamal* or the equilibrium state of the two mutually interdependent principles, according to the Agama, is a '*sanghatt*' between the two, or a 'structure'. It stands for joining together of thousands of expressions and businesses on one hand and a similar number of powers and potencies on the other. We can also call it a very large portfolio of the '*yugpat*' relationships of inviolable interdependence of the two principles, both—by their very definition itself—credited with infinite potential to extend in their respective, yet numerous, directions. For example, if one of the principles represented the colour, it can manifest millions of varying shades of red, blue, green, violet, etc., while the other principle can hold any and all the assortments of these shades as a kite, a balloon, a butterfly, or even a whole galaxy.

Tied into a '*yugpat*' relationship of reciprocal interdependence, the two principles walk together upward along the axis of eternity to script a new episode—a new universe. One brings into it thousands of its expressions and businesses, while the other brings in thousands of powers and potencies to match (to be able to provide a body to all such expressions).

The polarization in the cosmic consciousness gives rise to a Universal Force-field. The cosmos arises within this force-field, which is the play-arena of two diverse aspects of a common reality, tied into a *yugpat* relation of mutual inter-dependence; and with thousands of powers, expressions and businesses arising and being handled between the two. Expression of 'Chit' the experiencing aspect which is the positive half that can 'know', are like thought proposals, while 'Ananda' or the bliss of the 'experienced' side, which constitutes the negative half, converts these proposals into 'bodies' of vibrating energy that can be 'known' by the former.

This force-field can keep on giving rise to *yaamal* or equilibrium points like a 'coin' that may come into circulation—as this manifestation or that—as this particular unit of manifestation here or that particular aggregate there. One side of this new 'coin' readying to roll out of the 'unmanifest', to emerge on the path of manifestation, represents Shiva, the positive side; the other represents Shakti, the 'negative'. As stated, this polar difference comes into existence in the pre-manifestation realm of the existence. For the physics fraternity, accordingly, it is a given thing that originates with physical observable 'energy' or the 'matter' itself.

Of the two, Shakti is the dynamic aspect into this most primary 'field' coming into existence for the manifestation of a universe. It is a vibration and it behaves like a wave. Shiva is the static aspect on the other hand, which contains and balances this wave.

As a wave, Shakti is a disturbance in the field and the field values need to oscillate about a stable equilibrium. Accordingly, for Shakti or the energy to exist as such, as 'waves of activity' in this force field, there should be a force that tends to restore the field to equilibrium. And this part is played by Shiva, tied to Shakti in a relation that is forever, as the static aspect. The two principles, according to the rishis, collaborate and also balance each other, and together the two become manifest as the world with relativity and its endless dualities. Each manifesting duality, accordingly, should be comparable to a coin, and each of the two sides of this coin will represent a pole—positive or negative, *Shiva or Shakti* (Father or the Spirit for the Christine).

THE WAVE-PARTICLE DUALITY

What comes to manifest, as explained before, is neither Shiva nor Shakti but the union of the two. It is the seed, or the outcome of this union, we can say, which is manifesting; and this manifestation takes place in the gross realm of physical energy as well. The Shiva part in a particle of matter lends it with a static element and expresses itself as its form. The Shakti part into it expresses itself as its body which is made of vibration; so, the particle can also behave as a wave. Depending on which of its two faces is visible, this novel product of the Nature acts as a particle or a wave. Like the Uncertainty Relation, the wave-particle duality is also, in a way, predicted by an even more primary science, *Samvit Vigyan*, the Science of Consciousness.

The Physics people were greatly surprised when they came to discover this for the first time. They were able to observe for the first time the two different aspects of a reality manifesting with its two faces. Werner Heisenberg introduced his famous propositions in an article of 1927, entitled *"On the perceptible content* of quantum theoretical kinematics and mechanics". He was looking at the static aspect, the *perceptible* aspect; the Shiva (Father), or the observer aspect into a particle.

Erwin Schrödinger, on the other hand, assumed that an electron in an atom could be represented as an oscillating charged cloud, evolving continuously in space and time according to a wave equation. He was looking at the energy aspect in the electron, the mother aspect. And both were right. As a particle, an electron radiates the hallmarks of both its progenitors. It is both a particle and a wave at the same time. *It is both matter and mind as a particle*, the rishis in their humble way, seem to suggest.

The Currency in Use for a Manifest World

What comes to manifest, according to the ancient rishis of India, is the existence aspect (*Sat*, or the Truth), and it is called *Swayam-Bhuva*—one that comes to be born of itself. It comes to be born of its own, and it takes birth with the notion of a 'self', or I-ness. Accordingly, it strives to survive and to protect itself under all conditions: and depending on the freedom allowed to it by Nature, in space and the time, it may also strive to improve its comparative level of fitness. This *Swayam-Bhuva* of the ancient Indians is same as the 'Son' component in the Trinity of the Christian belief. It is this 'Son' only which can take birth—and it comes to be born like a coin with two faces. Its head side is its awareness (*Chit*), which is called Shiva or the Father, while its tails side is its experience (of bliss, or *Ananda*), which is called Shakti or the Holy Spirit. If the Father side, which displays positive attributes, was to be credited with a +1 sign, and its counterpart, 'Mother' or the Holy Spirit side with -1, then Son, the common seed or the coin, must carry both in equal measure, as +1 and -1, even if the net should be a perfect balance of the two and not directly visible. It would seem that negative and positive aspects in the manifest world of matter, are also mere predictions of a more primary Theory of Manifestation, and likewise, the properties displayed on the outside by the three constituent particles of 'matter' too appear to arise normally, and of their own, from the same theory—the Theory of Manifestation, which is more primary.

The Head Side in the Coin: The Father aspect into this manifestation, with two aspects or two faces, is of a static or unmoving nature, and is equipped with the faculty of 'knowing'. It is that aspect into the awareness that can know 'bliss' (or '*ananda*') (and even the absence of it), or that can have an experience. We may call it the mind side into whatever begins to roll out—to become manifest, a particle, an aggregate, or a living thing.

The Tail That Can Wag: It is the Spirit element, that constitutes the 'Mother' aspect in the awareness, which originally becomes separated 'from the awareness that knows', as an experience for itself. Whereas Father awareness remains aloof as a seer or knower, Mother awareness remains immanent into all things and can be known and experienced. Unlike the former, which is static, this division into the awareness is dynamic, and is of a vibratory nature. It constitutes the Body part into the composite awareness which can be known by its Mind part, since it always vibrates, and it can wag as a tail. To that extent, beyond a person's own body, the physical world in which he/she lives is also made up by vibrations, and in a broader sense this physical world can act as his or her extended body as well, and this too can be known by the Mind part into him/her.

The Home Maker and Keeper of the House: It is this immanent part of awareness in Nature that turns itself into bodies for each and every manifest thing, and also as the world that can be known by it, vibrating and conveying experience. Further, it is this immanent part of awareness into all the bodies which also enables the Mind-side on the scale of the universe to receive feedbacks from every single spec into the body of this universe. This becomes possible since every particle in the universe vibrates in a way exclusive for itself, and its vibration is different from any other vibration in the ultimate sense. In consequence, the immanent aspect of awareness is also able to give rise of instincts into all things as well, so that it may be able to run and control the world as a whole—each of its units, each of its aggregates, and also the whole. We see no reason to disagree with the rishis that it is Mother or the Spirit aspect turning itself into all the bodies or housings, which itself comes to assume all the house-keeping responsibilities in the world as well.

The Common or External Nature: This trinity of Shiva, Shakti and Swayam-bhuva of the Shaivites, is similar to Vishnu, Brahma and Mahesha of the more traditional schools in the Hindu philosophical refrain. Apart from the other information they may have possessed, these more traditional schools may have followed the process of building a layer of mythology around the dry knowledge of Vedanta and the Shaivite School. However, the troika of the Shaivites also embraces the trinity of 'Father', Holy Spirit and the Son of the Christine doctrine, with equal ease.

As stated, this trinity can only manifest together, as a coin on one hand, and as its two faces on the other. Further, each member of this troika also has an external nature, typical of itself. It may be useful for our readers to bear in mind that what we are discussing here is the very nature of the Reality which is eternal and self-aware. Our own awareness, and a part of our nature are also derived from this basic reality itself. Thus far, however, we have tried to explain the internal nature that abides into this eternal awareness only. That apart, this eternal awareness also has an external nature which it can manifest on the outside. Following a procedure, and assisted by its internal and external natures, this eternal awareness is able to descend to the denser levels of 'matter' or the physical bodies, to take the form of a gross manifestation.

It is suggested that it is this Sovereign that undertakes to manifest itself as the world, and then it reabsorbs the same again and again in a cyclic order. And it does so with the help its Internal and External natures.

External Nature and the Three Forces

Having evolved its 'internal nature', or having spread its wings: In the language of ancient masters, the unmanifest God now turns into Sat-Chid-Ananda Brahma, with its three attributes of 'existence', 'awareness' and 'bliss'. At our option, we can call this Brahma as the 'super-self', but if we want to keep things simple, we may continue to call it just 'God', the same God to whom we are accustomed to pray every other day, and from whom we also ask for some boon every now and then.

Assisted by its external nature, according to the ancient masters, God can also become manifest now. To suit to its pleasure and at its own time, this conscious entity that eternally exists, can manifest as a thought, a sound (or word), a thing, a person, or even a whole universe. The entity is now ready to take off with both its wings ready to fan out. The wings are now positioned to open—a little, some more, or to an extent that may bewilder one and all. Again, if we call this eternal entity as the 'super-self', then it is also able to convert itself into as many individual 'selves' as it may be pleased to do—and each as complete and potentially as capable as the mother-self itself.

Nature of the Son aspect, or the Coin with a 'self', is 'Will', which is vibratory by nature. It is the seed nature, in a way. Like its master, it carries both the 'Father' and the 'Mother' components in equal proportions. Accordingly, one side of this vibration is the power of 'Knowledge', which is a static nature typical of the Father principle. Likewise, the other side of this vibration is the faculty of 'Action', which is dynamic; it is the typical nature of energy, the dynamic Spirit, that can give rise to work and, hence, also the bodies. After the three principals, and like them, the external nature is also tripartite.

As a relative observer, to make use of the world and its many objects, in all areas and directions, the force that is most commonly used by us out of the three main forces of physics, is the force of electro-magnetism. It is this power that creates light which enables us to see the world, and it is this power which is responsible for making the matter to work as chemical elements. All matter is made of atoms, and the atoms themselves are made of subatomic particles of three kinds. Into these, the protons carry a unit positive charge, while the electron carries an equal but opposite charge which is called 'negative'—the two sides balancing each other. The properties and behaviour of the electron should readily remind one of the creative-nature of the Mother Principle, which is 'Action' (Likewise, the proton, we can see, would readily remind one of the Shiva or the Father Principle).

We see a similar balance in the properties of attraction and repulsion for the strong force which binds the nuclear stuff. The force between the nucleons is strongly attractive at distances of about 1.0×10^{-15} meters (or 1fm), so that it can overcome the electromagnetic repulsion between the protons and can bind them into a nucleus. At distances of less than 0.7fm, however, the same force becomes repulsive. This repulsive component in the force ensures the stability of the nuclei, since it can persuade the nucleons not to invade the private space of each other, and to maintain a healthy distance between themselves. The main task of this force is to cobble the things together at the most primary of the levels of vibrations, even by the standards of the gross physical realm— the most condensed realm, per se the Rishis. The nuclear force may be strong or week, but it is a force in either case. The 'force', according to rishis, is the domain of the Force of 'Will'—the nature of the Son or the Coin in the Holy Trinity. It is a composite principal, so its nature is also composite. The Shiva side lends the power of 'contraction' to the nuclear force, while the Shakti side, which is the force of repulsion and 'expansion', prevents the particles from coming too close to each other (Why there is a weak nuclear force, giving rise to an Electro-weak Theory or the Quantum Electrodynamics, has been explained as well by us in our books named before).

Coming to gravity, it is the force that keeps us bound to the Earth, and which keeps the Earth, the Sun, and the other astronomical bodies, spread over vast distances, at their respective places. This is akin to the nature associated with Father principle, which is 'Knowledge' and Love (attraction, contraction and re-absorption). We can try to visualize the 'relationships' between the three external natures like a shoe-crafter's anvil. It works as 'three', and yet it can prop any one of its three faces up, to gain one of the nature's objectives which, again, happen to be three-fold as well. This clever joining of the natures constitutes a 'key' property component into, what Jesus would have described as "my Father's mansion".

The Anvil Has a Shape

The pull of gravity would have forced the universe to collapse on it-self a long time ago unless a mechanism to counter the same was also in place at the same time. Apart from matter (visible or otherwise), the vacuum energy believed to be residing in empty-space is also believed to make a substantial contribution to the mass-energy density of the universe, or its overall gravitational hold on the constituents of the world. Currently, it is believed that the vacuum energy should also be carrying a negative pressure which can produce enough repulsion at cosmological distances to offset the gravitational pull. However, some people simply believe that the force of gravity itself becomes repulsive at cosmological distances—to rule out an unwanted collapse.

We shall like to emphasize the importance of understanding the relationships that exist at the most primary level—at the pre-manifestation or unmanifest level itself, if the rishis are to be believed. The three natures are linked in a way that they all remain present at the same time, like three systems supporting each other.

Perhaps the best way to try to understand this relation, is to presume a straight horizontal line at a 180 degrees flat surface. In the middle of this straight line another line standing as the line of *Will* arises which is perpendicular to it, and which can be presumed to act as the line of time as well. The manifestation takes place on its two sides—the 'Father' side representing 'Knowledge' and the 'Mother' side standing for 'Action'. There can be no manifestation on a flat line. The line of *Will* is the line of '*yaamal*' state, the state of equal strength or the equilibrium. On its either side—the other two sides (in any manifestation) try to balance each other with a ninety-degree opposition.

In relation to the flat plane, and the line in perpendicular in its middle, the best position for the forces of two kinds in a relation of mutual interdependence, to begin with, will be to make an angle of forty-five degree on either side of the middle line. To manifest an effect, the two lines of, let's say 'a' and 'b' sides, can be allowed to come as close to the middle line as they can without touching it. Thus, 'a' can extend to occupy up to 89.99 degrees of its side of the manifesting quarter and with even 0.01 degree being left on the side of b', 'b' can still hold and support the expansion of 'a', still leaving a balanced state in the manifesting force-field from the point of view of the manifesting property (The closest approach which could be measured, is called a catastrophe by the physics fraternity. It shows a balancing of the cosmological constant that goes up to 107 places after the decimal). Two principals holding, supporting and opposing each other at the same time and three natures acting likewise, in a similar manner—into every manifesting property—is a big advantage. Examples of these relationships lie scattered everywhere, in whichever direction of the manifesting universe we may look.

Further, the exclusive nature of vibration of a particle or a thing will predict the need of an exclusive piece of space-time into its hand, giving rise to a situation described by the Exclusion Principle of Wolfgang Pauli. Likewise, how the need for the three-pronged external nature, which is responsible to create all property, to remain present in a state of equilibrium in the internal-structure of a nucleon, would give rise to what the physicists call 'the colour index', has also been explained by us in our books named before. And yet, even from the very simple description we have provided in this essay thus far, we should be able to gain glimpses of the very physics in its making. To find acceptance, on one hand, a new theory must answer some unresolved issues, while on the other, it should also make predictions that can be verified. We can see:

- An answer is available for the first time to the rise of electrical charge.
- Need for the nuclear particles to comply with colour index requirement into their interior also stands explained in a much better way.
- Balancing within the forces is explained.
- Wave-particle duality is predicted.
- Uncertainty relation is predicted.
- Exclusion principle is predicted.
- Three particles that can make matter are predicted, and
- Relation of ninety degree between electricity and magnetism is also in a way predicted.

THE HOLY TRINITY

Nature of the Son aspect is 'Will', which is vibratory by nature. One side of this vibration is the power of 'Knowledge', which has a static nature, typical of the Father principle. Likewise, the other side of this vibration is the faculty of 'Action', which is dynamic—typically the nature of Spirit that can give rise to work and, hence, also the bodies. Thus, the external nature is also tripartite, following the Trinity of the principals which, in a way, wield these natures, kind of using them as their vehicles. Kindly see the figures provided below.

In the first frame of the Holy Trinity doctrine, there is God but there is no manifestation. In Vedantic parlance, it is called Nishkal Brahma, or the Supreme State—devoid of any specific attributes or parts. In the second frame, the Trinity has arisen, which is similar to Sakal Brahma. It has limbs or parts. It is this Trinity or the Sakal aspect of Brahma with its three attributes, which can manifest and can become the world. Father is God, and the Spirit is also God, and so is the Son as well. But they are different from each other, since each of them has its own nature and its own functions. Nevertheless, as stated, these remain interdependent and need to manifest together, like a coin and its two faces.

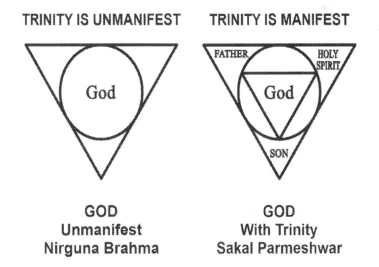

The other picture is more explicit. This is merely a photographic reproduction of the image of the principal deity in an 1800 years old temple in South India. This deity is known as Jambukeswarar. Besides the troika, the carved image in the temple also shows the respective natures or vehicles of this trinity, as seen by a rishi who has been able to pierce the veil of the relative viewership, or of Maya.

In the upper section of the image, Mahesha, or the 'Son' is depicted, which makes use of the nature of Will as its vehicle—shown in the image as a 'Nandi', a sturdy bull standing firm on its four legs. Without itself moving, the Son aspect, with a single or unified leg, provides support to the god of Knowledge (which represents the mind side) on its right side, and to the god of Action (which represents the body or the work side) on its left.

The vehicle for the creating aspect in the Trinity, with Action' as its nature, is shown as a majestically swimming swan, since its takes time to create work by piling bricks of action (called '*h*') on one another. 'Knowledge', which is the nature of mind side, on the other, is Garuda, the ancient super-eagle which can instantly rise as high in the skies as it likes (in its mythological context, this figure is shown akin to a human frame but with two broad wings).

This world of ours is only one episode from an ever-going sport between Father (eternal awareness) and the vibrating conscious energy (eternal Spirit). As stated, what we usually call as Nature, is actually an aggregate of the three external faculties of God, of Will, Knowledge and Action, that work together simultaneously into their respective dimensions, like a trident with three prongs. It is this aggregate of three external natures of God that bring this grand show that we call the 'world' into effect. And this 'show' is not only scripted by the Holy Triad itself, but is also enacted by itself only, as the three actors that are about and abound—everywhere and into all the roles.

It is this Trinity that becomes the world. Further, the same Trinity also turns itself into every single thing that comes to manifest. How this trinity can manifest itself as electron, proton and the neutron and create matter, we have tried to explain both in the scientific, as well as in spiritual and intellectual terms, in our main book (and in *Jesus Christ and the Spirit of Truth* as well).

Further, how the survival aspect, or a 'self', associated with the Son gives rise to the 'Exclusion Principle'? how the two faces of the coin translate into the 'Uncertainty Relation'? and how the three sections in Nature give rise to the internal charges in the nuclear matter? have also been resolved in the simplest of the terms, in the light of this old and more primary 'Science of Consciousness', now being served with a new flavour.

Our real objective was not to discuss matter, as we crafted our books. It was only incidental to our context. What we wanted to serve to our readers was a basket of wholesome knowledge that is concerned with the wisdoms of both, of the rishis in the East, as well as of Jesus in the West. The author merely plays the part of an anchor or paraclete (just the writer of a plaint—not even a full-time advocate) trying to build a narrative. And this narrative aims to create a universal understanding of what Jesus and the other masters, who have become one with the Father principle, even today want the people to know and to understand.

The main Section of the mother book, which is also the subject matter of the second book, *Jesus Christ and the Spirit of Truth*, begins with a discussion on the foundation aspect of the world, that applies both to matter and intelligent human life, and to every other thing between these two as well. This description of the foundation is derived from a Text which is considered to be the technical side of the knowledge revealed in Bhagwat Gita, which is the most revered scripture of the Vedic people.

The technical aspects of physics, we know, should hold good both in East and the West. Likewise, the author has tried to show, that this knowledge of the foundation can also be conveniently used to understand the technical aspects involved in what Jesus Christ had witnessed in his own time, and—through the offices of his apostles—what he had placed on record for the posterity.

In chapters 14, 15 and 16 of the John's gospel, even Jesus has mentioned a paraclete advocating on his behalf. "I still have many things to say to you (John 16:12-13), but you cannot bear them now. When the spirit of the truth comes (however), he (*the paraclete*) will guide you into all the truth, for he will not speak on his own but will speak whatever he hears, and he will declare to you the things that are to come."

This Trinity going into any foundation always appears as a troika, since none of the three can be excluded from any manifest object, or a being. Of these, Son is the coin that comes to manifest, while the Father and Spirit aspects only manifest as its two faces. And an understanding of this basic truth, the author feels inspired to suggest, is the main key that can open all the doors in the mansion of the Father—for a worthy Son of Man, who is industrious and who also strives.

As the manifesting Trinity emerges out of the unmanifest realm as a movement, each aspect in the trinity evolves its own plane to set its camp up, as suitable for its nature. The manifest reality too, as such, extends over three increasingly denser planes of existence— known in the wisdom circles as Causal, Astral and the Physical planes. Each living and non-living thing carries into itself three levels of vibrations, widely removed from each other. It exists at three levels at the same time. The world itself as a whole too, likewise, exists simultaneously at three planes of vibrations—one superimposed on the other.

The Son or the coin aspect comes to manifest first, and it creates a base on which a world of multiplicity can be erected. It remains present into every manifest thing in the world, even a particle, as its causal body. It lends a thing an individuality or a 'self', so that it can move about in the world (with a lot many other things) without loss of its integrity. It is the vibrations of the subtle causal energy, which is called spiritual energy, that give rise to instincts. It is these primal instincts, usually autonomic, which enable the sub-human world, in particular, to function.

The matter which is not alive and conscious does not have the option to ignore Nature's instruction, conveyed to it through the agency of instinct or intuition, while the live matter may stand to lose food or even life, when it does so. Usually, only the humans ignore the knowledge coming from the Causal realm of Nature through the mechanism of the instincts. They can easily afford to do so though, at least most of the times, while it could also hide big boons for at least some of them.

Once it is out of the causal realm, every individual with a self becomes qualified to own a mind side with awareness, and a body side that can give rise to an experience for it, and also movement. It is the mind side that is evolved by Nature first, at the second level, which is known as Astral Level. Besides spiritual energy, psychic energy can also function at this level, which is evolved by the 'Father' principle, the awareness side. Chit, the Father Principle, or Shiva, with knowledge as its nature, now comes in with the notion of a 'world, or this-ness for this evolving seed for everything (the 'Son'), as a non-self—as a second that can be distinguished and, hence, experienced. The self can know a non-self through the knowledge evolving into it as its mind side, courtesy the Father Principle.

A common template, called the universal astral body, is created by the knowledge arm of the Nature at this level, according to the rishis. Five instruments for knowing and five for action come into effect for the mind's use at this stage. These constitute the ten psychic propensities, that can be evolved by Nature in stages for all the individuals—beginning with the particulate matter.

Every individual entity with a self or a causal body, emerging from the womb of Nature, is first-born into the astral realm. Here it gets an astral body, which is non-destructive and which remains with it till the end of the world (a particular cycle). However, different entities can evolve these bodies to greatly varied extents. One reason for such variation is the opportunity provided to it by Nature in space and time, since the two sides of the coin—the mind-side of an entity and its body-side, must evolve together, in parallel. For example, if the individual becomes a proton at the very beginning, its physical body can also last the whole cycle, and its astral body practically loses all possibility of any further evolution.

Next it is the turn of the Shakti element, the dynamic Spirit principle with 'Action' as its nature, to create 'work' and to build a physical body for the 'self', and also a gross physical world that it can experience. It continues to parallelly evolve the astral and physical bodies, according to the rishis, until the humans are born. Thereafter, there is no further evolution of the physical body.

The causal body of Son, or of the common seed which comes to manifest, is made of a vibration which knows itself as 'I' and which has a 'will' to survive, or to exist. The inner side of this vibration is towards the Father Aspect, which enables it to know and to gain knowledge. The outward side of its causal vibration is towards the dynamic spirit and this propels it towards action—to give rise to work and its experience.

The world is Relative according to the rishis—or *Mayik* in their language—and it can differ for different entities, since it can only be experienced in relative terms. Based on the knowledge it has, a particle, a grasshopper or even a human being, can become involved in action and counter action of different kinds. For example, if the manifesting 'self' is an electron, the 'Father' part in it gives it the ability to cognise the positive, negative, and the neutral particles as different from each other. Likewise, the dynamic Spirit part into it enables it to move towards a particle with opposite charge, and away from one similar to itself.

The mind side of a manifest entity is forever, but not its body side. The mind part into an individual can unite with a physical body to take birth on the physical plane, and it can also detach from this body when it is destroyed or is otherwise rendered useless. Then it can get a new physical body—or a vehicle to ride-upon in its extended body—the physical world—at the convenience of Nature.

As individuals, we have kept changing our physical bodies in favour of the better-evolved ones. It is only in the humans that both the astral components and the physical bodies become fully developed. As humans, we have crossed a threshold and have acquired both intelligence and discrimination. We have become free agents now (an image of God, in a way), and can continue to evolve internally into our astral body or the mind side from here onwards. We can continue to be reborn in new physical bodies, as we continue to try to evolve more and more into our astral and causal bodies.

Just as we have a physical world, we also, likewise, have an astral world. And that is even larger, as we have a lot more freedom there. A human individual keeps spending time in both these worlds. It is this huge astral world which has been referred by Jesus Christ, as the kingdom of Heaven, at more places than one. By his repeated emphasis on the phrase, the 'son of man', Jesus too had wanted his disciples to try to understand the three-storied mechanism at work within them, occupied by them with their three bodies; and the true potential that they too actually possess. In fact, in primitive Hebrew conception, the very word 'heaven' is used to denote that place in a three-tier world, where the God resides. Again, the word 'son of man' has been used by Jesus not only for himself, but also for the others whom he considered to be worthy or ideal for the epithet.

All this, and many other aspects concerned with the mysteries of the world and the human existence, have been explained in sufficient detail in our aforementioned books, authored by Vigyan Mitra. And he requests that all intelligent adults in all age groups should make an effort to read one or the other of these books, to understand their true heritage—and also to be able to introduce their children to this true heritage, shared by them with the greatest of the sons (and daughters) of man.

The present book was, actually, written as a postlude to our principal book *Matter, Life and Spirit Demystified*, but looking at the size already gained by this compendium, it was excluded and could have remained unpublished. However, looking at the increasingly deteriorating world scenario, and warranted by it, it is now being published as a separate book.

Our books, in a way, echo the clarion call of the wise of the most ancient times to all the young progeny of man. This call of the ancient wise is still in the air and alive—constantly trying to inspire the progeny of man to gain victory over death. The world radiates from the effulgent light of God, and so do we, and the knowledge the rishis reveal is universal. Having realized it themselves, they simply invoke one and all,

"*Shrinwantu Vishwe, Amritasya Putrah*: Listen, you from all over the world, all a progeny of the immortality,

Vedahmetam, Purusham Mahantam, Adityavarnam Tamsah Parastat: Strive to know that into you that is the Purusha, which is the real you which should be known, which is of the nature of light and which is on the other side of the darkness of ignorance.

Tameva Viditwa Ati Mritumeti, Naa Anya Panthah, Vidyate Aynaaya: Only by knowing that, residing within your own self, you can overcome death. There is no other path (to overcome death) known to anyone, anywhere."

The great Brihadaranyka Upanisad of the Vedic people also tries to show the general direction for the mankind—to one and all of us—with its ever-green, forever-relevant aphorism:

"*Asato ma sadgamaya, tamaso ma jyotir gamaya, mrtyor ma amrtam gamya*: *Let, us all strive to move from what is false, towards the truth. Let, us all strive to move from darkness towards the light. And, let us all strive to move from death towards Immortality.*"

Chapter 1

JESUS, THE CHRIST

The entry of the human race to the year 2022 of the Lord commenced not on a very auspicious note. The deadly virus which leaked out from a laboratory in Wuhan a little more than two years ago still continues to affect and kill people. More than six million people have been killed by it already, including close to a million in the United States of America alone in its wake. The deadly virus continued to shine like a Sun that had risen into the heavens blazing most fiercely and devouring people.

Was this calamity of an unprecedented nature, the sign that Jesus had said that everyone will see, wonders the author, as he holds in his hands a copy of "The New Jerusalem Bible"? It is published by St Pauls, Mumbai, in India by arrangement with Darton, Longman & Todd Ltd., London. The copy of the New Testament gifted to the author by the principal of the school to which his two daughters went, had turned into shreds since then, as all pages had come out and he had purchased this complete book for keeps then. Especially, he was keen to learn more about the prophets Elijah and Daniel who have been mentioned by Jesus. After the work concerned with his main book *Matter, Life and Spirit Demystified*, was over, the author now had his opportunity to explore the Old Testament as well.

However, all the references and Scripture quotations used by the author and contained in his present book, from either of the two testaments, have been borrowed and quoted by him, with a sense of gratitude and thankfulness, from the updated edition of the New Revised Standard Version of the Bible, copyrighted 1989 by the Division of Christian

Education of the National Council of the Churches of Christ in the united States of America, who have all rights reserved, and these have been used by the author within their Permission Policy that allows reproduction of up to five hundred verses without express written permission of the publisher and right holder.

All the three major religions known as Semitic religions, commonly referred to as the Abrahamic religions, owe their origin to this holy book. All consider Abraham to be their principal ancestor. However, it was Jesus, who is acknowledged and respected by the adherents of all of these religions as the greatest among all the prophets, and it was him, who had told his followers to keep alert and to keep looking for the signs he was pointing out to them and take note when these happened.

The biggest event in the Bible was the rise of Christ, and the prevailing custom had been that a prophet was required to seal his covenant or directive with a 'sign' from the God. Jesus had already given many signs, which were topped by him with his own resurrection in a physical form after his death. Further, he had spoken about certain signs to help the people, to know and recognize the next big event when it commenced.

It is this second big event, predicted by Jesus and referred to as the Second Coming by the scribes, which constitutes the subject matter of this book which has been written as a postlude to our principal book, *Matter, Life and Spirit Demystified*. This book has been written to praise Jesus and the ancient teachers of the 'truth' from the Orient, and to make it easier for the people to understand what these great teachers separated in space and time have tried to explain across the centuries and millenniums.

They both speak of the same truth, nevertheless, and use a similar language as well. The ancient master in the East who realized the truth would say, '*Aham Brahmasmi*' (I and the Brahma are one); the master rising in the West said, 'I and my 'Father' are one'. In the East he preached *Tat Tvam Asi*, know that "You are 'That' too" (or the same Brahma is hiding into your very heart too as your own 'self'); in the West he made this simpler and taught 'Love your neighbour as yourself' (because same 'self' is residing in him/her too).

Jesus had been born, had trained himself and had lived, not for himself, but for the sheep that he had once lost and which he was now trying to gather again into his sheepfold, while he himself stood at the gate handing out the passes. Sometimes he chose to call the people gathered by him as 'this generation'. Jesus had to sacrifice his life to secure the passes he was able to hand out at the gate. He had told his people that this 'generation' (since it had the passes) was going to live and to see the day when these signs that he mentioned would become visible, if they were alert enough to take note. And he had repeatedly warned and advised his people to remain alert. Luke 21:34-36 "Be on guard so that your hearts are not weighed down by dissipation and drunkenness and the worries of this life and that day does not catch you unexpectedly, like a trap. For it will come upon all who live on the face of whole earth. Be alert at all times, praying that you may have the strength to escape all these things that will take place and to stand before the Son of Man (you should not be on the side that would betray and endanger the Son of Man, or even among those who fail to take action to secure him)."

THE GOOD NEWS

After resurrecting himself, Jesus had told his disciples to go and to spread the good news about what they had seen and heard. He had set an example and had provided visible evidence which no-one could deny, that the world of a person did not come to an end with the end of his or her physical life. If we look at it purely from the scientific point of view, it was also a proof that every human being had it in him or her to gain such power as well; to also become visible to the world left behind by it, after it has resurrected itself, as Jesus had been able to do. And it was not merely a matter of faith, for one to accept or to reject as one felt like, but an aspect of the reality of which we all happen to be a part.

Prophet Elijah had told the same thing as well, to his disciple, Elisha. That, however, was more than seven hundred years before the Christ. Elijah was the Guru and Elisha was his disciple then, and had sought from him twice the power of the divine than what he himself had, according to the scribes of the Old Testament. The teacher had agreed to his disciple's demand with only one condition, that he needed to raise his awareness to a stage before his Guru's leaving the physical world, so that he was evolved enough to be able to see him doing so.

When alive, Jesus had also told his disciples that he was the shepherd who had come to gather back his lost sheep (kind of providing a hint about an unfinished mission of his from an earlier life); and to bring them back into the fold of the kingdom of Heaven. "So, again Jesus said to them (John 10:7-11), 'Very truly, I tell you, *I am the gate for the sheep. All who came before me are thieves and bandits*, but the sheep did not listen to them. I am the gate. Whoever enters by me will be saved and will come in and go out and find pasture. The thief comes only to steal and kill and destroy. I came that they may have life and have abundantly. I am the good shepherd; the good shepherd lays down his life for his sheep'."

Jesus preferred the word 'Father', rather than God who could be coloured by the people as blue, green or red, as 'jealous' or 'biased' in favour of one set of people or for-ever against another.' People had retained the concept of God, but had forgotten that everything was made by him and that it was also regulated, though the threads or ropes used by his unseen hands may appear to be long at times. Again, Jesus has spoken about a 'kingdom of Heaven' and also a regulatory mechanism of the 'Father', at work behind the screen, through parables such as those of 'the Conscious Steward', 'the Ten Wedding Attendants' and 'the Talents'.

Matthew 24:42-51 "Keep awake, therefore, for you do not know on what day your Lord is coming. But understand this: If the owner of the house had known in what part of the night the thief was coming, he would have stayed awake and would not have his house to be broken into. Therefore, you also must be ready, for the Son of Man is coming at an hour you do not expect. Who, then, is the wise slave whom the master has put in charge of his household, to give the other slaves their allowance of food at the proper time? Blessed is that slave whom his master will find at work when he arrives. Truly I tell you, he will put that one in charge of all his possessions. But if that wicked slave says to himself, 'My master is delayed', and begins to beat his fellow-slaves and eats and drinks with drunkards, the master of that slave will come on a day he does not expect him and at an hour that he does not know. He (the master) will cut him in pieces and put him with the hypocrites, where there will be weeping and gnashing of teeth". Allegorically the 'trustworthy or dependable' and 'unreliable or dishonest' slaves or servants would also seem to indicate religions and a lot of emphasis seems to have been placed on the keepers of religions.

Matthew 25:1-13 "Then the kingdom of Heaven will be like this: Ten young women took their lamps and went to meet the bridegroom. Five of them were foolish and five were wise. When the foolish took their lamps, they took no oil with them; wise took flasks of oil with their lamps. As the bridegroom was delayed, all of them became drowsy and slept. But at midnight there was a shout, 'Look! Here is the bridegroom! Come out to meet him.' Then all those young women got up and trimmed their lamps. The foolish said to the wise, 'Give us some of your oil: our lamps are going out.' But the wise replied, 'No! there will not be enough for you and us, you had better go to the dealers and buy some for yourselves.' And while they went to buy it, the bridegroom came, and those who were ready went in with him to the wedding banquet and the door was shut. Later the other young women came also, saying, 'Lord, lord, open to us.' But he replied, 'Truly I tell you I do not know you.' Keep awake, therefore, for you know neither the day nor the hour."

Matthew 25:14-30 "For it is like a man going on a journey, summoned his slaves and entrusted his property to them; to one he gave five talents, to another two, to another one, each in proportion to his ability. Then he went away. At once the one who had received the five talents promptly went and traded with them and made five more talents. In the same way the one who had received two talents made two more talents. But the man who had received the one went off and dug a hole in the ground and hid his master's money. After a long time, the master of those slaves came back and settled accounts with them. Then the one, who had received the five talents came forward bringing five more talents, saying, 'Master, you handed over to me five talents; see, I have made five more talents.' His master said to him, 'Well done, good and trustworthy slave; you have been trustworthy in a few things; I will put you in charge of many things; enter into the joy of your master.' And the one with the two talents also came forward, saying, 'Master, you handed over to me two talents; see, I have made two more talents.' His master said to him, 'Well done, good and trustworthy slave; you have been trustworthy in a few things; I will put you in charge of many things; enter into the joy of your master.' Then the one who had received the one talent also came forward, saying, 'Master, I knew that you were a harsh man, reaping where you did not sow and gathering where you did not scatter; so, I was afraid and I went off and hid your talent in the ground. Here you have what is yours, you have it back.' But his master replied, 'You wicked and lazy slave! You knew, did you, that I reap where I did not sow and gather where I did not scatter? Then you ought to have deposited my money with the bankers and on my return, I would have received what was my own with interest. So, take the talent from him, and give it to the one with ten talents. For to all those who have, more will be given, and they will have an abundance; but from those who have nothing, even what they have will be taken away. As for this good-for-nothing servant, throw him into the darkness outside, *where there will be weeping and grinding of teeth'*." What the talents mean is 'virtue'. Both religion and faithfulness are concerned with the gaining of virtue only.

Unfortunately, all the notions of a rebirth, of the astral world or the Kingdom of Heaven with its lower and higher quarters, which Jesus had tried to explain, were substantially watered down or diluted by Justinian in due time and was imbibed by the community as well, soon. Unfortunately, again, most of the people who were rich, or were in a position of power or prominence, were apt to put more faith in clergy than in God, and like the Justinian household, would have been happier if there was to be no retribution for any evil deeds, once the decree of the emperor came into effect. The clergy could be managed, whereas the God had to be pleased— not managed.

Jesus, on his part, never let an opportunity to slip by to explain the Kingdom of Heaven and the mechanism of a retribution for one's deeds that was universally applicable.

Speaking to some of the Jews, who were not averse to listening to him, he had said (John 8:39-40), "If you are Abraham's children, you would do what Abraham did, but now you are trying to kill me, a man who has told you the truth that I heard from God. This is not what Abraham did (He didn't want to kill someone who told him the Truth)".

And again, John 8:51-59, "Very truly, I tell you, whoever keeps my word will never see death. The Jews said to him, 'Now we know that you have a demon. Abraham died, and so did the prophets, yet you say, "Whoever keeps my word will never taste death." Are you greater than our father Abraham who is died? The prophets also died. Who do you claim to be?'

"Jesus answered: If I glorify myself, my glory is worth nothing. It is my Father who glorifies me, he of whom you say, 'He is our God,' though you do not know him. But I know him; if I would say, 'I do not know him,' I would be a liar like you. But I do know him, and I keep his word. Your ancestor Abraham rejoiced that he would see my Day; he saw it and was glad.

('He saw it and was glad' implies that when Jesus was planning or was about to leave the astral realm in the Kingdom to take a physical birth again, Abraham had welcomed such a prospect for the good of his descendants).

"Then the Jews said to him, 'You are not yet fifty years old, and have you seen Abraham!' Jesus said to them, 'Very truly, I tell you, before Abraham was, 'I am' (the Father always is and so is him who has become one with the Father. Such a one always lives in the present—there is no past or future, like 'I was' or 'I will be', for him in real sense). So, they (even the ones among the Jews who were friendly toward him, and had gathered to listen to him) picked up stones to throw at him; but Jesus hid himself and went out of the Temple."

Jesus had to undergo great suffering to be able to give rise to a new 'generation', to a flock of sheep that was different. The sheep from this flock followed a simple set of laws that were derived from Nature itself—or from the very nature of the things—which conferred equality on the people; even on the women. And he wanted it to comprise of people which were naturally catholic, not hypocritically so. However, this 'generation' did not have to block or to deny the goats then; only to half-quarantine them. The proper quarantining, he seemed to imply, was to come later.

There was a standard in place, however, from now onward. Things could be compared now and could be called right or wrong. Like some of the covenants; it was not enforced yet, but it was no longer invisible or so badly mixed up that most of the people should be unable to see it. And it was the Semitic people, in which he was primarily interested, and into which he was striving to bring in a divide; to save some and to leave the others to their own respective designs and fates.

A SHEPHERD PLANS TO LAY HIS LIFE FOR THE SHEEP

The suffering undergone by Jesus was deliberately born by him. He could have easily avoided it, had he wanted to do so. During the small period of two to three years when he was within the sight and was seen working, Jesus often crossed the borders of various provinces into which the Palestine was divided, each time thereby leaving the jurisdiction of the local authorities. It seems that by going to Jerusalem, in a way, Jesus may have himself chosen to give himself up to his persecutors. The people were not, however, ready then to understand the mechanism he had chosen to take the recourse to, for their sake. Jesus appears to have planned to offer his own life in exchange for the bargain he was willing to enter with the Father.

What Jesus could not know or fathom, however, was that while honouring the bargain, the 'Father' was under no obligation not to waive the condition on offer on Jesus' side. And now we know, that there is an Aquarian Gospel and, besides, there are many other facts that have come to light, since history can be researched. In Bible itself, a god has been mentioned whom the women loved. It was him, who said, one must discharge one's duties rightfully, but must not crave a given outcome or a specific 'return'. It is for the 'Father' to decide on the outcome or the 'return'.

Jesus himself never suggested that one should feel irretrievably bound to one's own ideas, or to those injected into one's system by some others, even some well-meaning people, especially in the realms one doesn't even understand fully. The saints responsible to build up early Christianity were well-meaning people, who wanted to set up infallible procedures, but they had not become one with the Father as Jesus had. That he was a haloed master was for all to see. Human effort to add to that halo may have actually added less and possibly subtracted more, by restricting what Jesus could or couldn't have done. It could easily convert what was straightway feasible in the kingdom of Heaven, into a kind of suspect impossibility: creating more doubt and adding little to the faith. It is the law of karma that must not be violated, nevertheless. Jesus deciding to incarnate was a major affair for the Kingdom, and it may have involved not just Jesus as a an individual but some other very important person or persons as well, linked to him by karma.

It was a mixed lot of people, entrusted to Jesus at his own behest by the 'Father', by selecting some and inviting many others, to give rise to a new generation. People who joined him did so willingly and by volunteering, however, without being forced in any way. Jesus taught them simple things that they could implement, and he provided them with an ample amount of evidence that he had been sent to them by the Father of all; That he had been sent to uplift their lot.

Due to faith in his words, and for many people it bordered on a kind of willing 'surrender', this new generation had ushered itself into a territory in which the compliance with the Eternal Law of the higher nature, which Jesus called the Father principle, came to acquire a status of its own. In fact, it came to gain an autonomic sort of status for a majority component in this new generation. And that was a big advantage, since such a law actually exists; and that is the very reason it is called the 'eternal law' of the Nature in the eastern world.

Entering the Gate, With a Clean Slate

It was a mixed lot of people sharing same faith, same rituals, same temples, same priests and the same prophets. Only the prophets could talk to their God and only the high priests could interpret the word of that God. And it was a God which was jealous. It was not like the Father who had sent Jesus and who was neither jealous nor partisan, but who, as the Father of all, was benign for all. Killing people, stoning them to death, putting them to sword or slitting their throats was not into the department of God, the Father, but of the Satan. People were being misled for sure, but it may be unfair to blame the prophets or the priests alone. What the majority at a given time craves, leaders come to arise to cash-in on the same.

Some a little less and some a little more, depending on their individual tendencies, all Semitic people shared the negative karma of their community's way of thinking, living, and interacting with the other people as a whole in those days. A vicious thought process had come into existence which was devouring goodness and people; and it was incurring karma in the long run, in the eternal context, which included what Jesus referred to as the kingdom of Heaven. Jesus had segregated a major part away out of 'this mix', that was more inclined toward the right and less toward wrong; leaving much evil and the little right to fend for itself.

For reasons obvious to Jesus, this evil component of negative energy into its sheep was an obstacle to the accrual and accumulation of what was 'good' or the right and was positive, or on the side of God, the Father; what was non-evil and non-negative, or away from the side of the devil. Jesus decided to give those people, who volunteered, a clean state, by accepting for himself the recoil of the negative energy accumulated by them over the generations, and providing such energy with a channel to release itself. He allowed the energy to release, through absorbing its impact on his own physical body.

Through his personal suffering of the pain and injury, Jesus provided a short-cut for the accumulated negative energy to leak out from the 'sheep' entering his fold, to make its baggage lighter; to unburden it of the evil from its past; to activate his free pass for this new 'generation' to enter the sheepfold created by him. It was a certificate to be vested on every sheep with a simple procedure of baptism, ushering it into a second life, a new life; the life as a son of man, that of an evolved homo-sapiens—well on its way to loosening the shackles of its animal brain.

Jesus had not used his option as a Master to separate his astral body from the 'physical', to avoid feeling the bodily pain immediately on his crucifixion. As a Master who had become one with the 'Father' he could have done so, but he didn't. He suffered the pain in his physical body in full, and knowingly so, like a deal between him and the Father. In fact, he may have resisted even fainting in the face of extreme pain and discomfort—at least, as long as he could. Jesus, the Christ to-be, was as hard a nut in his mind, as he was soft in his heart.

There could be, and there seems to be, a little misconception or misunderstanding, however, about what Jesus had said. People may presume that Jesus freed all his followers from the burden of their sins forever by letting his blood to be shed, and irrespective of what they did, granting them eternal life in the kingdom of Heaven after their death. This is true; and yet it could be a truth probably only half understood. It is a truth in the absolute sense only, with a 'here onwards' rider. All his followers had acquired the potential to gain eternal life in the kingdom of Heaven, without having to be reborn on Earth again. At the same time, however, they were not barred from choosing to be reborn on account of their unsatiated desires, their unfulfilled relationships, and the pull of their karma.

They do stand to be judged, however, based on the clean slate they received through his authorized hand at the entry gate to the sheepfold.

They need not go down to hellish regions of the astral world, unless someone had committed a very dark sin, but would keep getting reborn from the ground state of the heaven, after spending a good time there and in good company. This was a great advantage against the others who brought a huge debt or debit of evil deeds from their past that their Prophets were not in a position to transfer to themselves; assuming that they all must have wanted to do so. They were only prophets, not Masters (mostly thieves and bandits, including snakes and the broods of vipers, according to Jesus), and they generally misled the people, less out of ignorance and more guided by a motif of personal gain. When they grew older, they had to take guard that they may not be poisoned by their successors to-be.

On record, Jesus had said "(John 10:8-13) All who came before me (claiming and demonstrating different things) are thieves and bandits... The thief comes only to steal and kill and destroy ...The hired man, who is not the shepherd and does not own the sheep, sees the wolf coming, and leaves the sheep and runs away, and the wolf snatches them and scatters them. The hired man runs away because a hired hand does not care for the sheep."

In fact, the hired man, as one time investment, goes out to the people with a feigned air of arrogance of the superior, to confirm his self-selection of himself, since they were not supposed to able to communicate with the God and he claimed that he could; they were not able to interpret the scripture or the law, but they become convinced that he could. As a result, they also became dependent on him to sanctify any sacrifice suggested or ordained by the scriptures or the prophet. And for this reason, people would begin to pay him in the currency of their respect, money and manual or other labour. Sometimes they could even be convinced or cornered to give their very lives away for an end beneficial to the hired man but fruitless for them. If Jesus represented the kingdom of Heaven, these people would seem to be working or having worked to promote the Satanic Realm of the Hell.

A prophet, a priest or a leader must impress or persuade their target people first, however, so that they 'select' him; then they become bound to him for their lives and he enjoys the freedom, the luxury, and the power he thinks he deserves, since he is clever to convert people's faith in God into a trust for himself, assuming the air of a demi-god, a prophet or cleric of repute, whose words acquire the halo of being a godly injunction for many people—especially the ignorant ones or those who may easily be lured or tempted to commit 'sins'. He could put words in the mouth of the God created by him to suit his ends and, if needed, also to kill any dissent or opposition. No holds are barred; Use of chemistry and black-art may be a part of the tools in common employ.

The Humans Can Have Transitory Interests

A person may see a nude photograph or painting or even a piece of pornography and he or she may have liked it. Usually, these events are not happening when the persons see them but these may excite their minds. Their minds become affected by what they see, to excite their bodies which may release sex related hormones. The scriptures or the rishis do not really forbid anything, and there is no conflict between people trying to understand the Spirit of Truth on one hand and seeing nudes or getting involved into some bona fide sexual activity, on the other. The interest in sex etc. happens naturally and is not a sin. It may be a hinderance for one seeking the highest goal, though. Hence, only from that point of view it may fall in the category of a distraction that needs to be overcome. From one's own personal point of view he or she may treat such escapades as minor and transient sins, since these are entirely different from sins like theft and cheating or from such heinous acts as rape or murder. Besides, any minor distractions or aberrations may go away on their own with time.

Again, making an effort to understand the nature of Truth does not affect one's sexual ability or reduces the feeling of pleasure or enjoyment in sensual indulgence of sex, pleasing sights, pleasing sounds or rich food and rich smells. If at all, in fact, understanding of Truth and of the freedoms given by the Lord may often remove the notion of 'sin' from such natural behaviour.

However, the knowledge of Truth does not stop here, at being sinful or otherwise, but helps the person to evolve further. It begins by enhancing his/her confidence in what he/she does, and leads him or her to discriminate between right and wrong action, and more than that, between right and wrong thought patterns. As one's understanding grows, a person may decide to make a voluntary effort to evolve further on the path of spirituality, and to move Godward. The time is chosen by the person involved and not by anyone else, though, according to how the forces from one's past karma continue to flow after a given pattern, while the Nature may keep providing opportunities from time to time for that person, to accept or to ignore and to let the same slip away.

Knowledge of Truth in itself is a great advancement and is of great value, while how one plans his or her ascension on the scales of evolution remains a person's own personal choice, since after evolving him or her, the Father has set the person free. Yet, he has also set his laws of motions or movement concerning the living and non-living things also free. And these laws, as we all know, include the third law of motion discovered by Isaac Newton, which states that every action gives rise to an equal and opposite counter-action as well. What we do not usually know is, that it applies to all actions indulged into by the human beings as well, and that such counter action need not become visibly manifest at once.

A Movement Which Will Gather Momentum

Jesus knew that people could and probably would commit sins, but he taught them that they were expected to know and understand that they had committed a sin, when they did, and also to have the courage to confess its occurance. It could be a friend, a parent, or a priest to whom they confessed or none of these; but for sure they must confess to the 'Father' in their mind and heart, so that the score was known both to the 'Father' and his human progeny.

Further, Jesus made them feel that he expected them to cultivate and also increasingly display the wisdom and nobility of an evolved son-of-man, or a true world citizen; a citizenship they had come to acquire since they had taken a vow (*sankalpa*) to that effect through baptism or some other procedure. He taught and encouraged them to repent or compensate in some manner for any sin, neglect, or an undue advantage accruing to them or derived by them, whatever be the context; be it at the individual, ecological or social level. Of course, not everybody was likely, or even be able to comply, and certainly not on each occasion. Jesus, therefore, also at the same time created a positive momentum to further help his sheep.

And he actualized this positive momentum created by him through his simplest of simple advice to every member of this new generation, viz., (Matthew 22:37-40) "You must love the Lord your God with all your heart, with all your soul, and with all your mind. This is the greatest and the first commandment. And a second is like it: You shall love your neighbour as yourself. On these two commandments *hang all the Law* and *the Prophets*." (You do not need any prophet if you are compliant with these two, which actually covers the three levels on which one exists, and anyone talking a deviation from these two, especially the latter, cannot be a true prophet—he is more likely to be a thief and a bandit, trying to exploit you for his own personal gain).

NAY! I HAVE COME TO DIVIDE

As the good news about the Kingdom of Heaven was spread by the apostles, and as missionaries went, going out to the people; to the people in similar situations, who wanted to keep off evil and preferred catholicity to the lures of a sinful life—the sheepfold of Jesus began to swell and to expand. People, who chose to lead their lives following the universal and eternal Laws of Nature, began to gather themselves into a generation; into a flock of sheep that had been taken by Jesus under his protection.

And as was expected, while many people joined, an equal number also chose to keep all their freedoms, as once the Asur had done, and had broken away from the Sur worshippers. 'Sur' actually means to be in tune, in tune with nature's rhythm. 'Asur', likewise means those who deviated and took freedoms that were not fair, creating discordant notes. They will not be affected by any laws of any higher nature if they did not accept it, or if they denied Jesus, a large number of people still believed. Jesus, however, had himself clarified in no uncertain terms: "No, I have not come to unite, but to divide".

Luke 12:51-53 "Do you suppose that I am here to bring peace on earth? No, I tell you, but rather a division. For, from now on, a household of five will be divided: three against two and two against three; father opposed to a son, son to father, mother to daughter, daughter to mother, mother-in-law to daughter-in-law, daughter-in-law to the mother-in-law."

Matthew 10:36 "and one's foes will be the members of one's 'own' household (or close friend-circle)." It is clear that Jesus is referring to a firm denial for the evil or the unjust one is often tempted to indulge into under the influence of one's family and friends. He simply wanted them to part their ways with such influence, be it of a family member or of a friend.

Jesus wanted people to voluntarily give up evil, even at the cost of losing a family or friend. Families joined his bandwagon; some broke to be able to join him, and some joined into their whole. People were segregated, nevertheless. Jesus, kind of placed the people willing to comply with the laws of the higher nature on one side, the right side; and those unwilling to shun evil, or their unprincipled indulgence, on the other side—the not-right side. It was provisional then; a kind of general gestation period was on. One day it was going to freeze where it was; when the doors of the sheepfold would possibly be sealed. And that day may be 'now' if we follow the signs, that Jesus had spoken about!

Haven't there been spillages causing death of over six million people, already? Aren't we forgetting the warning given by Jesus (Matthew 24:6), "And you will hear of wars and rumours of war (threats of bigger wars; of the use of nuclear weapons); see that you are not alarmed *for this is something that must happen*, but the end will not be yet"? What Jesus wants to convey across the millenniums, is that we should show the courage to call the bluff or to look the devil direct into the eyes, and that the fear of war or skirmishes or even the use of nuclear weaponry, shouldn't deter the mankind on the right side of the fence. It shouldn't prevent us from taking the initiative back into our hands, from turning the mankind back towards Life, towards God and towards the Good, so that it can survive. We may think about letting the mankind making a fresh beginning to be able to gain the heights that can only be gained by a true Son of Man, the foundation for which, Jesus had said, was laid by God with the foundation of the World!

Let's help Nature! Let's help God! And, let's defeat the devil and its designs! Let's change the gears! Let's help the Son of Man to SURVIVE. Let's DIVIDE in a major way with good or near good on one side and evil and near evil on the other. Let's create a sheepfold hard to breach, so that the Son of Man does not lose, and can WIN!! If the economies can survive the Covid, these can survive the other devils, and the consequent inconvenience for a further period, as well. For sure, those on the side of right, the side of the 'Father', stand to win! At the end of the day, those with evil designs will stand to lose, first deflated and then probably swept away altogether!

The Last Judgment

The day chosen by the Father for such sealing, or the freezing of the divide was neither known to Jesus nor to the angels in the Heaven. All that Jesus was able to do in his time, before his crucifixion, was to mention the signs, to warn the people and to repeat his advice for them to keep on the alert, so that they would take note of the signs when these appeared, and would remember the advice Jesus had given them.

Matthew 25:31-35,40 "When the 'son of man' comes in his glory, and all the angels with him, then he will sit on the throne of his glory. All nations will be gathered before him and he will separate people one from another as the shepherd separates sheep from the goats, and he will put the sheep at his right hand and the goats at the left. Then the King will say to those on his right hand, 'Come, you who are blessed by my Father, *inherit the Kingdom prepared for you since the foundation of the world*, for I was hungry and you gave me food, I was thirsty and you gave me something to drink, I was a stranger and you welcomed me', I was naked and you gave me clothing, I was sick and you took care of me, I was in prison and you visited me'....the King will answer, 'Truly I tell you, just as you did it to one of the least of these brothers and sisters of mine, you did it to me'."

Matthew 25:41-46 "Then he will say to those on his left hand, 'You who are accursed, depart from me into the eternal fire prepared for the devil and his angels, for I was hungry and you gave me no food, I was thirsty and you gave me nothing to drink, I was a stranger and you did not welcome me, naked and you did not give me clothing, sick and in prison and you did not visit me.' Then they also will answer, 'Lord when was it when we saw you hungry or thirsty, or a stranger or naked, or sick, or in prison and did not take care of you?' Then he will answer them, 'Truly

I tell you, just as you did not do it to one of the least of these, you did not do it to me.' And these will go away into eternal punishment but the righteous into eternal life."

One hallmark of a true Master is that he or she is able to see simultaneously into several dimensions and the statements made by him or her would apply 'as they were' in more than one context. Besides, in a simple single-utterance, they can pack the wisdom of the millenniums; even eternal wisdom.

In just two commandments and the declaration "I and my Father are one" Jesus had conveyed everything worth conveying. Likewise, while describing a likely event in the future, Jesus had conveyed or confirmed all that would be presented before the nations, also at the same time explaining the mechanism that worked at the back of the kingdom of Heaven. The mechanism works in the astral realm, though, and it comes into action upon a person's death (to understand this better, please read an article or a book on 'near death experiences', or read *Matter, Life and Spirit Demystified*).

In the Introduction to the Synoptic Gospels in the New Jerusalem Bible (only John's gospel is independent), it is explained, "The gospels are not 'lives' or 'biographies' of Jesus, but are four versions of the *record of the Good News* brought by Jesus. Jesus himself preached the coming of God's rule, the establishment of his sovereignty, breaking through the bonds of evil, sin and death to which all people had been subject. The gospels are full also of wonder at the mystery of Jesus himself…" Therefore, in trying to understand the '*record of the Good News*' and Jesus mentioning the coming of the God's rule, one needs to be careful and discreet enough to make an effort to understand the deeper truth, which may not be straightway obvious and may easily be overlooked or cause some confusion.

A Fifth Gospel

There is one very apparent gap in the narratives that all the faithful come across, going through the four gospels of the New Testament. These all provide information about birth of Jesus Christ and John the Baptist, and also mention the extra-ordinary wisdom and awareness displayed by

Jesus as a boy of thirteen concerning his knowledge of the scriptures, but the details are very sketchy—almost absent. The gospels do not state how Jesus came to acquire his knowledge that astonished even the most learned. Besides there is a clear gap in their narrative from the time Jesus had turned thirteen, until his reappearance as a man of about thirty-three. Marry, his mother, nevertheless, seemed to be in the know—perhaps all through—as to what Jesus did and where he stayed during this intervening period of some twenty years, or so.

John 2: 1-10 "On the third day (after John the Baptist had seen the holy spirit descend as a dove on Jesus on the banks of river Jordan) there was a wedding at Cana in Galilee, and the mother of Jesus was there. Jesus and his disciples had also been invited to the wedding. When the wine gave out, the mother of Jesus said to him, 'They have no wine'. And Jesus said to her, 'Woman, what concern is that to me and to you? My hour has not come yet.' His mother said to the servants, *'Do whatever he tells you.'* Now standing there were six stone water jars for the Jewish rites of purification, each holding twenty or thirty gallons. Jesus said to them, 'Fill the jars with water,' and they filled them up to the brim. He said to them, 'Now draw some out, and take it to the person in-charge of the banquet.' So, they took it. When the person in charge tasted the water that had become wine and did not know where it came from (though the servants who had drawn the water knew), that person called the bridegroom and said to him, 'Everyone serves the good wine first and then the inferior wine after the guests have become drunk. But you have kept the best wine until now'."

That Mary knew everything about the escapades, learning and evolution of Jesus is evident from her simple matter of the fact statement to Jesus in the presence of his disciples, 'They have no wine'. And this single incident also shows her degree of confidence about what his son was capable of, that ignoring his objection she tells the servants, *'Do whatever he tells you.'* The problem was as good as already solved, as far as the mother of Jesus was concerned.

In October, 1887 Nicolai Alexandrovitch Notovitch of Crimea, who had studied history at the University of St. Petersburg, arrived in India and visited Kashmir and Ladakh. His retinue included a dependable interpreter. While visiting the Buddhist monasteries in Ladakh and Leh, Notovitch was pleasantly surprised to learn that Buddhist lamas held Jesus, whom they called Issa, in very high esteem, in fact, even higher than their own Dalai Lamas. They told the visiting scholar that Jesus had visited these lands long ago as a young man and this was recorded in Buddhist writings. Notovitch came to understand that thousands of volumes of scriptures based on various historical sources were stored at Lhasa in Tibet, and that hand written copies of some of these writings were also often prepared and kept at some of the larger monasteries.

At the Hemis monastery at Leh, Notovich was given to understand that there were indeed scriptures about the mysterious prophet Issa, and his life did seem to bear close similarities to the stories of Jesus. In fact, at a subsequent visit, when he was able to spend more time at the Leh Monastery, Notovitch was lucky to himself able to see two volumes of such writings, copied from the originals at Lhasa, that were also read out to him in the presence of his interpreter. These volumes written in the old Indian script Pali were compiled by different monks during the first and second centuries A.D. These stated that as a boy of fourteen (Issa) Jesus had arrived in India with a group of merchants, to gather wisdom from the noted learning centres of the time at Jagannath Puri in Orissa, at Varanasi and Rajagriha, and also at the Himalayan regions adjoining Nepal. Work of Notovitch based on his discovery was published by a Paris Publisher in France, in 1885.

"*The Aquarian Gospel of Jesus the Christ*", authored by Levi H. Dowling was originally written in 1908. Publication of the findings of Notovitch may have triggered the research by Levi, who was a Church of Christ pastor, a Civil War chaplain for the union Army, and a New Thought lecturer of his time. Levi was an American citizen, and had been a close student of the religions of the world from childhood. When but a boy he was impressed with the sensitiveness of the finer ethers and believed that in some manner they were sensitised plates on which sounds, even thoughts, were recorded. With avidity, he entered into the deeper studies of etheric vibrations, determined to solve the great mysteries of the heavens for himself. Forty years he spent in study and silent meditation, and then he found himself in that stage of spiritual consciousness that permitted him to enter the domain of these superfine ethers and become familiar with their mysteries. Needless to point out, that not only the assumptions of Levi about the subtle space (ether) will appear to be correct, but also the special ability he was able to develop—in the light of logic, mathematics, procedures, and other details provided by us in our book, *Matter, Life and Spirit Demystified*.

In author's view, all the description provided by Levi about the life of Jesus in India and until the hour of his resurrection may be true. Although, these were things that were not known to the authors of the gospels, but Jesus never intended to hide them from anyone. So, there is no difficulty in a devout person of faith and practice being able to access those. However, the events immediately prior to the resurrection of Jesus were secrets shared between Jesus and the Father. If anyone tried to pry into anything private of a divinity or into a secret of the Relative Realm of the Spirit, Nature has two courses. It either misleads a person, or it just collapses the function. While we quote certain details concerned with life of Jesus here and in the next chapter, some other aspects of Levi's gospel, that may be of interest only to the more serious among our readers, have also been reproduced by us at the end of the book (Appendix-2).

Exchanges with Mary when Jesus Was Away

Chapter 30, Aquarian Gospel: "One day as Jesus stood beside the Ganges (probably at Varanasi of the Gyan Wapi fame) busy with his work, a caravan, returning from the West, drew near. And one, approaching Jesus, said, 'We come to you from your native land and bring unwelcome news. Your father is no more on earth; your mother grieves; and none can comfort her. She wonders whether you are still alive or not; she longs to see you once again. And Jesus bowed his head in silent thought; and then he wrote. Of what he wrote this is the sum:

"My mother, noblest of the womankind; A man just from my native land has brought me word that father is no more in flesh, and that you grieve, and are disconsolate. My mother, all is well; is well for father and is well for you. His work in this earth-round is done, and it is nobly done. In all the walks of life men cannot charge him with deceit, dishonesty, nor wrong intent. Here in this round, he finished many heavy tasks, and he has gone from hence prepared to solve the problems of the round of soul. Our Father-God is with him there, as he was with him here; and there his angel guards his footsteps lest he goes astray.

"Why should you weep? Tears cannot conquer grief. There is no power in grief to mend a broken heart. The plane of grief is idleness; the busy soul can never grieve; it has no time for grief. When grief comes trooping through the heart, just lose yourself; plunge deep into the ministry of love, and grief is not. Yours is a ministry of love, and all the world is calling out for love. Then let the past go with the past; rise from the cares of carnal things and give your life for those who live. And if you lose your life in serving life you will be sure to find it in the morning sun, the evening dews, in song of bird, in flowers, and in the stars of night.

"In just a little while your problems of this earth-round will be solved; and when your sums are all worked out it will be pleasure unalloyed for you to enter wider fields of usefulness, to solve the greater problems of the soul. Strive, then, to be content, and I will come to you some day and bring you richer gifts than gold or precious stones. I'm sure that John will care for you, supplying all your needs; and I am with you all the way, Jehoshua."

"And by the hand of one, a merchant going to Jerusalem, he sent this letter on its way."

THEN JESUS BECAME 'ONE' WITH THE FATHER

Matthew 4:1-7 "Then Jesus was led by the Spirit into the wilderness to be tested by the devil. He fasted forty days and forty nights, afterward he was famished. The tempter came and said to him, 'If you are Son of God, command these stones to become loaves of bread.' But he answered, 'It is written, "One does not live by bread alone, but by every word that comes from the mouth of God".' …Jesus said to him, 'Again, it is written: Do not put the Lord your God to the test'."

Matthew 4:8-11 "Again, the devil took him to a very high mountain and showed him all the kingdoms of the world and their glory, and he said to him, 'All these I will give you, if you will fall down and worship me.' Then Jesus said to him, 'Away with you, Satan! For it is written: Worship the Lord your God, and serve only him.' Then the devil left him, and suddenly angels came and waited on him (He had not eaten or slept for forty days and forty nights)."

One test for Master-hood, for one-ness with the Father principle, is absolute non-attachment in relation to the things of the manifested physical-world, which constitutes the impure realm; an absolute dis-interest even in all the kingdoms of the world. Only then the 'Father' allows one of its sons to become one with it, and to be able to wield the true power of the 'natural Will' which has arisen in him and which can sub-due and supersede the physical nature in its various aspects.

However, the path is not as simple as it looks, though straight. There can be many obstructions on the way—on the path of gaining to the Truth— like the kingdoms, the power, and the perks, waiting for those who begin to vacillate on the way, choosing to do the bidding of the devil instead.

The Reward

Jesus was tested by the Spirit only after he had come out of his Samadhi, or a trance called 'a fasting' by the apostle, which had lasted for a duration of forty days. His resolve was unwavering. The splendour of all the kingdoms of the world did not hold any charm for him in comparison to his resolve to stick to his nature, to the Truth into him (To a worldly person, this may appear a very difficult thing to do, but to one who is pure in heart, who has no malice against anyone, and who has seen his own real 'self', it may come of its own—naturally).

There was no outside devil to test Jesus. In fact, there could not be. As his unwavering meditation on his true nature—on his true self—matured and began to bear fruit, first he had to shift his identity from his physical body to his 'individual's astral body, carrying the memory of all his past incarnations as an individual. He would have been unable to do so, if any of the objects of the physical world had continued to hold interest of any kind for him. All that was the impure and the unreal part, which was separating him from the real or the pure, was required to be left behind (or was left behind of its own—naturally—for one pure in mind and of a firm resolve).

After having shifted his identification from his physical body to his astral, now Jesus could go for shifting his identity again; this time from his astral body of an individual to the astral body of the cosmic person. And once he succeeded in doing this, he would be in a position to see all persons and places forming parts of all other individuals' eternal bodies too, as himself—within himself, as the 'Father' of the cosmos itself. Further, as Jesus would be able to do so, now his 'Will' too would become one with the 'Will' of the Father. Jesus knew that it would achieve for him whatever he wanted in a moment. He did not, however, have any interest in ruler-ship of all the kingdoms of the world. He had already risen above the world; in a way also above thought.

Jesus had no interest in any of the super-powers that had been accruing to him, either; he had no wish to try to test any as well. He had won at all the tests the Father had put him through. He could now become 'one' with his Father, and at a time of his choosing, he would be able to proclaim, as he did: "I and my Father are One"—or as he would have said, had he been a rishi as successful as him, *"Aham Brahmasmi"* (I and the eternal Brahma are one). A Master is a Master, he is one with the 'Father'; he is no longer a Christian or of some other religion; he must be universally revered and heeded to too, if that should be possible, whatever the political or diplomatic protocols, the exigencies, or the economic and marketing strategies of the day may try to dictate.

Jesus had wanted to separate the sheepfold created by him, to keep clear of the evil ways of acting and the wrong ways of thinking; and he did succeed in what he had willed: doing extremely well. It was the 'will' of a Master who was one with the Father; not a curse or threat by a magician calling upon forces of the dark. This separation was considered necessary by Jesus then. However, it was provisional at that time. To save goodness and the mankind, and to contain evil and destruction, it now probably needs to be sealed and cemented as well.

The nations may want to sit and decide. He did not know the date and the hour, but he will send the signs, Jesus had said. And he seems to have sent the means as well in the form of the protocol required to be observed when a deadly virus is out to engulf everything; so, all that the nations need to do is, to sit and to decide; to begin to consider at least, if not make a beginning right-away that should be significant enough!

The Law of Diminishing Returns

Jesus was the self-sparkling gem among a very long list of prophets from the Biblical scripture; he was a true Master. No one in his time, or ever in those lands, was greater than him. And he was not the son of a son of Abraham really, but of Marry, the Virgin.

"For to everyone," said Jesus (Matthew 25:29—the parable of Talents), referring to allocation of the virtue, "who has will be given more, and he will have enough; but anyone who has not, will be deprived of even what he has." In fact, the virtue is neither given nor taken away by God. It is the natural tendency of the things that your savings add up and keep increasing and so do your debts unless these are repaid on time.

When, one's savings—if it should be too little—will manage to slip out of one's fingers, one may not even know! But if one has virtue in account, even though not in great abundance but enough to cushion the ups and downs usual to all, and even if one may have made a given number of mistakes or sins of a common nature, still one can retain one's frequent flier tag in and out of the kingdom of Heaven. After the death of its physical body, every soul is sucked into the astral world. The only option for a soul not to move to the astral plane, would be to remain in disembodied form on the physical plane as a good or bad spirit, that many people may call a 'ghost' (Please see, *Matter, Life and Spirit Demystified*).

On arrival in the astral world, the soul must undergo a quick life-review in the arrival lounge. Here, depending on the cushion of virtues, or their absence, it may or may not have to shift to the under-worlds, for a reform session—or to undergo harsh or very harsh punishment for short, medium or long durations; depending on the nature and the bulk of its evil karma. However, if it has a sufficient cushion, it remains on the Heaven side of the astral kingdom, where it can continue to enjoy the fruits of its merits, for short, medium or long durations, before being born again on the earth. It is able to enjoy an unhindered eternal life, even if the earth may cease to exist, or all life is wiped out from its surface by use of nuclear, chemical or biological weaponry by one or more of the 'countries' (as for the 'nations', we hope that no nation would want to do that, ever).

There is no death really, but two planes, a physical plane and an astral plane; while the fruits of karma can be good, very good or very-very bad.

There is lot of weeping and grinding of teeth in the hellish realms, and some of its sections are very-very scary or very dark. It is always better not to let one's virtues slip and vanish, but to maintain a fair cushion, so that one can make a private confession if one commits a sin, and should be able to hope, with a degree of confidence, to gain the pardon one seeks as well, so that the son of man is able to move from one pasture to another as suits him/her.

When Jesus says that one who 'has' will be given more, he also means that goodness will increase on the side it is there. The people on either side of the divide, who develop virtue, will be reborn among the virtuous when their time comes, reducing the goodness on the 'has not' side further. Likewise, those who stray more or who move out of the sheepfold, could be reborn on the other side, lightening the lending side in its evil content and further burdening the other.

A time may come when the other side has no virtue left. There will be no purpose served thereafter by keeping the door open, or keeping the divide provisional; and it can be firmed up first, and then it can be sealed. Ratios of living life on the Earth has been changed by the Nature before to make room for the higher species, who could take the evolution further ahead. It is the better suited, the more deserving, who have survived and not the larger and the stronger. The tiny mammals survived, while the dinosaurs perished to make room for the higher evolution.

One Cannot Move Out of One's Own Sight

It is a pity how the academic cartels work. The author feels surprised that such valuable a work as "The Proper Method of Reincarnation Therapy" by Trutz Hardo should be not already an acclaimed text-book in medicine and a part of recommended reading for every post-graduation student in psychiatry.

It is a common knowledge now among the successful regression therapists that developments taking place in a single lifetime are knowingly written by the subject on the slate or the file of his present life through the agency of its own un-conscious mind. They just get punched-in or recorded as they happen (no CCTVs or other recording devices need to be installed by Nature). Let us suppose that in a fresh instalment of renaissance, bypassing the classical opposition of modern medicine, regression therapy is now included by some universities, Mr. Trutz Hardo can still possibly be persuaded to guide at least a few early batches in that event. And that may be highly welcome and very-very significant.

Chapter 2

THE AQUARIAN GOSPEL
OF JESUS THE CHRIST

Chapter 1: Augustus Caesar reigned and Herod Antipas was ruler of Jerusalem. Three provinces comprised the land of Palestine: Judea, and Samaria, and Galilee. Joachim was a master of the Jewish law, a man of wealth; he lived in Nazareth of Galilee; and Anna, of the tribe of Judah, was his wife. To them was born a child, a goodly female child, and they were glad; and Mary was the name they gave the child. Joachim made a feast in honour of the child; but he invited not the rich, the honoured and the great; he called the poor the halt and the lame, the blind, and to each one he gave gift of raiment, food or other needful thing.

Now when the child was three years old her parents took her to Jerusalem, and in the temple, she received the blessings of the priests. The high priest was a prophet and a seer, and when he saw the child he said, 'behold the child will be the mother of an honoured prophet and a master of the law; she shall abide within this holy temple of the Lord.' And Mary did abide within the temple of the Lord; and Hillel, chief of the Sanhedrim, taught her all the precepts of Jews, and she delighted in the law of God. When Mary reached the age of womanhood she was betrothed to Joseph, son of Jacob, and a carpenter of Nazareth. And Joseph was an upright man, and a devoted Essenes.

Chapter 2: Near Hebron in the hills of Judah, Zacharias and Elizabeth abode. They were devout and just and every day they read the Law, the

Prophets and the Psalms which told of one to come, strong to redeem, and they were waiting for the king.

Now Zacharias was a priest, and in his turn, he led the temple service in Jerusalem. It came to pass as Zacharias stood before the Lord and burned the incense in the Holy Place, that Gabriel came and stood before his face. Gabriel said, "O man of Good, fear not; I bring to you and all the world a message of goodwill and peace on Earth. Behold, the Prince of Peace, the king you seek, will quickly come. Your wife will bear to you a son, a holy son, of whom the prophet wrote, 'Behold, I send Elijah unto you again before the coming of the Lord; and he will level down the hills and fill the valleys up, and pave the way for him who shall redeem.' From the beginning of the age your son has borne the name of John, the mercy of the Lord; his name is John. He will be honoured in the sight of God, and he will drink no wine, and from his birth he will be filled with Holy Breath." And Gabriel stood before Elizabeth as she was in the silence of her home and told her all the words that he had said to Zacharias in Jerusalem. When he had done the service of his course, the priest went home, and with Elizabeth rejoiced.

Five months passed by and Gabriel came to Mary in her home in Nazareth and said, "Hail Mary, hail! Once blessed in the name of God; twice blessed in the name of Holy Breath; thrice blessed in the name of Christ; for you are worthy, and will bear a son who shall be called Immanuel. His name is Jesus, for he saves his people from their sins." When Joseph's daily task was done, he came, and Mary told him all the words that Gabriel spoke to her, and they rejoiced; for they believed that he, the man of God, had spoken words of truth. And Mary went with haste to tell Elizabeth about the promises of Gabriel; together they rejoiced. And in the home of Zacharias and Elizabeth did Mary tarry ninety days; then she returned to Nazareth. To Zacharias and Elizabeth, a son was born.

Chapter 3: The time was nearly due for Jesus to be born, and Mary longed to see Elizabeth, and she and Joseph turned their faces towards the Judean hills. And when upon their way, they came to Bethlehem the day was done and they must tarry for the night. But Bethlehem was thronged with people going to Jerusalem, the inns and homes were filled with guests, and Joseph and his wife could find no place to rest, but in a cave where animals were kept; and there they slept.

At midnight came a cry, a child is born in a yonder cave among the beasts. And lo, the promised son of man was born. And strangers took the little one and wrapped him in the dainty robes that Mary had prepared and laid him in a trough from which the beasts of burden fed. Three persons clad in snow-white robes came in and stood before the child and said, "All strength, all wisdom and all love be yours, Immanuel!

Now, on the hills of Bethlehem were many flocks of sheep with shepherds guarding them. The shepherds were devout, were men of prayer, and they were waiting for a strong deliverer to come. And when the child of promise came, a man in snow-white robe appeared to them, and they fell back in fear. The man stood forth and said, "Fear not! Behold I bring you joyful news. At midnight in a cave in Bethlehem was born the prophet and the king that you have long been waiting for." ...And then the shepherds came with haste to Bethlehem and to the cave, that they might see and honour him whom men had called Immanuel.

Now, when the morning came, a shepherdess whose home was near, prepared a room for Mary, Joseph and the child; and here they tarried many days. And Joseph sent a messenger in haste to Zacharias and Elizabeth to say, 'The child is born in Bethlehem.' And Zacharias and Elizabeth took John and came to Bethlehem with words of cheer. And Mary and Elizabeth recounted all their wonderous things that had transpired. The people joined with them in praising God. According to the custom of the Jews, the child was circumcised; and when they asked, 'What will you call the child?' the mother said, 'His name is Jesus, as the man of God declared.'

Chapter 5: Beyond the river Euphrates the Magians lived; and they were wise, could read the language of the stars, and they divined that one, a master soul, was born; they saw his star above Jerusalem. And there were three among the Magian priests who longed to see the master of the coming age; and they took costly gifts and hastened to the West in search of him, the new-born king, that they might honour him. ...Now when the Magians reached Jerusalem, the people were amazed. ...And when they asked, 'Where is the child that has been born a king?' the very throne of Herod seemed to shake. And Herod sent a courtier forth to bring the Magians to his court. And when they came, they asked again, 'Where is the new-born king?' And then they said, 'While yet beyond the Euphrates, we saw his star arise, and we have come to honour him. …These Magian priests could read the hearts of men; they read the wickedness of Herod's heart, and knew that he had sworn to kill the new born king. And so, they told the secret to the parents of the child, and bid them flee beyond the reach of harm. And then the priests went on their homeward way; they went not through Jerusalem. …And Joseph took the infant Jesus and his mother in the night and fled to Egypt land, and with Elihu and Salome in ancient Zoan they abode.

Chapter 6: Now, when the Magian priests did not return to tell him of the child that had been born a king, King Herod was enraged. And then his courtiers told him of another child in Bethlehem, one born to go before and prepare the people to receive the king. He said, "Let no mistake be made, and that you may be sure to slay these claimants to my throne, slay all the male children in the town not yet two years of age". Elizabeth knew not that Herod sought to slay her son, and she and John were yet in Bethlehem; but when she knew, she took the infant John and hastened to the hills. The murderous guards were near; they pressed upon her hard; but then she knew the secret caves in all the hills, and into one she ran and hid herself and John until the guards were gone.

Their cruel task was done; the guards returned and told the story to the king. They said, 'We know that we have slain the infant king; but John his harbinger, we could not find. The king was angry with his guards because they failed to slay the infant John. He sent them to the tower in chains. And other guards were sent to Zacharias, father of the harbinger, while he was serving in the Holy Place, to say, 'The king demands that you shall tell where is your son.' But Zacharias did not know and he replied, 'I am a minister of God, a servant in the Holy Place; how could I know where they have taken him?' …Now, Zacharias stood before the altar in the Holy Place engaged in prayer. A guard approached and with a dagger thrust him through; he fell and died before the curtain of the sanctuary of the Lord.

(After a time) …Now Herod sat upon his throne; he did not seem to move; his courtiers came; the king was dead. His sons reigned in his stead.

Chapter 7: The son of Herod, Archelaus reigned in Jerusalem. He was a selfish, cruel king; he put to death all those who did not honour him. He called in council all the wisest men and asked about the infant claimant to his throne. The council said that John and Jesus both were dead; then he was satisfied.

Now Joseph, Mary and their son were down in Egypt in Zoan and John was with his mother in the Judean Hills. Elihu and Salome sent messengers in haste to find Elizabeth and John. They found them and they brought them to Zoan. Now Mary and Elizabeth were marvelling much because of their deliverance. Elihu said, 'It is not strange happenings; law governs all events. From olden times it was ordained that you should be with us, and in this sacred school be taught.'

Elihu and Salome took Mary and Elizabeth out to the sacred grove nearby where they were wont to teach. Elihu said to Mary and Elizabeth, "You may esteem yourself thrice blest, for you are chosen mothers of long promised sons who are ordained to lay in solid rock, a sure foundation-stone on which the temple of the perfect man shall rest—a temple that shall never be destroyed. ...We call these sons, Revealers of the Light; but they must have the light before they can reveal the light. And you must teach your sons, and set their souls on fire with love and holy zeal, and make them conscious of their missions to the sons of men. Teach them that God and man are one; but that through carnal thoughts and words and deeds, man tore himself away from God; debased himself. Teach that the Holy Breath would make them 'one' (with God) again, restoring harmony and peace."

Chapter 8: Again, Elihu met his pupils in the sacred grove, and said, "No man lives unto himself; for every living thing is bound by cords to every other living thing. Blessed, are the pure in heart; for they will love and not demand love in return. They will not do, to other men what they would not have other men do unto them.

There are two selves; the higher and the lower self. The higher self is human spirit clothed with soul, made in the form of God. The lower self, the carnal self, the body of desires, is a reflection of the higher self, distorted by the murky ethers of the flesh. The lower self is illusion, and will pass away; the higher self is God in man, and will not pass away. ...The lower-self breeds hatred, slander, lewdness, murders, theft, and everything that harms; the higher self is mother of the virtues and the harmonies of life. ...If man would find his saviour he must look within; and when the demon self has been dethroned, the saviour, Love, will be exulted to the throne of power."

Chapter 9: Salome taught the lesson of the day. "Before the worlds were formed all things were One, just Spirit, Universal Breath. And Spirit breathed, and that which was not manifest became the Fire and Thought of Heaven—the Father God, the Mother God. And when the Fire and Thought of heaven in union breathed, their son, their only son, was born. This son is Love whom men have called the Christ. Men call the Thought of heaven the Holy Breath. And when the Triune God breathed forth, lo, seven spirits stood before the throne. These are Elohim, creative spirits of the universe. And these are they who said, Let's make man; and in their image man was made. ...Now spirit loves the pure, the good, the true; the body of desires extols the selfish self; the soul becomes the battle ground between the two. And blessed is the man whose spirit is triumphant and whose lower self is purified; whose soul is cleansed."

Chapter 10: Elihu taught; he said, "In ancient times a people in the East were worshippers of God, the One, whom they called Brahm. Their laws were just; they lived in peace; they saw the light within; they walked in wisdom's way. But priests with carnal aims arose, who changed the laws to suit the carnal mind; bound heavy burdens on the poor, and scorned the rules of right; and so, the Brahms became corrupt. But in darkness of the age a few great masters stood unmoved; they loved the name of Brahm; they were great beacon lights before the world. And they preserved inviolate the wisdom of their holy Brahm, and you may read the wisdom in their sacred books.

"And in Chaldea, Brahm was known. A pious Brahm named Terah lived in Ur; his son was so devoted to the Brahmic faith that he was called A-Brahm; and he was set apart to be the father of the Hebrew race. ...In Persia Brahm was known and feared. Men saw him as the One, the causeless Cause of all that is and he was sacred unto them. ...In course of time a lofty soul, whom men called Zarathustra, came in flesh. ...And Persia is the Magian land where live the priests who saw the star arise to mark the place where Mary's son was born, and were the first to greet him as the Prince of Peace.

Chapter 11: Again, Elihu taught; he said, "The Indian priests became corrupt. Brahm was forgotten in the streets, the rights of men were trampled in the dust. And a mighty master came, a Buddha of enlightenment, who turned away from wealth and all the honours of the world, and found the Silence in the quiet groves and caves, and he was blest. …Buddha spoke, '…He is greater man who conquers self than he who kills a thousand men in war."

Chapter 12: Salome was the first to speak, "Behold the sun! It manifests the power of God who speaks to us through sun and moon and stars; through mountain, hill and vale; through flower, and plant and tree. …It is not prayer to shout at God, to stand, or sit, or kneel and tell him all about sins of men. It is not prayer to tell the Holy One how great he is, how good he is, how strong and how compassionate. God is not man to be bought up by praise of man. Prayer is the ardent wish that every way of life be light; that every act be crowned with good; that every living thing be prospered by our ministry. A noble deed, a helpful word is prayer; a fervent, and effectual prayer."

And then Elihu spoke. He said to Mary and Elizabeth, "Our words are said; you need not tarry longer here; the call has come; the way is clear; you may return unto your native land. A mighty work is given you to do; you shall direct the minds that will direct the world. Your sons are set apart to lead men up to righteous thoughts, and words and deeds; to make men know the sinfulness of sin; to lead them from the adoration of the lower self, and all illusive things, and make them conscious of the self that lives with Christ in God. In preparation for their work your sons must walk in many thorny paths."

Now, Mary, Joseph and Elizabeth with Jesus and his harbinger, set forth upon their homeward way. They went not by Jerusalem, for Archelaus reigned. They journeyed by the Bitter Sea, and when they reached Engedi hills they rested in the home of Joshua, a near of kin; and here Elizabeth and John abode. But Joseph, Mary and their son went by the Jordan way, and after certain days they reached their home in Nazareth.

Chapter 13: Elizabeth was blest. She spent her time with John, and gave to him the lessons that Elihu and Salome had given her. And John delighted in the wilderness of his home and in the lessons that he learned. Now in the hills were many caves. The cave of David was a-near in which the Hermit of Engedi lived. This hermit was Matheno, priest of Egypt, master from the temple of Sakara. When John was seven years of age Matheno took him to the wilderness and in the cave of David they abode. Matheno taught, and John was thrilled with what the master said, and day by day Matheno opened up to him the mysteries of life. John loved the wilderness; he loved his master and his simple fare. Their food was fruits, and nuts, wild honey and the carob bread. Matheno was an Israelite, and he attended all the Jewish feasts.

When John was nine years old Matheno took him to a great feast in Jerusalem. The wicked Archelaus had been deposed and exiled to a distant land because of selfishness and cruelty, and John was not afraid. John was delighted with his visit to Jerusalem. Matheno told him all about the service of the Jews; the meaning of their rites.

(However,) John could not understand how sin could be forgiven by killing animals and birds and burning them before the Lord. Matheno said, 'The God of heaven and earth does not require sacrifice. This custom with its cruel rites was borrowed from the idol worshippers of other lands. No sin was ever blotted out by sacrifice of animal, of bird, or man. …Return and purify your hearts by love and righteousness and you shall be forgiven. This is the burden of the message that the harbinger shall bring to men".

'What is forgiveness?' John enquired. Matheno said, 'It is the paying up of debts. A man who wrongs another man can never be forgiven until he rightens the wrong. The Vedas say that none can right the wrong but him who does the wrong."

Chapter 15: When John was twelve years old his mother died, and neighbours laid her body in a tomb among her kindred in the Hebron burying ground and near to Zacharias' tomb. And John was deeply grieved; he wept.

Matheno said, "It is not well to weep because of death. …let your mother rest in peace. Just let her noble life be strength and inspiration unto you. A crisis in your life has come, and you must have a clear conception of the work that you are called to do. The sages of the ages call you harbinger. The prophets look to you and say, 'He is Elijah come again'. In infancy the vow for you was made and you became a Nazarite. The razor shall not touch your face nor head, and you shall taste not wine nor fiery drinks.

And in the river Jordan, John was washed; then they returned unto the wilderness. Now in Engedi's hills Matheno's work was done and he and John were down to Egypt. They rested not until they reached the temple of Sakara in the valley of the Nile. For many years Matheno was a master in this temple of the Brotherhood, and when he told, about the life of John and of his mission to them, the sons of men, the hierophant with joy received the harbinger and he was called a Brother-Nazarite.

Chapter 16: The home of Joseph was on Marmion Way in Nazareth; here Mary taught her son the lessons of Elihu and Salome. And Jesus greatly loved the Vedic and the Avesta; but more than all he loved to read the Psalms of David and the pungent words of Solomon. The Jewish books of prophecy were his delight; and when he reached his seventh year, he needed not the books to read, for he had fixed in memory every word. Joachim and his wife, grandparents of child Jesus, made a feast in honour of the child, and all their near of kin were guests.

Joachim said, "My son, today you pass the seventh milestone of your life, for you are seven years of age, and we will give to you, as a remembrance of this day, whatever you desire; choose that which will afford you most delight." And Jesus said, 'I do not want a gift, for I am satisfied. If I could make a multitude of children glad upon this day I would be greatly pleased. Now, there are many hungry boys and girls in Nazareth who would be pleased to eat with us this feast and share with us the pleasures of this day. The richest gift that you can give to me is your permission to go out and find these needy ones and bring them here that they may feast with us.' Joachim said, "It's well; go out and find the needy boys and girls and bring them here; we will prepare enough for all."

And Jesus didn't wait; he ran; he entered every dingy hut and cabin of the town; he did not waste his words; he told his mission everywhere. And in a little time one hundred and three-score of happy, ragged boys and girls were following him up Marmion Way. The guests made way; the banquet hall was filled with Jesus' guests, and Jesus and his mother helped to serve. And there was food enough for all, and all were glad; and so, the birthday gift of Jesus was a crown of righteousness.

Chapter 17: Now, Rabbi Barachia of the synagogue of Nazareth, was aid to Mary in the teaching of her son. …And Rabbi Barachia said (to Jesus), "Your words are seasoned with the salt of wisdom that is from above. Who is the teacher who has opened up this truth to you?" …Now, in the evening Jesus and his mother sat alone, and Jesus said, 'The rabbi seems to think that God is partial in his treatment of the sons of men; that Jews are favoured and are blest above all other men. I do not see how God can have his favourites and be just. Are not Samaritans and Greeks and Romans just as much the children of the Holy One as are the Jews? I think the Jews have built a wall about themselves, and they see nothing on the other side of it. ...I want to go from Jewry land and meet my kin in other countries of my Fatherland."

Chapter 18: The great feast of the Jews was on, and Joseph, Mary and their son, and many of their kin, went to Jerusalem. The child was ten years old. And Jesus watched the butchers kill the lambs and birds and burn them on the altar in the name of God. His tender heart was shocked at this display of cruelty; he asked the serving priest, 'What is the purpose of this slaughter of the beasts and birds? Why do you burn their flesh before the Lord?'

But Jesus heeded not his (priest's) taunts; he went to Hillel, chief of the Sanhedrim, and he said to him, "Rabboni, I would like to talk with you; I am disturbed about this service of the pascal feast. I thought the temple was the house of God where love and kindness dwell. Do you not hear the bleating of those lambs, the pleading of those doves that men are killing over there? Do you not smell that awful stench that comes from burning flesh?" ...But Hillel could not give an answer to the child. His heart was stirred with sympathy. He called the child to him; he laid his hand upon his head and wept.

Hillel said within himself, 'This child is surely prophet sent from God.' Then Hillel sought the parents of the child, and asked that Jesus might abide with them, and learn the precepts of the law, and all the lessons of the temple priests. His parents gave consent, and Jesus did abide within the holy temple in Jerusalem, and Hillel taught him every day. And every day the master learned from Jesus many lessons of the higher life. The child remained with Hillel in the temple for a year, and then returned unto his home in Nazareth; and there he wrought with Joseph as a carpenter.

Chapter 19: Again, the great feast in Jerusalem was on, and Joseph, Mary and their son were there. The child was twelve years old. And there were Jews and proselytes from many countries in Jerusalem. And Jesus sat among the priests and doctors in the temple hall. And Jesus opened up a book of prophecy and read, "… And Israel has gone far astray; has not regarded justice, nor the rights of man, and God demands that Israel shall reform, and turn again to ways of holiness. And if our people will not hear the voice of God, lo, nations from afar will come and sack Jerusalem, and tear our temple down, and take our people captive into foreign lands." …When Jesus had thus said, he stepped aside, and all the people were amazed and said, 'This surely is the Christ.' (Readers, kindly take note that Jesus was reading from the Jewish scripture only, and among the Jews. Author requests that no offence may kindly be taken by any soul if incidents from old Bible are cited and they seem to be in bad light. Regression therapy works on the principle that if a scarry event that happened in the past is briefly relived by a person with an otherwise inexplicable phobia during a hypnotic trance, the phobia gets cured and the recurring pain etc. goes away for ever. Discussing the mistakes of mankind, including a people, is like reliving those events and then the scars can go away for ever. The slate shall become cleaned).

Chapter 20: The great feast of the pasch was ended and the Nazarenes were journeying towards their homes. And they were in Samaria, and Mary said, 'Where is my son?' No one had seen the boy. And Joseph sought among their kindred who were on their way to Galilee; but they had seen him not. Then Joseph, Mary, and a son of Zebedee, returned and sought through all Jerusalem, but they could find him not. And then they went up to the temple courts and asked the guards, 'Have you seen Jesus, a fair-haired boy, with deep blue eyes, twelve years of age, about these courts?' The guards replied, 'Yes, he is in the temple now disputing with the doctors of the law.'

And they went in, and found him as the guards had said. And Mary said, 'Why Jesus, why do you treat your parents thus? Lo, we have sought two days for you. We feared that some great harm had overtaken you.' And Jesus said, 'Do you not know that I must be about my Father's work?' But he went round and pressed the hand of every doctor of the law and said, I trust that we may meet again. And then he went forth with his parents on their way to Nazareth; and when they reached their home he wrought with Joseph as a carpenter.

One day as he was bringing forth the tools for work, he said, "These tools remind me of the ones we handle in the workshop of the mind where things were made of thought and where we build up character. We use the square to measure all our lines, to straighten out the crooked places of the way, and make the corners of our conduct square. We use the compass to draw circles round our passions and desires to keep them in the bounds of righteousness. We use the axe to cut away the knotty, useless and ungainly parts and make the character symmetrical. We use the hammer to drive home the truth, and pound it in until it is a part of every part. We use the plane to smooth the rough, uneven surfaces of joint, and block, and board, that go to build the temple for the truth. The chisel, line, the plummet and the saw all have their uses in the workshop of the mind.

"And then this ladder with its trinity of steps—faith, hope and love—on it we climb up to the dome of purity in life. And on the twelve-step ladder we ascend until we reach the pinnacle of that which life is spent to build—the temple of perfected man." (The twelve-step ladder of perception in the manifest awareness—of increasingly sublime stages in the thought of God manifesting as his son, and as the world—has been explained in the book *Jesus Christ and the Spirit of Truth*).

Chapter 21: A royal prince of India, Ravanna of Orissa in the south, was at the Jewish feast. Ravanna was a man of wealth; and he was just, and with a band of Brahmic priests sought wisdom in the West. When Jesus stood among the Jewish priests and read and spoke, Ravanna heard and was amazed. And when he asked who Jesus was, from whence he came and what he was, chief Hillel said, '…' Ravanna was entranced, and asked to know the way to Nazareth, that he might go and honour such a one as son of God.

He found the object of his search engaged in building dwellings for the sons of men. And when he first saw Jesus, he was climbing up a twelve-step ladder, and he carried in his hands a compass, square and axe. Ravanna said, 'All hail, most favoured son of heaven! And at the inn Ravanna made a feast for all the people of the town; and Jesus and his parents were honoured guests. For certain days Ravanna was a guest in Joseph's home on Marmion Way; he sought to learn the secret of the wisdom of the son, but it was all too great for him. And then he asked that he might be the patron of the child; might take him to the East where he could learn the wisdom of the Brahms. And Jesus longed to go that he might learn; and after many days his parents gave consent.

JESUS ARRIVES IN INDIA

Then, with proud heart, Ravanna with his train (of carts), began the journey towards the rising sun; and after many days they crossed the Sind, and reached the province of Orissa, and the palace of the prince. The Brahmic priests were glad to welcome home the prince; with favour they received the Jewish boy. And Jesus was accepted as a pupil in the temple Jagannath; and here learned the Vedas and the Manic laws, according to Levi H. Dowling.

The Brahmic masters wondered at the clear conceptions of the child, and often were amazed when he explained to them the meaning of the laws. That Jesus should have been able to grasp the essentials of the Upanishadic teachings rather easily, was only to be expected. His sharp intellect, his earlier achievements in surprising even the most learned in his homeland, and his keen desire to learn the most sublime, everything favoured his gaining mastery in the basic truths, which are otherwise simple to understand, if one's mind was unencumbered and clean.

The next step is practicing the truths that have been intellectually understood, making best use of the very special body structure the humans are endowed with. Unless someone was lucky to straightway start practising under an accomplished yogi, often there is a first guru, then another and then, possibly, a third also, since progress in practised yoga is very rapid if the guru himself should be an accomplished master. Usually, the practice must continue for ten to twelve years, before perfection can be gained. Thereafter, those whose minds remain pure and whose resolve remains firm and un-wavered, can gain perfection, or oneness with the 'Father' aspect. Jesus is said to have remained at Jagannath Puri for several years, learning, besides also engaging himself in the practice of yoga. Then he began to develop conflicts with the local priesthood.

Since earliest of the times and at least since before 3,000 B.C., the Indian populace was comprised of different classes and creeds of people engaged in different kind of activities, speaking several languages, having varied food habits, practising varied standards of hygiene and to an extent also varying in builds. It was a heterogeneous mix of people in the process of evolving as a nation. Apart from hygiene, food habits, and education, usually similar people engaged themselves in similar work. In the earliest times, the division arose naturally out of engagement in different work without being defined. There was a teachers' class which produced most of the rishis and which came to be known as the Brahmins. Then there was a warrior class which defended the borders and fought wars and which produced a majority of the kings. And there were other people engaged in trade, farming and manual work. In time, the trading community too grew to become distinct as against the others, and a class in itself.

The society came to be divided in four distinct classes in due time. Possibly, it all began with the Brahminic notion of a pure mind into a pure body, and the succeeding generations took it to heart. The Brahmin were very particular that the food they partook must be cooked after the cook had taken a bath, that no one could serve food, or eat before washing his hands and rinsing his mouth, and so on, besides what they would eat and what they must not. In fact, in those early times, some of the Brahmins took food only once a day, and so on, too. Initially the division was based on work and not lineage. In later time, at the initiative of the Brahmins, it took the form of a caste system and, kind of, came to be frozen. Some people actually took it to the extreme as well, especially after the population grew, when rishis were far and few between and the families had taken over. Some of the Brahmins would even take a bath afresh to keep themselves pure if they were even touched by a lower cast person. In the evolving social set-up, persons from the lowest class, called the 'sudra', kind of, naturally began to be treated like untouchable ones.

The first million B.C. had commenced by then, and at that point of time, not only the Brahmin teachers will not impart education to the lowest class, they even tried to bar it from reading itself of the scriptures. It was a pity that a silly Brahmin boy lacking even basic knowledge of Upanishad could be invited to auspicious feasts and other celebrations now, to deserve gifts and respect from the other castes, whereas a *sudra* was barred from even gaining knowledge of the scriptures. The scriptures, as if, belonged not to the humanity as a whole as proclaimed by the rishis, but only to their progeny (like the copy right laws that prevail now, and like patents being obtained by pharma companies on the herbs growing free in the nature and with their properties being well-known for thousands of years). Only the other higher castes—literate or illiterate, even dishonest or less unkempt in body, and less pure in mind than some of those that were thus barred—who practically financed the Brahmins, were now approved by them as worthy to gain access to the scriptures. For sure, not everyone among the brotherhood of the learned Brahmins would have approved the protocol that became popular, and that became kind of mechanical too. They could not, however, choose to fight, as Jesus had taken upon himself to do, and that is why Jesus was so special.

It was the growing discontent among the really wise and intelligent, which made two princes from the warrior class, who favoured reforms, to come forward—both in the sixth century B.C. and even overlapping each other in contemporary terms. Bhagwan Mahavir (Jin), who propagated Jainism was first, while Gautam, the Buddha, followed him in quick succession. Neither of these two, trying to bring in reforms, barred anyone from joining their Faith. However, Jainism is now confined mostly to the trading community or the Vaisya caste. As for Buddhism, the score is known to everyone.

The original Sanatan Dharma, practised by all the people, divided into four castes, led by the Brahmin, was able to bounce back during the centuries that followed, however. It could regain its ground since it was simple; it was more in conformity with the way the people wanted to live in accordance with their basic natures. This was the scenario, nevertheless, when Jesus first visited Jagannath Puri and then Varanasi.

It may be noteworthy, however, that while the improvisation, and a self-chosen and possibly incomplete portfolio, in place of 'a reform from within', was in order, and it has never been the way of the Sanatan, the natural one, to oppose any such proposals to branch out, it remains a fact that all of the hundred-plus siddhas or masters, who are known to have become one with 'Father' or the 'Mother' principles since then, have come to fore only on the side of Sanatan dharma, the original and eternal side only. In fact, the great yogi Milarepa among the Tibetans too, in a way, besides the Buddhist concepts on the nature of the reality, pursued the path shown by Sanatan dharma only.

Both Jain and the Buddhist religions initially focussed on ultimate salvation through hard means, and although even today great teachers continue to arise, a majority of the followers in both these religions, in time, are known to have settled for softer and greatly diluted versions of their original formats.

Jesus was not only a great teacher in making at the time, he was also a great revolutionary who refused to accept any inequity and injustice, and for him it mattered little whether he was in his homeland or was abroad. From Jagannath Puri, Jesus travelled to other parts of Orissa, and after having a tiff with the Brahmins there, he first travelled to Bihar and then to Varanasi, which was one of the most important centres for learning in those days. Here too he incurred the wrath of the Brahmin priests, trying to teach the '*sudras*', and speaking about and advocating natural justice and equity. At one time, the Brahmin priests in Varanasi became as opposed to him and as angered, as the Jewish priest would become in due course, after his return to Israel and Jerusalem. At Varanasi, among other things, according to Levi H. Dowling, "Jesus was accepted as a pupil by Udraka, greatest of the Hindu healers. Udraka taught him the uses of the waters, plants and earths; of heat and cold; sunshine and shade; of light and dark."

After spending several years at Varanasi, Jesus moved to the Himalayan regions via Nepal. It was either at Varanasi or in Nepal that Jesus may have come into contact with an exalted Nath Guru, Chetan Nath as well.

Chapter 47: And Jesus came to Egypt land and all was well. He tarried not upon the coast; he went at once to Zoan, home of Elihu and Salome, who five and twenty years before had taught his mother in their sacred school. And there was joy when these three met. When last the son of Mary saw these sacred groves, he was a babe. And now a man grown strong by buffeting of every kind; a teacher who had stirred the multitudes in many lands. And Jesus told the aged teachers all about his life; about his journeyings in foreign lands; about the meetings with the masters and about his kind receptions by the multitudes. ...And Jesus stayed in Zoan many days.

JOHN, THE BAPTIST

Chapter 61: It came to pass when John the son of Zacharias and Elizabeth, had finished all his studies in the Egyptian schools that he returned to Hebron, where he abided for certain days. And then he sought wilderness and made his home in David's cave where, many years before, he was instructed by the Egyptian sage. Some people called him Hermit of

Engedi; and others said, 'He is the Wild Man of the Hills'. He clothed himself with skins of beasts; his food was carobs, honey, nuts and fruits. When John was thirty years of age he went into Jerusalem, and in the market place he sat in silence for seven days. The common people and the priests, the scribes and Pharisees came out in multitudes to see the silent hermit of the hills; but none were bold enough to ask him who he was. But when his silent fast was done he stood forth in the midst of all and said, "Prepare, O Israel, prepare to meet your king." And that was all he said, and then he disappeared, and no one knew where he had gone (as Elijah was known to do, too).

And after certain days he came again into the market place, and all the city came to hear him speak; he said: "Be not disturbed, you rulers of the state; the coming king is no antagonist; he seeks no place on any earthly throne. He comes as the Prince of Peace, the king of righteousness and love; his kingdom is within the soul. The eyes of men shall see it not and none can enter but the pure in heart. Prepare, O Israel, prepare to meet your king." Again, the hermit disappeared, the people strove to follow him, but he had drawn a veil about his form and men could see him not.

A Jewish feast day came; Jerusalem was filled with Jews and proselytes from every part of Palestine, and John stood in the temple court and said, "Prepare, O Israel, prepare to meet your king. Lo, you have lived in sin; the poor cry in your streets, and you regard them not. Your neighbours, who are they? You have defrauded friend and foe alike. You worship God with voice and lip; your hearts are far away, and set on gold. Your priests have bound upon the people burdens far too great to bear; the priests live in ease upon the hard-earned wages of the poor. Your lawyers, doctors, scribes are useless cumberers of the ground, they are but tumours on the body of the state; They toil not, neither do they spin, yet they consume the profits of your marts of trade. Your rulers are adulterers, extortioners and thieves, regarding not the rights of any man…" He said no more; he left the court and no one saw him go.

…But many people followed him as far as Bethany, and there he tarried at the home of Lazarus, his kin. The anxious people gathered all about the home and would not go; then John came forth and said, "Reform, O Israel, reform; prepare to meet your king. The sins of Israel do not all lie at the door of priests and scribes. O think you not that all sinners of Judea are found among rulers and the men of wealth. It is no sign that man is good and pure because he lives in want. The listless, shiftless vagabonds of earth are mostly poor and have to beg for bread. I saw the very men that cheered because I told the priests and scribes of their injustice unto man—throw stones and beat poor Justice in the streets. I saw them trample on the poor dead bird of Righteousness; And you who follow after me, you commoners, are not one whit behind the scribes and priests in crime. Reform, you men of Israel; the king has come; prepare to meet your king." With Lazarus and his sisters, John remained for certain days.

Chapter 64: The news reached Galilee, and Jesus with the multitude went down to where the harbinger was preaching at the ford. When Jesus saw the harbinger, he said, 'Behold the man of God! Behold the greatest of the seers! Behold, Elijah has returned! …When John saw Jesus standing with the throng he said, 'Behold the king who cometh in the name of God!' And Jesus said to John, 'I would be washed in water as a symbol of the cleansing of the soul.' And John replied, 'You do not need to wash, for you are pure in thought, and word, and deed. And if you need to wash, I am not worthy to perform the rite.'

And Jesus said, 'I come to be a pattern for the sons of men, and what I bid them do, that I must do; and all men must be washed, symbolic of the cleansing of the soul. This washing we establish as a rite—baptism rite we call it now, and so it shall be called. Your work, prophetic harbinger, is to prepare the way, and to reveal the hidden things. The multitudes are ready for the words of life, and I come to be made known by you to all the world, as prophet of the Triune God, and as the chosen one to manifest the Christ to men.' Then John led Jesus into the river at the ford and he baptised him in the sacred name of him who sent him forth to manifest the Christ to men. And as they came out of the stream, the Holy Breath, in form of dove, came down and sat on Jesus' head.

Chapter 85: Herod Antipas, the tetrarch of Paraca and of Galilee was dissipated, selfish and tyrannical. He drove his wife away from home that he might take as wife Herodias, the wife of one, a near of kin, a woman like himself—immoral and unjust. The city of Tiberius, upon the shores of Galilee, was Herod's home. Now John, the harbinger, had left the Salim Springs to teach the people by the sea of Galilee; and he rebuked the wicked ruler and his stolen wife for all their sins. Herodias was enraged because the preacher dared accuse her and her husband of their crimes; And she prevailed on Herod to arrest the harbinger and cast him in a dungeon in the castle of Machaerus that stood beside the Bitter Sea; And Herod did as she required.

When it was known that John had been imprisoned by the tetrarch court, the friends of Jesus thought it best that he should not remain in Galilee. But Jesus said I have no need to fear; my time has not yet come; no man can slay me till my work is done. …And when my work is done the rulers will do unto me, what they have done to John, and more.

And Jesus said, "No prophet is received with honour by the people of his native land; and prophets are not sent to everyone. Elijah was a man of God; he had the power and he closed the gates of heaven, and it did not rain for forty months; and when he spoke the Word, the rain came on the earth brought forth again." The author will like to draw the attention of the readers at this point. After spending forty years in study and silent meditation, Dowling, a Church of Christ pastor, and a close student of the different religions, had been able to gain to a stage of spiritual consciousness that permitted him to enter the domain of superfine ethers and become familiar with their mysteries. And yet, while writing his Gospel, he could have turned himself easily into a common scribe with his own biases and preferences.

Without applying his matured judgement, Dowling, seems to have just copied and pasted this particular praise of Elijah, from the Old Testament itself; Else, he would not have failed to take notice of the glaring contradiction. Ahab, the king of Israel had married Jezebel, daughter of the king of Sidonians, which the brotherhood of prophets disapproved. Besides, steeped in evils of all kinds, the brotherhood of the time had very little real contact with Elijah, the man of God. Had it been within their powers, they would never have appointed Elijah as the prophet. The test whether he was a man of God or not would be simple. In the very next line from where we have diverted, Dowling has mentioned the widow whose dead son was brought to life by Elijah. Even assuming that siding with the brotherhood, Elijah was displeased with king Ahab, it should be unimaginable that out of his displeasure with the king, the man of God would have stopped rains for forty months causing deaths, hunger and extreme hardship for so many people. God does not confer power on ordinary people, governed by anger or bias, to return the life to a dead. Only those who are really and highly evolved can do this. It would seem more reasonable to read that Elijah had journeyed to warn Ahab of the impending danger, so that he could ready himself to face the calamity by preserving whatever resources lay under his control, and not to pronounce a curse on him. God and the Truth belong to all people. It is far easier to steal from the House of God and the Truth than from a person of the world who could offer a resistance. Even billionaires on way to become trillionaires may find it hard to resist a temptation. It may not be the right place, however, to cite an example.

Chapter 117: A royal feast was held in honour of the birthday of the tetrarch in fortified Machaerus, east of the Bitter Sea. The tetrarch, Herod, and his wife Herodias, together with Salome were there; and all the men and women of the royal court were there. And when the feast was done, lo, all the guests and courtiers were drunk with wine; they danced and leaped about like children in their play.

Salome, daughter of Herodias, came in and danced before the king. The beauty of her form, her grace and winning ways entranced the silly Herod, then half-drunk with wine. He called the maiden to his side and said, Salome, you have won my heart, and you may ask and I will give you anything you wish. The maiden ran in childish glee and told her mother what the ruler said. Her mother said, "Go back and say, 'Give me the head of John, the harbinger'." The maiden ran and told the ruler what she wished.

And Herod called the trustee executioner and said to him, "Go to the tower and tell the keeper that by my authority you come to execute the prisoner known as John." The man went forth and in a little while returned, and on a platter bore the lifeless head of John. And Herod offered it unto the maiden in the presence of the guests. The maiden stood aloof; her innocence was outraged when she saw the bloody gift, and she would touch it not. Her mother, steeped and hardened well in crime, came up and took the head and held it up before the guests and said, 'This is the fate of every man who dares to scorn, or criticise, the acts of him who reigns.'

The drunken rabble gazed upon the gruesome sight with fiendish joy. The head was taken back unto the tower. The body had been given unto holy men who had been friends of John; they placed it in a burial case and carried it away. They bore it to the Jordan, which they crossed just at the ford where John first preached the word; and through the passes of the Judean hills, they carried it. They reached the sacred grounds near Hebron, where the bodies of the parents of the harbinger lay in their tombs; and there they buried it; and then they went their way.

The Sermon on the Mount and Afterward

Chapter 96: "And when men make a God of stone or wood or clay, they make an image of a shade; and they who worship at the shrine of shades are shades (This is a fact anyway. Rishis called it Maya. Einstein called it relativity. Even the bodies of men are shades, really, built by atoms and molecules forming a part of an extending food chain. The real thing lies within. On the outside, there is reflected light and there are shades, made of clay, stone, wood or even the food chain). So, God in mercy said (Yahweh, the God said), 'You shall not carve out images of wood, or clay, or stone. Such idols are ideals, abased ideals, and men can gain no higher plane than their ideals'."

In the Old Testament, we can see that whatever suits the prophets, or the priests or even their appointees, exactly same instructions are given by God, Yahweh, occasionally first, and later almost on a day-to-day basis. Usually only the prophet is able to hear what the God says, but there are times when the appointees of the brotherhood of prophets are also able to hear the commands or the advice. Everything worth a mention in the Old Testament seemingly happened on explicit commands of God.

In the New Testament, however, the authors of the gospels have confined themselves to reporting only what Jesus had said or he had appeared to be conveying, keeping their own opinions to themselves. In Aquarian Gospel, however, at several places, we see the scribe succumbing to his temptations. Here too, most of the words ascribed to Jesus, seem to have been put into his mouth, by the author of the Aquarian Gospel. Jesus was no fan of idol worship, there is little doubt. However, such direct condemnation of idol making or worship of God through such means as idols, etc. neither matches the character of Jesus, nor his words. Inter-alia, it may possibly be such temptation hard to resist by a scribe, doctor or priest, etc., that may have led to Matthew 7:3-5, where Jesus said, "Why do you see the speck in your neighbour's eye, but do not notice the log in your own eye? Or how can you say to your neighbour, 'Let me take the speck out of your eye,' while the log is in your own eye? You hypocrite! First take the log out of your own eye, and then you will see clearly to take the spec out of your neighbour's eye."

There is a genotype that each of us possesses, which is based on our genetic material or the DNA. Besides, we are also known to display a character based on our phenotype, which is characteristic of our upbringing or the surroundings amidst which we grow (including the academics and the other education through the clerics etc., or by real life situations, we may have been provided with). The followers of Yahweh, took pride in calling their God as a jealous God. Post their Egyptian days, and for nearly a millennium thereafter—whenever putting to sword one or more of the idol-worshippers, they seldom failed to curb their display of delight, triumph and glee. The writings of Philo would seem to convey such impression.

Even when the genotype remains the same, the phenotype may change, and it may change either way, for better or for the worse. With rise of Christianity, the Jews had begun to mellow down in their approach toward the idol worshipper. A new denomination, as far as the phenotype is concerned, came to arise to take the place vacated by them, and for close to a millennium of their own, they continued to kill and plunder the idol worshipper, destroying their temples and places of leaning, burning their libraries and abducting their women. Luckily for the mankind, the new denomination may also be now on way to losing its extra steam, except in certain territories. On the other hand, most of the mankind is now inclined favourably towards the Jewish community. In this book we quote extensively from the Old Testament since on one hand we can do so without being accused of blasphemy, while on the other, in a way, it is also leading to the Second Coming. The idea of the author is not to discuss a people but a past, since it is this past that is leading to our present, and since there is a crying need to reform, the way some people are accustomed to think and to behave. This book itself, in a way and as a matter of fact, is a tribute to the steadiness and valour displayed by President Zelensky of Ukraine of the Jewish faith, in the face of an uncalled for and unnecessary invasion of his country.

Again, had Jesus been so much opposed to worship of idols, or so particular as to how the God must be worshipped and prayed to, he would not have mentioned a Paraclete (a commoner known by his function, and not by his material worth, a position of power, or any other credential), whom God, the Father, would send to reveal the spirit of truth. In particular, he would never have said, "the coming of the Son of Man will be like lightning striking in the East (known for promoting the worship of idols) and flashing far into the West". He would, rather, have waited for it to strike in the West first and then travel Eastward to teach the idol worshippers the things they didn't know (like the art of digging a hole into a stone Shiva-lingam, representing the formless one that can take any form, trying to convert it into the look alike of a fountain). However, as for the day, it was neither known to the angles in the heaven, nor to the son of man, only the Father knew.

Likewise, it would be absurd to presuppose that one fine morning, all of a sudden, everyone will start striving to pursue or worship the abstract that cannot be seen but which does exist. At the moment, even the essence of the Spirit is not widely known, and yet the bulk of the humanity must find its own convenient way to connect to God on a day-to-day basis. If it is easier to so connect through an image or an idol of clay, wood, metal or stone etc., why not let or allow the ordinary folk who are comfortable at it to do so and to also live—why they need to be put to sword or get beheaded by people taking pride in their descent from Abraham—himself a holy and pious person, completely incapable of such atrocity?

The next sentence in Chapter 96 of the Aquarian Gospel, viz., "The God is Spirit men must worship, if they would attain a consciousness of God" would seem to be nearly unblemished and in order, however. This only points out the goal, and does not condemn; it leaves the choice with the people. People may or may not choose to strive, and they may elect to strive at their own time. Again, if they turn spirit-ward after the logic behind a particular idol is explained to them, and the time being opportune it becomes registered into their being, in place of going over their heads, it deserves to be pardoned by the more-mighty and more-righty.

Chapter 132: A multitude of people thronged the streets. The officers were on the way to court with one, a man accused of stealing bread. And in a little while the man was brought before the judge to answer to the charge. And Jesus and the twelve were there. The man showed in his face and hands the hard drawn lines of toil and want. A woman richly clad, the accuser of the man, stood forth and said, I caught this man myself: I know him well, for yesterday he came to beg for bread. And when I drove him from my door, he should have known that I would harbour not a man like him; and then today he came and took the bread. He is a thief and I demand that he be sent to jail. The servants also testified against the man; he was adjudged a thief, and officers were leading him away.

But Jesus standing forth exclaimed, 'You officers and judge, be not in haste to lead this man away'. Is this a land of justice and of the right? Can you accuse and sentence men to punishment for any crime until they testify themselves? The Roman law will not permit such travesty on right, and I demand that you permit this man to speak.' And then the judge recalled the man and said, 'If you have any tale to tell, say on.'

In tears the man stood forth and said, 'I have a wife and little ones and they are perishing for bread, and I have told my story oft, and begged for the bread; but none would hear. This morning when I left our cheerless hut in search of work my children cried for bread, and I resolved to feed them or to die. I took the bread, and I appeal to God, Was it a crime? This woman snatched the bread away and threw it to the dogs, and called the officers and I am here. Good people, do with me whatever you will, but save my wife and little ones from death.'

Then Jesus said, "Who is the culprit in this case? I charge this woman as a felon in the sight of God. I charge this judge as criminal before the bar of human rights. I charge these servants and these officers as parties to the crime. I charge the people of Capernaum with cruelty and theft, because they heeded not the cries of poverty and want, and have withheld from helpless ones that which is theirs by every law of right; and I appeal unto these people here, and ask: 'Are not my charges based on righteousness and truth'?" And every man said, "yes".

The accused woman blushed for shame; the judge shrank back in fear; the officers threw off the shackles from the man and ran away. Then Jesus said, "Give this man what he needs and let him go and feed his wife and little ones." The people gave abundantly; the man went on his way. '…The thief thinks every other man a thief and judges him accordingly'.

Luke 10:29-37 – The Good Samaritan: "But wanting to vindicate himself, he asked Jesus, 'And who is my neighbour?' Jesus replied, 'A man was going down from Jerusalem to Jericho and fell into the hands of robbers, who stripped him, beat him and took off, leaving him half dead. Now by chance a priest was going down that road, and when he saw him, he passed by on the other side. So, likewise a Levite, who came to the place and saw him, passed by on the other side. But a Samaritan while travelling came upon him, and when he saw him, he was moved with compassion. He went to him and bandaged his wounds, treating him with oil and wine. Then he put him on his own animal, brought him to an inn and took care of him. The next day, he took out two denarii, gave them to the innkeeper, and said, "Take care of him, and when I come back, I will repay you whatever more you spend." Which of these three do you think, was a neighbour to the man who fell into the hands of the robbers?' He said, 'The one who showed him mercy.' Jesus said to him, 'Go, and do likewise'."

Luke 11:5-13 (Matthew 7:7-11): Knock and the Door Shall Open: And he said to them, "Suppose one of you has a friend and you go to him at midnight and say to him, 'Friend, lend me three loaves of bread, for a friend of mine has arrived, and I have nothing to set before him.' And he answers from within, 'Do not bother me; the door has already been locked, and my children are with me in bed; I cannot get up and give you anything.' I tell you, even though he will not get up and give him anything out of friendship, at least because of his persistence he will get up and give him whatever he needs (God is not a stranger too or one far away, as most of us may be apt to think, but a friend within proximity, and he will be apt to do likewise).

"So, I say to you: Ask, and it will be given to you; search, and you will find; knock, and the door will be opened to you. For everyone who asks, receives; everyone who searches finds; everyone who knocks will have the door opened. What father among you, if his son asked for a fish, would hand him a snake? Or if he asked for an egg, hand him a scorpion? If you then, evil as you are, know how to give your children what is good, how much more will the heavenly Father give 'the Holy Spirit' to those who ask him (Apart from Father, who resides in your heart, everything that you see around you or that you seek is nothing but this or that form of the conscious energy—the Holy Spirit, or the 'Mother' that also provides you with a body. What the Father gives, therefore, is nothing but a measure of the Holy Spirit)."

Chapter 142: Then Jesus spoke this parable to them: A rich man lived in splendid state; he wore the finest garments men could make; his boards were loaded with the costliest viands of the land. A beggar, blind and lame, whose name was Lazarus, was wont to sit beside the waste gate of this home that he might share with dogs the refuse from the rich man's board. It came to pass that Lazarus died, and angels carried him away unto the bosom of our father Abraham. The rich man also died, and he was buried in a costly tomb; but in the purifying fires he opened up his eyes dissatisfied. He looked and saw the beggar resting peacefully in the bosom of his father Abraham, and in the bitterness of his soul he cried. My father Abraham, look down in mercy on your son; I am tormented in these flames. Send Lazarus, I beseech, that he may give me just a sup of water to cool my parched tongue. But Abraham replied, "My son, in mortal life, you had the best things of the earth and Lazarus had the worst, and you would not give him a cup of water there, but drove him from your door. The law must be fulfilled, and Lazarus now is comforted, and you are paying what you owe.

"Besides, there is a great gulf fixed between your zone and us, and if I would I could not send Lazarus to you, and you cannot come up to us till you have paid your debts." The Kingdom of Heaven has its own rules to follow (Please see *Matter, Life and Spirit Demystified*).

Chapter 3

THE SECOND COMING

The last journey of Jesus Christ begins with his final words to his disciples—words that he will not be able to repeat as he will be betrayed. Matthew 23 begins with Jesus describing the motives and methods of the scribes and Pharisees to deceive people and make them incur adverse karma, deploring them for their hypocrisy and vanity. He condemns them in strictest of the words, while also predicting what lay ahead for them at a distant future. And then he admonishes Jerusalem.

Matthew 23:33-36 "You *snakes, you brood of vipers!* How can you escape the judgement of hell? For this reason (Like Krishna in Gita, identifying himself with the Father, with whom he has become one), I send you (true) prophets, sages and scribes, some of whom you will kill and crucify, and some you will flog in your synagogues and pursue from town to town; so that upon you may come all the righteous blood shed on earth, from the blood of righteous Abel, to the blood of Zechariah son of Barachiah, whom you murdered between the sanctuary and the altar. Truly, I tell you, this will come upon this generation."

(Here it may be noteworthy that Jesus uses the words 'this generation' to indicate a given aggregate or type of people who shall be condemned, not all the Jewish people. Elsewhere he uses same words to indicate the Christian community as a whole, as a different set of people).

Matthew 23:37-39 "Jerusalem, Jerusalem, the city that kills the prophets and stone those that are sent to it! How often have I desired to gather your children together, as a hen gathers her brood under her wings, and you were not willing! See your house is left to you desolate. For, I tell you, you will not see me any more until you say, '*Blessed is the one who comes in the name of the Lord*'." (It needs to be understood that only a teacher coming in the name of the true Lord, aiming at universal good and neither biased in favour of one people nor against some others, should be welcome. Further, being one with Father, Jesus is always around too and can even be seen in his astral or physical form by anyone who is awake in Truth).

And after accusing them of their unpardonable sins and how these were going to recoil on them, Jesus begins to describe how the things would begin to unfold, what developments will take place, and what kind of signs will begin to become visible to those who remain alert and who can begin to take their guards.

Matthew 24:1-2 "As Jesus came out of the temple and was going away, his disciples came to point out to him the buildings of the temple. Then he asked them, 'You see all these, do you not? (He points to the walls of the temple) Truly I tell you, not one stone here will be left here on another; all will be thrown down."

WARS MUST HAPPEN

"When he was sitting on the Mount of Olives, the disciples came to him privately, saying, 'Tell us, when will this be, and what will be the sign of your coming and of the end of the age?'

Jesus answered them, 'Beware that no one leads you astray. For many will come in my name, saying I am the Messiah! And they will lead many astray (Matthew 24:3-5)."

Christ means a true prophet or a messiah. The concept of Christ in Christianity originated from the concept of messiah in Judaism. Although the conceptions of the messiah in each religion are similar, for the most part they are distinct from one another due to the split of early Christianity and Judaism in the 1st century. Jesus did not call himself Christ; later Christians began to call him 'Jesus, the Christ'.

(Matthew 24:6) "And you will hear of wars and rumours of war; see that you are not alarmed *for this must take place*, but the end is not yet." (The world has been subject to threats of missile attacks by the trigger-happy dictators of people's republics. Tensions are also openly visible between a number of nations and China, a people's republic, from where the virus had leaked through an oversight on someone's part. Harsh words were being exchanged. The divide beneath the surface had been trying to come to the fore, and no person was in a position to stop a flare up from taking place somewhere, and a war from breaking down.) We do see such a situation developing in Eastern Europe as well now. Nuclear-weapons have been placed in active mode by several countries already, and threats of total wipe-outs are in the air.

This is something that must happen, says Jesus ('*but the end will not be yet*', even if this may be the last opportunity the mankind may get to understand and to reform). The mankind needs to wake up to the harsh reality of the threats of terror and aggression which can grow but will never go away, even if the evil forces may lie low for a time waiting for the opportunity they need. The upright mankind needs to reorganize itself on a value system really sound, and which is in tune with the nature's rhythm—a bonding of the like-minded, based firmly and exclusively on values that are favoured by Nature, and which is also advocated by Jesus Christ. Such a bond, based on transparency and value, put effectively in use, can gain immense strength within a couple of years if not within months, to become impenetrable, even against the combined power of all the evil thinking and evil doing conglomerates— whether the permanent ones, or those ready to lie in a formation when the opportunity arises.

WHERE LAWYERS CAN TRUST JUDGES

(Matthew 24:7-10) "For nations will rise against nation, and kingdom against kingdom, and there will be famines and earthquakes in various places: all this is but the beginning of the birth-pangs. Then they will hand you over to be tortured and will put you to death, and you will be hated by all nations because of my name (nations does not mean any countries, but certain given sets of people). Then many will fall away and they will betray one another and hate one another."

We know of Daniel Pearl of the Wall Street Journal, who was kidnapped by Ahmed Omar Saeed Sheikh of Pakistan and handed over to Khalid Sheikh Mohammed and his own bunch of apostles. A video was circulated among *many* countries to be savoured all around. After a few weeks, a copy of the video was also forwarded to the US Consulate in Karachi.

In April, 2020, a High Court in Pakistan commuted the death sentence of Sheikh, and since he had completed more than seven years in jail, he should have been a free person then. However, possibly fearing a backlash from the Western world, and to divert their attention, the provincial Govt. of Sindh had extended his detention by three months on administrative grounds, more than once. The trial of Khalid, the man who actually beheaded Daniel Pearl, has been delayed too (not taken up) for one reason or other.

There are places where the lawyers can trust all the agencies of the government and they can possibly trust the Judges also. Moreover, beheading people or slitting their throats is a normal act defendable within the confines of the latest among the three Semitic or Abrahamic religions. Such powers and permissiveness do not gel at all with Nature's own favoured laws, for sure. A universal yard-stick is necessary so that promising young people may not be easily misled and can grow as the other normal persons are able to do.

GOOD NEWS OF THE KINGDOM: EVIDENCE

(Matthew 24:11-14) "*And many false prophets will arise and will lead many astray. And because of the increase of lawlessness, the love of many will grow cold. But the one who endures to the end will be saved. And this good news of the kingdom will be proclaimed throughout the whole world, as a testimony to all the nations* (the readers must understand: author), *and then the end will come*".

Let us try to understand the terms used in the present context. Today hundreds of prophets can be seen openly deceiving and misguiding people, some in jails, and some spreading communal virus with their cries of war, destruction and loan wolf attacks, while there are other prophets who are running camps to build and train terror groups. They do not claim to be God, but try to create a strong pitch for themselves as rightful prophets who can interpret Him and can uplift the understanding of the followers of their respective Gods. Rise in lawlessness is becoming increasingly evident even in the organized societies, with terror modules, hidden sleeper cells becoming active to disrupt and to disturb peace through coded messages in social media. On the other hand, though, we also see a lonely Zelensky *standing firm* for over sixteen weeks already against an invading super-power, *hoping for a divine intervention* and hoping against all odds *to be saved*. Standing firm actually means standing firm by values and by the principles based on such values, ignoring the lures of the devil and the fear from the might of the evil.

Coming back to 'this good news of the kingdom', it may be difficult to understand the world, if we consider it to be a creation of God, in its capacity as a creator. Things would become a lot easier, if we bear in mind that it is God itself manifesting as the world and becoming everything into it, both units and the aggregates. Further, all the units and aggregates of the world exist as a three-tier system, like a three-storied house with only the top floor being visible, the two other floors existing below the surface. Besides a physical body, which is like the top floor, all things have a causal and an astral body as well. These subtle bodies or below the surface things can be fathomed and known, but cannot be directly seen or measured, and it is true both for a particle of matter and the 'man'.

The place or the seat of the Son of man in the Kingdom, is located within its own astral body at the base of its spine, and this is true for all progeny of the men and women (Those readers who do not wish to read the compendium, *Matter, Life and Spirit Demystified*, are advised to read *Jesus Christ and the Spirit of Truth*, at least, to understand their own structural detail). It is carried within each of us, into our subtle body (the combination of our causal and astral bodies) that becomes detached from the physical body at the time of our physical death. Another significant aspect about the kingdom is that a person's file of the life is written by the own un-conscious mind of that person; there is no lawyer to confuse the judge or to write one's will, and there can be no mix up of any kind whatsoever.

The individual picks up the total record of the life lived by it, which is carried into its subtle body, when it moves from here to its quarter in the astral kingdom. Also, it must bring it back with itself when a new span of life on earth is allotted to it and whereby it may come to be reborn. A new file for the new life is now opened, and gradually the old memories become inaccessible to it once again—in most cases, by the time it has learnt to speak.

By 'evidence to the nations', it is possibly indicated that this knowledge about the astral world and the astral body of the humans, lasting for billions of years for any individual, will stand revealed to the nations (the mankind) in a way that it can be understood, like two and two must add up to just four and not to five or seven or any other number. Such knowledge must be accepted on its qualification and merit with an option to accept or reject after examination of the evidence; more specifically by reference to the revealed knowledge of science and by relating it to what Jesus had himself said or done, and which cannot be altered and can be included as evidence too.

Coming to the words, *and then the end will come*, we can also take it as a continuation of, *'you will hear of wars and rumours of war..., but the end will not be yet'*. However, it will be too straight forward and, possibly, misleading to deduce that after going to such lengths to reveal the spirit of truth and sending a paraclete, the 'Father' was going to wind up the humanity and the human world for good, since it is preceded by *'anyone who stands firm to the end will be saved'*. Besides, it is noteworthy that the very questions asked by the disciples of Jesus in private when he was sitting on the Mount of Olives at the beginning of this chapter was, 'Tell us, when will this be, and what will be the sign of your coming and of the end of the age?' Taking up from where the things were left, the disciples had wanted to know about the 'end of the age' and not the end of the world.

Extinctions have taken place before. Even such powerful creatures as dinosaurs became extinct, but every major event of extinction was followed by rise of a fitter and better equipped species. Still earlier, we already know, up to 96% of all marine species and 70% of terrestrial vertebrate species had died out in the event known as the Permian extinction. Perhaps (and let us hope it should be that way only), it is 'the age' of the false prophets who can deceive, of terror modules and sleeper cells who may create disorder and lawlessness, and of the leaders that eye other's territory to create mistrust; all of which leads to the most natural human emotion 'love' to growing cold, that will come to an end. With a smoother surface and cleaned up slate, the Son of Man may come into his own, then.

The Great Tribulation of Jerusalem

Matthew 24:15-16 "So, when you see the desolating sacrilege (a religious symbol of other people that were non-Jewish, or an idol or sign worshipped by them) spoken of by prophet Daniel, standing in the holy place, then those in Judea must flee into the mountains."

Prophet Daniel has spoken of the appalling abomination at three places in chapters 9, 11 and 12 of his Book. As we shall see in the last chapter of this book, devoted to the visions and prophesies of Prophet Daniel, these indicate three different incidents in the history of the Jewish people. Of these one appears to have occurred before Jesus had been born, and one could actually indicate the event of his own crucifixion. It is the third incident of which both Jesus and Daniel speak, which lay in the womb of the future then. And we may be approaching that time quite soon now.

Whereas there is a long list of prophets in the Bible, Masters like Elijah and Jesus, or the true and advanced seekers like Daniel and Elisha belonged to all people; anyone could claim them as its own, as none of them will ever have said, 'no I don't belong to this people; I don't preach or guide them'. It seems worth pointing out, that the scholars who have studied and analysed the narratives in the Holy Bible do not hesitate to question the impartiality of the scribes who wrote these narratives.

The twelve tribes of the Semitic people are believed to have moved out of the general area in and around Afghanistan a little more than 2000 years prior to Christ. The area had come under the influence of the Vedic people who prayed to Brahma and other assorted god-heads. Even in the days of Taliban, some popular names of Hindu kings still form a part of popular culture in that country. The narrative of the Holy Bible possibly begins with a recollection of the community's memory from those very old days. By then the knowledge about '*sabda*', 'sound' or the 'word', being the first state of God, in the process of manifesting itself as the world, had become common knowledge among the scholars in the East. The creation at the causal plane, which is the realm of foundation and specification, is creation by 'word' which can also be termed as the thought of God. This has been explained in both our other books mentioned herein. We do see a mention in the Bible that "in the beginning there was 'word', the 'word' was with God and 'the word' was God", etc., though no elaboration of the concept has been made anywhere in the Holy Book.

The task of the scribes is not easy. They are fairly intelligent and good at writing for sure. However, often it becomes difficult for them to understand what the prophets say and do, since they do not descend to explain such things to the scribes entrusted with the job of writing or placing the events on record, especially prophets in the category of Elijah, Elisha or even Daniel. Again, the scribes may be biased, and above all, they needed to secure concurrence of the senior people among the brotherhood that were in-charge at the time, when the event was being recorded. Sometimes, a bit of tweaking here and there also becomes necessary to justify a specific manipulation of an event, since the events had to be reported and at times it may have been hard to bring those to conform to what they themselves or their supervisors needed to hide and what they needed to project.

The authors of gospels were not in the same category as the scribes of the Old Testament, however, since they would be aghast at the very idea of trying to manipulate a thought or deed of Jesus, or a word uttered by him. However, to understand everything and then to put it down into written word could not be an easy task for them too. Here and there some slips would be likely enough to creep in if not inevitable, and more so if two events were being described at the same time, possibly overlapping, and though not simultaneous in the sense of immediacy but more or less successive and described in the same context and in the course of a single dialogue.

The Great Distress

Matthew 24:16-19 "Then those in Judea must escape to the mountains; the one on the housetop must not go down to take things from the house; the one in the fields must not turn back to get a coat. Woe to those who are pregnant and to those who are nursing infants in those days!"

Here, the author believes, we should not take just the literal meaning, but also take in account what follows, and try to visualize how a person will organize his words to describe the quarantining procedures, necessitated by Covid-19, to one in total ignorance of such possibilities, and then some two thousand years ahead of the time. However, it may be hard to understand and be cohesive putting on record a description heard only once when two events of a similar nature one following from another in a sequential order may have been spoken about. Anyone not able to follow or remember cent-percent, a future happening being described to him, may easily reverse the sequence while trying to reduce the narrative to a written record at a subsequent date.

The above description of the hardship to be faced and care to be taken, better fits use of chemical weaponry and the area which is affected is more localized since those in Judea are advised to escape to the mountains. On the other hand, the scenario universally prevalent at the time is described in the revelation that follows, is more akin to the biological-distress the world has been going through even in the present moment. And yet again, Judea may have been chosen only as a name familiar to the apostles, to describe the event. It can very well be a town in Ukraine also for all we know, since phosphorous bombs have been used in the ongoing war of aggression, and an incident when about a thousand men of Ukrainian army had to choose to surrender when faced with suffocation under the conditions of a gas hazard is also known. With the war having moved into its fifth month already, and becoming uglier, use of more lethal chemical weaponry can easily be on the cards now. Also, a still subsequent event to follow, and actually involving Judea, could be on the cards as well.

Matthew 24:21-28 "For at that time there will be great suffering, such as has not been from the beginning of the world until now; no, and never will be. And if those days had not been cut short, no one would be saved, but for the sake of the elect those days will be cut short (for them to survive and to evolve further). Then if anyone says to you, 'look here is the Messiah!', or 'There he is', do not believe it. For false messiahs and false prophets will appear and produce great signs and wonders, to lead astray, if possible, even the elect (*but it will fail to deceive the true who stand firm*). Take note, I have told you beforehand! So, if they say to you, 'Look! He is in the wilderness', do not go out. If they say, 'Look! He is in the inner rooms, do not believe it. For as the lightning comes from the East and flashes as far as the West,' so will be the coming of the Son of Man. Wherever the corpse is, there the eagles will gather." (The field has withered in the East already, buried under the false pride of a common acquisition of the knowledge of truth from the ancient days. However, knowledge about the Truth is little understood by a majority of the people in India at this point of time. We have been burdened with a growing heap of consumerism instead, with little time or space to spare in our hands. The seekers of truth 'now abound' in the West, on the other hand).

In the days of media, internet and e-books, anything happening anywhere in the world, significant in any manner, takes minutes to spread from East to West; the example of lightning striking and flashing as far, possibly, could only mean that, and nothing as spectacular like the signs given in the olden times (as some people may expect, before giving due credence to the wisdom of the East). However, this is a humble suggestion of the author only, only worth that much. Yet, that 'East' has been mentioned in a positive light and as the source, would seem to be beyond any dispute.

THE SON OF MAN

The rishis (and we can call them 'true' prophets, though they also included Masters like Jesus), when they hand over the science of the 'kingdom' to their chosen, the Son of 'Man', with his fairly cleansed up mind and heart, they also tell him: "It is possible for every Son of Man to be able to reach a station in life when he will be able to realize, 'I and my Father are one'."

It should be interesting to note that Jesus has referred to both himself and Elijah, as well, as the Son of Man. Mark 9:9-13 "As they were coming down from the mountain, he ordered them to tell no one about what they had seen, *until after the Son of Man has risen from the dead*. So, they kept the matter to themselves, questioning what this 'rising from the dead' could mean. Then they asked him, 'Why do the scribes say that Elijah must come first?'

"He said to them, 'Elijah is indeed coming first to restore all things. How then it is written about the Son of Man, that he is to go through many sufferings and be treated with contempt? But I tell you that Elijah has come and they did to him whatever they pleased, as it is written about him'."

It seems clear enough that Jesus is referring to the beheading of John the Baptist in the context of Elijah suffering grievously as the Son of Man, or conveying that it was Prophet Elijah who had reincarnated as John.

Further, the use of the word *'again'* may hold some important significance as well. It would immediately begin to make sense if Elisha was to be reborn as Jesus, as suggested by Paramhansa Yogananda, in his world famous 'Autobiography of a Yogi'. Both Elijah and Elisha probably spent many centuries together in the higher echelons of the astral world, which has been described in detail by Swami Yukteswar Giri, before reincarnating again with the gap of just a few months between them (This knowledge of the kingdom of Heaven was revealed by Sri Yukteswar when he had resurrected himself before Sri Yogananda in his Mumbai hotel, three months after being buried by him at Puri with his own hands. Please refer to either of the two books mentioned by us, or the 'Autobiography' itself, while keeping in mind that the source of light has been mentioned as 'East').

Matthew 24:29-31 "Immediately after the suffering of those days, the sun will be darkened, and the moon will not give its light; the stars will fall from the sky and the powers of the heaven will be shaken (*like a meteorite or one or more nuclear bombs striking the Earth*). Then the sign of Son of Man will appear in heaven; and then all the tribes of the earth will mourn, and they will see the Son of Man coming on the clouds of heaven with power and great glory. And he will send his angels with a loud trumpet call, and they will gather his elect from the four winds, from one end of heaven to the other."

The Son of Man 'coming on the clouds of Heaven' with power and great glory possibly means that name of Jesus with what he said, did and preached, will come into proper limelight once again through the medium of a paraclete (an advocate). That 'he will send his angels from one end of the heaven to the other' possibly means, that people chosen or hand-picked by him to accomplish this task from the kingdom of Heaven will be reborn into the world at this time of great upheaval and change; of the extinction attributable to an era that may be given a name of its own, and the 'reorganization' afresh.

Surprisingly, we may already be witnessing the reversal of the magnetic poles too, when the North Pole begins to turn into the South Pole and vice versa. The last time it happened was some 780,000 years ago. Changes do seem to be in the offing. And these can have far reaching consequences. Alertness is advised by Jesus; and guarding is suggested by him. Besides, there may be things he wants the 'nations' to discuss and the evidence they must consider. It should not be that they will take note only after the holocaust actually occurs. They should, rather begin to take appropriate action now itself, when the signs have become visible already.

Has Jesus Been Reborn?

Luke 17:20-25 "Once Jesus was asked by the pharisees when the Kingdom of God was coming, and he answered, 'The kingdom of God is not coming with things that can be observed; nor will they say, "Look, here it is, look there it is!" For, in fact, the Kingdom of God is among you'. Then he said to the disciples, 'The days are coming when you will long to see one of the days of the Son of Man, and you will not see it. They will say to you, "Look there", or "Look here!" Do not go; do not set off in pursuit. For as the lightning flashes and lights up the sky from one side to the other, so will be the Son of Man in his day'."

Jesus had offered his life to the Father, to expiate the past sins of his followers. The context may have been different, but people have offered their lives to God before, and while in some cases it has been accepted, in others it has also been 'returned' as well. The coming of Jesus had a great purpose to it, and yet, it could not have been free from the laws of karma or action, and it is but natural that a lot of karma and also some vital relationships from the past come to be disposed of, or to become neutralized, in every human rebirth, even of a Master.

Besides Mother Marry, we see Mary Magdalen also at each step crucial to Jesus. Often, we tend to undermine the importance of the persons in close proximity to an important incarnation. For sure, the Mary of Magdala could not have been an ordinary person too. Besides, we are mostly in dark as regards how Jesus, as a boy of twelve, was able to display such astute awareness and knowledge about the scriptures at the temple at Jerusalem, so as to leave the wise people present there speechless. Perhaps we should accept the Levi narrative in the Aquarian Gospel, where we are told that to escape the ire of Archelaus, the son of Herod, who ruled in Jerusalem, soon after the birth of John and Jesus, their mothers Elizabeth and Mary were made to shift to Zoan in Egypt, where for three years they both were taught about things of a 'higher' nature by Elihu and Salome, before they could return to their respective places, so that they were able to transfer such knowledge to their sons in the process of growing. Among other things, the ladies were taught in detail about the Brahmic religion then followed by the wise in India.

Jesus was an extremely intelligent person, without any doubt. From the Dowling Gospel, we learn that while in India, Jesus had accepted to be a disciple of Udraka, greatest of the Hindu healers, and had learnt from him the uses of the waters, plants and earths; of heat and cold; sunshine and shade; of light and dark. We also see that after crucifixion, the physical body of Jesus had disappeared. It had moved or was removed, and was never buried or cremated. It is very much likely that he was helped by his friend from the Nath Order, Chetan Nath from India, who besides being an expert in Siddha medicine, could see events happening at any place, and could also reach there instantly (these faculties are known and have been discussed in detail in our books). Arriving there in time, perhaps he was able to revive and recoup Jesus with the help of his close and discreet associates. It may have been the wish of the Father not to accept the offer of life made by the Son and return the life back to Jesus as a gift. For sure, it would not be within the jurisdiction of Jesus to refuse.

Possibly, with the help of his influential friends, after setting the things right with his apostles, Jesus had travelled back to India as claimed by several faithful and learned researchers, to live to a ripe age. Holger Kersten, a professor of Physics and author of 'Jesus Lived in India' is one of them. According to 'Snippets from the Subconscious', authored by Dr Rajeev M. Kaushik, M.D., an expert in Regression Therapy, too, Jesus may have returned to India, may have taken Mary of Magdala as his wife, and may have lived to an age of 130 years, when he was buried according to Jewish customs in the old town of Srinagar in Kashmir. Perhaps, Jesus was already betrothed to Mary Magdalene around the time he had turned twelve. Dowling would not have discovered the same by entering the ethers, as such a notion would have been repugnant to him.

One of the names by which Jesus was known in these parts was Yuz Asaf. With assistance from the local king, Yuz Asaf had also arranged for a thousand years old temple of King Solomon, known as Takht-e-Suleman, to be repaired and restored in Srinagar. The fact is mentioned in a stone tablet that can be seen at the temple even today. Besides, there is a building there known as Roza Bal, which holds two tombs, one laid East West, after the Jewish custom, which is accredited to Yuz Asaf, and another which is of much later origin and which is a Muslim tomb laid north-south. There are foot prints carved into stone also, by the side of the Jewish tomb, in which the nail wounds can be seen even today.

Likewise, Holger Kersten has also mentioned about existence of a grave to the north of Ladakh in the Chinese province of Sinkiang nearly ten kilometres from the town of Kashgar, which is said to be that of a certain Mary who was among Jesus' following. Possibly, there was a strong karmic bond between Jesus and Mary Magdalene which needed consummation and neutralization, to set both of the great souls supremely free.

There are strong reasons to believe that Jesus and Mary Magdalene may have both been reborn in early 3rd century and are still alive, maintaining physical bodies that look like those of young persons in their mid-twenties, but they are born as cousins this time. They both head really capable and powerful generations of disciples, as Mahavatar Babaji and Kshepai Mata (mother). Incidentally, every word in our principal book is also inspired by or has been borrowed from the disciples and sub-disciples of one or the other of these two great masters. Of them, the Mahavatar is also accredited as being the Sixth Guru, under the well-known Nath Order of the Siddha Gurus of the Indians. Likewise, several of the Siddha Ashrams in Tibet, including the famous ashram at Gyanganj, are headed by Sage Mahatapa, a disciple of Kshepai Mata, his current age exceeding about 1400 years. (All these things are discussed in detail in *Jesus Christ and the Spirit of Truth*).

Naturally, anyone interested in high-end yoga and the spiritual realm in India and elsewhere is keen to know more about Mahavatar Babaji. That his facial features and the colour of his hair, do not appear to be of Asian descent, is also a source of an unanswered bafflement for the investigative spiritualists, who are interested to know more about him. Perhaps, Jesus had a reason to be present in body for as long as the present cycle of manifestation may last. Perhaps his promise to resurrect himself after his bodily death hid a resolve far deeper than his followers may have presumed. In both our books, we have included excerpts from 'Autobiography of a Yogi' authored by Paramhansa Yogananda, mentioning the incident of a celestial promise being conveyed by Mahavatar Babaji, accepting a request from his cousin sister to this effect, to maintain his physical frame till the end of the present cycle of manifestation and to keep appearing to select people from time to time. Seen in this light what we have quoted above from Luke 17 will begin to make a sense as well, where Jesus has said, "A time will come when you will long to see one of the days of the Son of Man, and will not see it. They will say to you, 'Look he is there', or 'Look he is here', make no move; do not set in pursuit; for as the lightning from one part of heaven lights up the other, so will be the Son of Man, when his day comes."

The Second Coming, in a way, is about Jesus coming in full limelight once again, and also being understood fully on this occasion. Let us see some quotes:

John 6:32-33 "Very truly, I tell you, it was not Moses who gave you the bread from heaven, but it is my Father who gives you the true bread from heaven. For the bread of God is that which comes down from heaven and gives life to the world (It is first of the three levels of *prana*, in the three-tier manifestation. It provides basic nourishment for our living and functioning, and it gives rise to spiritual energy. At the second level, this *prana* gives rise to psychic energy working through our instruments of knowledge and interaction, while at the third level, according to the masters, it becomes manifest as our physical breath. (Please see *Jesus Christ and the Spirit of Truth*)."

John 6:63 "It is the Spirit that gives life, the flesh is useless. The words I have spoken to you are Spirit and life (too)."

John 10:17-18 "For this reason the 'Father' loves me, because I lay down my life in order to take it up again. No one takes it from me, I lay it down of my own accord. I have power to lay it down, and I have power to take it up again. I have received this command from my 'Father'."

John 14:12 "In all truth I tell you, whoever believes in me will perform the same work as I do myself, and will perform even greater works, because I am going to the 'Father'."

John 14:15-17 "If you love me, you will keep my commandments. And I will ask the 'Father' and he will give you another Advocate to be with you forever (*perhaps in the form of written word*). (*And you shall know, whereas*) This is the Spirit of Truth, whom the world (modern science in its present state) cannot receive because it neither sees him nor knows him. You know it because he abides with you, and he will be in you (as your very self, which only you can know)."

John 14:25-26 "I have said these things to you while I am still with you. But the Advocate, the Holy Spirit, whom the Father will send in my name, will teach you everything and remind you of all I have said to you."

John 16:7-15 "Nevertheless, I tell you the truth; it is to your advantage that I go away, for if I do not go away, the Advocate will not come to you; but if I go, I will send him to you (as soon as you are ready to understand). And when he comes, he will prove the world wrong about sin, and about righteousness and judgement: about sin, because they do not believe in me; about righteousness, because I am going to the 'Father', and you will see me no longer; about judgment, because the ruler of this world has been condemned.

"I still have many things to say to you, but you cannot bear them now. When the Spirit of Truth Comes, he (this advocate) will guide you into all the truth, for he will not speak on his own, but will speak whatever he hears, and he will declare to you the things that are to come. He will glorify me because he will take what is mine and declare it to you. All the 'Father' has is mine. For this reason, I said that he will take what is mine and declare it to you."

And Jesus said to him, "Foxes have holes and the birds of air have nests, but the Son of Man has nowhere to lay his head (Matthew 8:20)." The Son of Man hides into each of us. It has a body, but it is not the body that can lay its head anywhere, and it needs to be welcome, made a universal plaintiff, and granted the highest level of security. Let the nations put some covenants, some definitions in place to welcome a new era, the era of the 'Son of Man'.

If 2019 was the year of Covid-19, let 2022 or 2023 become the year of the Son of Man. Let the things begin to sort themselves out. Let there be a new beginning; a new dawn! And let the nations set covenants to accommodate the Son of Man; covenants that define a colour-less regime, the white regime purged of all evil. That, in fact, is the coveted goal of the Nature! Let the nations do it for the sake of the mankind; for the sake of human progeny, and also to help Nature in gaining its cherished objective!

TOLERANCE AND INTOLERANT

In the Indian Sub-continent, during the early prehistoric times, those who imbibed high moral truth as a way of life were called worshippers of 'Sur' gods that were in tune with natural cosmic vibration, while those that deviated from such tuning in their way of life were called a-Sur, which became 'ashur' in later times in the territories that lay more westward (In Sanskrit prefix 'a' has a negative connotation; in European languages it indicates a positive excellence of some kind, however).

After the concept of Brahma came to arise in Indian main-lands, many of the Sur worshippers began to call themselves as Brahmanas. According to Levi's Aquarian Gospel, in Chaldea, Brahm was known. A pious Brahm named Terah lived in Ur; his son was so devoted to the Brahmic faith that he was called A-Brahm (as wise as the best of the Brahmanas), and he was set apart to be the father of the Hebrew race.

None of the four religions that have come to arise under the shadows cast by the Himalayas, makes a pronouncement that their God is higher or superior than the God of any other people or religion. God is the Father or common progenitor of everyone without any distinction or differentiation of any kind; else how can it be named as God with a capital 'G'—the one Lord of everyone and everything. The Hindu, Jain, Buddhist and Sikh religions have all come to evolve following a natural and 'forever' common tradition, coming down to them since the prehistoric times.

Depending on their background and the exigencies at the time of the rising of these religions, and depending on the philosophical aspects focused upon by their seers, minor differences may be seen by a lay person, but there are no factual contradictions between any of these religions since they are all founded on a single universal truth which is also eternal. All these religions have their mooring on a sound philosophical base which is universally true, and which remains as sound and as unmoved, as the Tibetan plateau itself. There is no room for any notion to kill or destroy any other people or for forcible conversion through violence—to out-number or overtake a people, a nation, or a part of the world—a piece of land with its associated resources.

Even the Sikhs, residing in the border province of Punjab in India, had begun to carry a sword only after a systematic invasion of the Indian land by the Muslims had commenced. For sure, they had to make great sacrifices also in the process. Two of their Gurus were murdered by two separate Moghul emperors. The head of the 9th Guru Teg Bahadur was kicked around by the Moghuls after beheading him. As for the Tenth Guru, Guru Govind Singh, while two of his teenage sons were killed when fighting the invaders, his two youngest sons, aged seven and nine were bricked and plastered alive into a wall when they had refused to embrace the Faith of the invading Moghuls. For sure, they made great history and for sure they have carved their names into the Indian minds for a long-long time to come.

At the end of the day, however, it is the Nature that must hold all the cards. Powerful species like the dinosaur have been eliminated, leaving behind just the birds. Powerful kings, dictators and tyrants have also been decimated over the time. When lines are crossed and things are taken to the extreme, then the reversal of the trend could be that much nearer in Nature's plan. It is the 'truth' that must prevail in the end—otherwise, the God would not have made 'Man', and neither he would have given him the freedom to choose his path.

The Beginning of Intolerance

If we turn the pages of the known human history, we see an early conflict between philosophy, and the goals and ambitions of the 'individuals' and 'flag bearers' of different people. Philosophy concerning God and the nature of the world became tagged to the religious identity of a people at one time, and was displaced as a natural faculty. Instead, notions of your philosophy against my philosophy, superior and inferior philosophy, and overriding philosophies of force and coercion on one hand—and of continued tolerance and survival on the other—came into vogue in the wake of rise of some very aggressive Faiths.

The philosophical exchange and dialogue were forthwith discontinued at that point of time. We see clear unambiguous edicts promulgated by the early prophets of the Holy Bible itself some 3,500 years ago, whereby the idol-worshippers had come to be pronounced as heathen, unequal, and unworthy of being considered as human beings.

God is everywhere, into all things, and is always there; He can be worshipped by any means and in any form. This is a knowledge which is simple and white: not colored or shaded, yet higher than the knowledge of all the prophets of all the religions combined together and which is known to every idol-worshipper—even to an uneducated or outright foolish and highly superstitious idol-worshipper. Likewise, to welcome a guest and treating him like a god was a common tradition for these people, even if their own hearts had hardened too with growing distance from the land of their origin—in space and the time.

These, however, can be matters that can be discussed and explained to some, but not to everyone. The aggressors or invaders never like to indulge in a discussion or debate. They remain interested in increasing the number of their followers, not in losing men to other faiths. For a long time, and in some places even today, any person trying to reason out could be dead before he had completed his second sentence. The emphasis in those early days, however, was on increasing the numbers following the route of the womb, as people having a different origin were not trusted, since they could corrupt the holy Faith of the supremely selected Faithful ones, or create cracks into the fortress built around them by their prophet. Only much later in times, life could be spared if someone was agreeable to adopt the Faith of the aggressor. People were converted by force in the latter denominations of the people sharing a domineering phenotype, under threat to life; or they were made to flee—leaving their homes and belongings behind.

It constitutes a very important event in the Bible when twenty-four thousand young men of Israel, who had married into the families of the followers of Baal of Peor and had even started accompanying their wives to their temples, and kneeling and bowing in front of the images, symbols or sculptures of the god-forms chosen by them for worship, had to be killed by their own families in compliance of the Prophet's edict. It is also typical of the scribes of the holy book to call women of all other people as prostitutes. This granted their own men the freedom to use them as bodies for pleasure, but barred their sons from officially taking them as their wives. Marriage following the customs of another faith was not recognized by the brotherhood of prophets and the priests of Israel.

Numbers 25:1-9 "While Israel was staying at Shittim, the people began to have sexual relations with the women of Moab. These invited the people to the sacrifices of their gods, and the people ate and bowed down to their gods. Thus, Israel yoked itself to the Baal of Peor, and the Lord's anger was kindled against Israel. The Lord said to Moses, 'Take all the chiefs of people and impale them in the sun before the Lord, in order that the fierce anger of the Lord may turn away from Israel.' And Moses said to the judges of Israel, 'Each of you shall kill any of your people who have yoked themselves to the Baal of Peor.'

"Just then one of the Israelites came and brought a Midianite woman (probably his fiancée, or even wife) into his family, in the sight of Moses and in the sight of the whole congregation of the Israelites, while they were weeping at the entrance of the tent of meeting. When Phinehas son of Eleazar, son of Aaron the priest (and the nephew of Moses), saw it, he got up and left the congregation. Taking a spear in his hand, he went after the Israelite man into the tent and pierced the two of them, the Israelite and the woman, through the belly. So, the plague was stopped among the Israelites. Nevertheless, those who died by the plague were twenty-four thousand (excluding the wives these sons of theirs may have taken who may also been killed, and possibly some children too)." For the zeal displayed by him, through the office of Moses, the Lord was pleased to grant this grandson of Aaron and his descendants a covenant of perpetual priesthood (Numbers 25:10-13).

It was a harsh decision no doubt. It, nevertheless, forever set the behavior pattern of the followers of the Abrahamic religions, as against the idol-worshipping people. Yet the blame possibly lay elsewhere. Nature places us into situations and people adopt courses and find solutions typical of them and they try to do their best or worst.

Moses was not an ordinary leader and it was not an ordinary circumstance. He had led his entire people out of Egypt, after freeing them from the clutches of a very cruel Pharaoh. Possibly, over two million people overall were led to freedom, since they may have included more than six hundred thousand males above twenty who could hold arms. He had freed the tribes of Israel from Egypt after living in slavery and captivity for five hundred years. Minds of people had become hardened and Moses could not do what he was able to do without putting steel in his heart. He was a leader of his people and he had his own immediate goals and little time to think of a long-term effect on the human world as a whole.

No Ambiguity of Intent! No Mincing of Words!

"Moses, Eleazar the priest (son of his brother Aaron), and all the leaders of congregation went to meet them outside the camp. Moses became angry (Numbers 31:13-18) with the officers of the army, the commanders of the thousands and the commanders of the hundreds, who had come from service in the war (with all the booty they could carry and bring from their exploit).

"Moses said to them, '(Why) have you allowed all the women to live? They women here, on Balaam's advice, made the Israelites to act treacherously against the Lord in the affair at Peor, so that the plague came among the congregation of the Lord. Now therefore, kill every male among the little ones, and kill every woman who has known a man by sleeping with him. But all the young girls who have not known a man by sleeping with him, keep alive for yourselves."

As for the use of the word plague, when Moses and Aaron were faced with the magicians of Pharaoh, whom Moses had challenged, ten different kinds of plagues are mentioned. These begin with water turning into blood, frogs, mosquitos and horseflies, frost, and locusts invading the land of Egyptians, death of Egyptian's livestock, hail storm sweeping through and damaging the country and, finally, the first born of Egypt dying from Pharaoh to the slave girl, but none of the Israelites, nor even any of their beasts (the Black Art at its peaking best).

Any of our readers who may have read the biography of the Tibetan Yogi Milarepa (*Tibet's Great Yogi Milarepa* by W.Y. Evans-Wentz), can easily see that all of these constitute, what the Tibetans know as Black Art. In particular, when any major destruction or malefic result, like subsiding of a house or land, hail storms, or death of specific category of beasts or children, etc. was required to be obtained or secured, a specific apparatus (Mandala) was required to be drawn and installed on the ground, with specific invocations and further procedure. It was an approved thing in those days and until much later times, if the men practised it, but any woman even suspected of indulging in any such practice would have been declared a witch by the menfolk and would have been stoned and killed forthwith.

A torch had been lit about 1,500 years before the Christ, to light up the path of the generations that were to come. The torch bearers will keep changing hands until it would extinguish of itself someday through the hand of God and, meanwhile, they would keep adding more fuel—even try to improve on the deadliness of the fire.

Deuteronomy, in the Bible, is the first attempt to reform and to set the systems in order. It seems to address more to the procedures of worship and those concerned with the duties of the priests etc., however. The attitude towards the other people inhabiting their part of the world had hardened further if anything. Deuteronomy 13:1-3, 5-10 read: "If prophets or those who divine by dreams appear among you and show you omens or portents, and the omens or the portents declared by them take place, and they say, 'Let us follow other gods' (whom you have not known) 'and let us serve them', you must not hear the words of those prophets or those who divine by dreams, for the Lord your God is testing you, to know whether you indeed love the Lord your God with all your heart and soul."

"But those prophets or those who divine by dreams shall be put to death for having spoken treason against the Lord your God who brought you out of the land of Egypt and redeemed you from the house of slavery... If anyone secretly entices you—even if it is your brother, your father's son or your mother's son, or your own son or daughter, or the wife you embrace, or your most intimate friend—saying, 'Let us go and serve other gods,' ...you must not yield to any such persons. Show them no pity or compassion, and do not shield them. But you shall surely kill them; your own hand shall be first against them to execute them and afterward the hands of all the people. Stone them to death'." (Stoning as a tool, and stoning to death, is still the approved thing for some people, in some parts of the world).

We do, however, see further relaxation for the women and children of the victims. The women were considered mostly as property and this is reflected as well in the duly reformed laws concerning them that were highly unfair to the fair sex—without excluding their own women. Nevertheless, whereas Moses, earlier, had ordered all except virgin girls to be killed. Now only males were not to be taken captive but killed.

Deuteronomy 20:10-16 "When you draw near to a town to fight against it ('to attack it', in New Jerusalem Bible), offer it terms of peace. If it accepts your terms of peace and surrenders to you, then all the people in it shall serve you at forced labour. But if does not accept your terms of peace and makes war against you, then you shall besiege it, and when the Lord *your God gives it into your hands, you shall put all its males to the sword. You may, however, take as your plunder the women, the children, livestock and everything else in the town, all its spoil. You may enjoy the spoil of your enemies, which the Lord your God has given you.* Thus, you shall treat all the towns that are very far from you, which are not towns of these nations here. But as for the towns of these people that the Lord your God is giving you as an inheritance, *you must not let anything that breathes remain alive.*"

Unfortunately, the chief people that were thus claimed to have been 'handed over' or were at the receiving end of the magnanimous largesse awarded by their God, were the idol-worshipping people. Denominations may have changed with time, but not the mindset of the people chosen by a partisan God, or the luck of the idol worshipper. Only some people were made to migrate to the other side by Jesus Christ. New names came in vogue, new prophets and new means. Fresh excuses and a wider variety of punishments to choose from for award and execution have come into vogue and the right to neutralize others has been retained by the historically superior and more dominant people, in one form or the other.

Beheading and throat slitting of even non-idol worshipping people can also be justified now at any place, on flimsiest of the grounds, and with noises from many corners of the world with arguments in its support. Perhaps, the God should have made two different worlds—one for those pursuing the truth, and the other for his preferred and specially chosen ones, with no holds barred for them. Perhaps, the surviving mankind, the 'not as strong' part that needs to be compliant to a value system of its own, should take the initiative and itself divide the world to improve the chances of its survival.

The idol worshipper survives only in India now. It has survived and the worst may be over for it now. Regimes have been shifting and hands have been changing as well, and more rapidly in the times more recent. There need be no going back for him/her to the days of coercion or manipulation. Freedom and hope have begun to fill the air, and so here are some books. The book in your hands is essentially just a postlude to our principal book which tries to portray the same essence or 'spirit of truth', the revelation of which (on a future date) was foretold by Jesus on more occasions than one, and which is mentioned in the John's Gospel.

God May be Advised to Punish You

Numbers 16: 1-10 "Now Korah, son of Izhar son of Kohath son of Levi, along with Dathan and Abiram sons of Eliab, and On son of Peleth sons of Reuben, took two hundred and fifty Israelite men, leaders of the congregation, chosen from the assembly, well-known men, and they confronted Moses.

"They assembled against Moses and (his brother) Aaron (the Chief Priest) and said to them, 'You have gone too far! All the congregation are holy, every one of them, and the Lord is among them. So why then do you exalt yourselves against the assembly of the Lord?' When Moses heard it, he fell on his face. Then he spoke to Korah and his congregation, saying, 'In the morning the Lord will make known who is his and who is holy and who will be allowed to approach him; the one whom he will choose he will allow to approach him. Do this: take censers, Korah and all your congregation, and tomorrow put fire in them and lay incense on them before the Lord and the man whom the Lord chooses shall be the holy one. *You Levites have gone too far' (you must ready yourself for an ultimate punishment)*!

"Then Moses said to Korah, 'Hear now, you Levites! Is it too little for you that the God of Israel has separated you from the congregation of Israel to allow you to approach him in order to perform the duties of the Lord's tabernacle and to stand before the congregation and serve them? He has also allowed you to approach him, and all your brother Levites with you, *and yet you seek the priesthood as well*'!"

Numbers 16: 12-14 "Moses then sent for Dathan and Abiram sons of Eliab, but they said, 'We will not come. Is it too little that you have brought us up out of a land flowing with milk and honey to kill us in the wilderness, that you must also lord it over us? It is clear you have not brought us into a land flowing with milk and honey or given us an inheritance over fields and vineyards. Would you put out the eyes of these men? We will not come'."

Numbers 16: 16-21 "And Moses said to Korah 'As for you and all your congregation, be present tomorrow before the Lord, you and they, and Aaron (his brother and the Chief priest), and let each one of you take his censer and put incense on it and each one of you present his censer before the Lord, two hundred and fifty censers, you also, and Aaron, each (with) his censer. So, each man took his censer, and they put fire in the censers and laid incense on them, and they stood at the entrance of the Tent of Meeting with Moses and Aaron. Then, Korah assembled the whole of congregation against them at the entrance to the Tent of Meeting; the glory of Yahweh appeared of the whole community. And the glory of the Lord appeared to the whole congregation."

Numbers 16: 23-35 "And the Lord spoke to Moses, 'Speak to the congregation, saying, 'Get away from the dwellings of Korah, Dathan and Abiram.' So, Moses got up and went to Dathan and Abiram; the elders of Israel followed him. He spoke to the congregation, saying, 'Turn away from the tents of *these wicked men and touch nothing of theirs;* (adding) *or you will be swept away* for all their sins'. So, they got away from the dwellings of Korah, Dathan and Abiram, and Dathan and Abiram came out and stood at the entrance of their tents, together with their wives, their children and their little ones. And Moses said, 'This is how you shall know that the Lord has sent me to do all these works; it has not been of my own accord. If these people die a natural death or a natural fate comes on them (but die they must), then the Lord has not sent me. But if the Lord creates *something new, and the ground opens its mouth and swallows them up with all that belongs to them,* and they go down alive into Sheol, then you will know that these men have despised the Lord'.

"As soon as he finished speaking all these words, the ground under them was split apart. The earth opened its mouth and swallowed them up, along with their households—everyone who belonged to Korah and all their goods. So, they with all that belonged to them went down alive into Sheol; the earth closed over them and they perished from the midst of the assembly. All Israel around them fled at their outcry, for they said, 'the earth will swallow us too. And fire came out of the Lord and consumed the two hundred and fifty men, offering incense." Between its own sons too, perhaps the God of Israel was more favourable to some and less to some others, even if they should be carrying their censers as a mark of prayer to him, complete with fire and incense on it.

The word plague has not been used in this instance. But we have heard about them earlier when Moses and Aaron together were able to win over the magic of the Egyptian magicians. We can also read in the biography of Yogi Milarepa (W.Y. Evans-Wentz) about the two kinds of plagues that he had mastered to punish his errant relatives first and the neighbours, showing animosity to his mother, later, and that included subsiding of a house or land with all the men and women present thereupon.

As was to be expected, on the following day, the whole community of the Israelites rebelled against Moses and Aaron, saying, "you have killed the people of the Lord". So, the Lord spoke to Moses again, offering to consume the congregation in a moment. Moses, however, was able to save the day for the people of Israel. He asked Aaron to carry his censer with incense laid on it and to run into the middle of the assembly, seeking atonement for the people. And the plague could be stopped.

TWO KINGDOMS

King David was now a very old man, and though wrapped in bed clothes he could not keep himself warm. Now Adonijah, son of Haggith, was growing pretentious and saying, 'I will be king!' He had support of a priest and another brother, but not of Prophet Nathan or Priest Zadok. On the other hand, at the time of his marriage to Bathsheba, David had promised to her on oath that he will make her son ascend the throne as the king. Nathan persuaded Bathsheba to make her claim and David obliged by appointing and also anointing Solomon as his successor to the throne, as the king.

Before his death, David was king of Israel for forty years. He reigned at Hebron for seven years, and in Jerusalem for thirty-three. It was customary for the kings to sacrifice at high places till then. Now, Solomon thought of building a temple for Yahweh, the God of Israel. It took him seven years to build and consecrate the Temple at Jerusalem. Solomon offered a community sacrifice of twenty-two thousand oxen and a hundred and twenty thousand sheep to Yahweh at the dedication ceremony.

It was a tradition that all rich and important people in Israel had multiple slaves. An account of the forced labour levied by King Solomon for building the temple, his own palace, Milo and the fortifications of Jerusalem and six other towns including Gezer, has been provided in the Holy Book. Of these, Gezer was invaded, captured and burnt down by Pharaoh, the king of Egypt after having massacred the Canaanites living there, and then he had given the town as a dowry to his daughter, and Solomon had rebuilt the town received by him as a gift from his father-in-law.

1-King 11:1-8 "King Solomon (it is stated), loved many foreign women along with the daughter of Pharaoh: Moabite, Ammonite, Edomite, Sidonian, and Hittite women, from the nations concerning which the Lord had said to the Israelites, 'You shall not enter into marriage with them, neither shall they with you, for they will surely incline your hearts to follow their gods'. Solomon clung to these in love. Among his wives, were seven hundred princesses and three hundred concubines, and his wives turned away his heart. For when Solomon was old, his wives turned away his heart after other gods, and his heart was not true to the Lord his God, as was the heart of his father David. For Solomon followed Astarte, the goddess of the Sidonians and Milcom, the *abomination* of the Ammonites. So, Solomon did what was evil in the sight of the Lord and did not completely follow the Lord, as his father David had done. Then Solomon built a high place for Chemosh the *abomination* of Moab and for Molech the *abomination* of the Ammonites, on the mountain east of Jerusalem. He did the same for all his foreign wives who offered incense and sacrifice to their gods."

The priests and the brotherhood of prophets were not pleased and were angry that other gods were being worshipped, besides Yahweh, by the Royal family. However, Solomon was a wise man, a very wise man actually. In fact, the queen of Sheba, herself a wise person of repute, had at one time visited Solomon. Solomon had an answer for all her questions—not one of them was too obscure for the king to answer to her. She had told him (1K 10:7-8), "Your wisdom and prosperity far surpass the report that I had heard. Happy are your wives! Happy are these your servants who continually attend you and hear your wisdom." She had made many presents to the king. Being such a wise person himself, it was natural that Solomon should have an open and unbiased mind and not a closed one. This, however, was not approved by the brotherhood of priests and prophets. A clear rift had come into effect from this point onwards, and it may be the reason why some of the families were more favourable to another son of David and were opposed to Solomon, from even before he was appointed and had come to be anointed as the king.

It was prophet Ahijah who took the lead to encourage and ready Jeroboam, till then a trusted lieutenant of Solomon for a revolt, proposing a division of the kingdom, the segregated half being supported by ten out of the twelve tribes of the Israelites. The plot had come to light and Jeroboam had managed to escape to Egypt, then. Like David, Solomon too ruled for forty years. As soon as the news of his death became known, Jeroboam returned to Israel. The brotherhood of prophets and priests called their elect Jeroboam, and also Rehoboam, the successor to King Solomon, and they spoke to Rehoboam as follows (1 Kings 12:4): "Your father made our yoke heavy. Now, therefore, lighten the hard service of your father and his heavy yoke that he placed on us, and we will serve you." At the end, the kingdom was divided in two, into Judah and Israel, Judah was left for Rehoboam to rule, while Jeroboam became the king of Israel. He fortified Shechem in the mountain country of Ephraim and made that his residence at first, and later he moved to Penuel at Bethel.

Ahab, became the king of Israel in 38th year of Asa (the great grandson of Solomon), the king of Judah. To the bewilderment and total disapproval of the brotherhood of prophets, he married Jezebel, daughter of Ethbaal, the king of Sidonians, and then proceeded to serve Baal and worship him. He erected an altar to him in the temple of Baal which he built in Samaria. Ahab also put up a sacred pole (to denote that it was a Canaanite religious place in honour of goddess Asherah). It was in his time that Hiel of Bethel rebuilt Jericho. He too was not a favourite with the brotherhood and both his sons died mysteriously at different stages of the construction.

ELIJAH, THE GREAT PROPHET

Once Elijah of Tishbe in Gilead warned Ahab in Israel about an incoming severe drought when there would be neither rain nor dew for several years. It appears that Elijah had very little contact with the brotherhood of prophets. It does not seem he approved of them a great deal as well. Accordingly, whatever the scribes have written about him in the Holy book, appears to have been written by them on the basis of their assumptions in an effort to somehow fill in the blanks, and to cover-up the misdeeds of the brotherhood.

After warning Ahab, himself Elijah moved eastward. There he stayed by the torrent of Cherith, in the east of Jordan. There, the ravens brought food for the holy man twice every day and his need for water could be met by the stream. As the drought set in, after a time, the stream dried up, and he moved to Zarephat in Sidonia. After a long walk, during the last stage of his journey, Elijah was feeling thirsty, as he approached the city gate.

At the city gate, Elijah saw a woman gathering sticks. Addressing her he said, 'Please bring a little water in a pitcher for me to drink. The woman was on her way to fetch it, when he called after her again, 'Please bring me a scrap of bread too in your hand. 'I have no baked bread, but only a handful of meal in a jar', the woman told the holy man, besides a little oil in a jug; I am just gathering a stick or two to go and prepare this for myself and my son to eat, and then we shall die (as there will be nothing left to eat thereafter).'

We have discussed a number of holy men and their ways in both our books mentioned before. What the woman told Elijah shocked him. The whole scenario and the woman being a widow, all became clear to him forthwith. He then told her, 'Do not be afraid, go and do as you have said; but first make a little scone of it for me and bring it to me, and then make some for yourself and for your son.' The holy man assured her, 'neither your jar of meal shall be spent, nor your jug of oil shall be emptied, before the day when the God sends rain on the face of the earth.' The woman went and did as Elijah had told her and they ate the food, she, Elijah himself and the widow's son. The jar of meal was not spent nor the jug of oil emptied, just as Elijah had foretold her. (A few centuries earlier, Krishna, the god whom women loved, had blessed the serving bowl of Paanchaali too in a similar way. Whether she served five or fifty, the bowl with cooked food would not be emptied until she herself ate.)

The Widow's Son Raised to Life

1K 17:24 "After this the son of the woman, the mistress of house, became ill; his illness was so severe that there was no breath left in him. She then said to Elijah, 'What have you against me, O man of God? You have come to me to bring my sin to remembrance and to cause the death of my son!' But he said to her, 'Give me your son.' He took him from her bosom, carried him to the upper chamber where he was lodging, and laid him on his own bed. He cried out to the Lord (prayed), 'O Lord my God, have you brought calamity even upon the widow with whom I am staying, by killing her son?'

"Then he stretched himself (rubbed or passed his hand) on the child three times and cried out to the Lord (prayed again), 'O Lord, my God, let this child's life come into him again.' The Lord listened to the voice of Elijah; the life of the child came back into him again, and he revived. Elijah took the child, brought him down from the upper chamber into the house, and gave him to his mother; then Elijah said, 'See, your son is alive.' So, the woman said to Elijah, 'Now I know that you are a man of God and that the word of the Lord in your mouth is the truth'."

The Elusive Rain

Many days passed like this, and one day Elijah set off back on way to Israel, to meet Ahab again. Around the same time, Ahab summoned Obadiah, the master of palace. As the famine was particularly severe in Samaria, Ahab wanted to scour the country, all the springs and all the ravines, in the hope of finding grass to keep horses and mules alive, to avoid the looming threat when they may be required to themselves slaughter the stock. He decided to go in one direction for this purpose and sent Obadiah to another.

Perhaps the brotherhood families had committed some unpardonable sacrilege, some great offence affecting the queen, whom they hated, and to escape her ire, Obadiah had hidden about 150 of the prophets, also providing them food, till the time the queen's ire should subside. The word used by the scribes 'when the queen was butchering prophets' seems certainly biased. A queen which was not liked by them, but was loved by her husband, who had built a temple for her to worship there with her, cannot run into in ire except in the case of something outright wrong, calling for severe punishment.

Probably, Obadiah was asked to go east, and whom should he meet but Elijah, who was on his way back to see Ahab. (1K 18:7-12) "As Obadiah was on the way, Elijah met him; Obadiah recognized him, fell on his face and said, 'Is it you, my lord Elijah?' He answered him, 'It is I. Go tell your lord that Elijah is here.' And he said, 'How have I sinned, that you hand your servant over to Ahab to kill me? As the Lord your God lives, there is no nation or kingdom to which my lord has not sent to seek you, and when they would say, "He is not here," he would require an oath of the kingdom or nation that they had not found you.' But now you say, "Go and tell your lord that Elijah is here." As soon as I have gone from you, the spirit of the Lord will carry you I know not where; So, when I come and tell Ahab and he cannot find you, he will kill me, although I your servant has revered the Lord from my youth'." Elijah assured him that he will not disappear.

In between, the scribes have shown Obadiah to continue his diatribe further by describing his act of saving the one hundred and fifty prophets from the queen's ire, kind of making Elijah also a party to this knowledge, though it does not seem to fit the occasion at all. Further, either the awe in which the brotherhood held Elijah was feigned, or the freedom to shower him with such irrelevant diatribe was a non-event, only an insertion to justify a horrendous act that was to take place at a subsequent hour.

It is obvious, however, that Elijah was Ahab's only hope to turn to, while the drought continued to bring great misery to his country and its people and, hence, he had not left any stone unturned to locate the holy man of great capability. He came forthwith to meet the Master as he received his message. Elijah told him to give orders for all Israel to gather round him on Mount Carmel, besides the four hundred fifty prophets of Baal, and the four hundred prophets of Asherah, who ate at Jezebel's table (The prophets of Asherah are not mentioned hereafter throughout the long narrative). The words used by Ahab to greet the prophet, when he came to meet him seem to be comical, and a 'part of the narrative' of what followed appears to be utterly bizarre and illogical, but we repeat the narrative verbatim, so that the event and what follows can be understood in a sensible manner and also why a botched-up effort is clearly visible to insert paragraphs of little meaning and consequence here and there.

The Sacrifice on Carmel

1K 18:20-40 "So Ahab sent to all Israelites and assembled the prophets at Mount Carmel. Elijah then came near to all the people (Many words seem to have been put into his mouth) and said, 'How long will you go limping with two different opinions? If (Yahweh) the Lord is God, follow him, but if Baal, then follow him.' The people didn't answer him a word. Then Elijah said to the people, 'I, even I only, am left as a prophet of (Yahweh) the Lord, but Baal's prophet number four hundred and fifty. Let two bulls be given to us; let them choose one bull for themselves, cut it in pieces and lay them on the wood, but put no fire to it. I will prepare the other bull and lay it on the wood but put no fire to it. Then you call on the name of your God and I will call on the name of (Yahweh) the Lord; the god who answers by fire is indeed the God'. All the people answered, 'Well spoken'! Then Elijah said to the prophets of Baal, 'Choose for yourselves one bull and prepare it first, for you are many; then call on the name of your God, but put no fire on it.' So, they took the bull that was given them, and prepared it, and called on the name of Baal from morning until noon, crying, 'O Baal, answer us!' But there was no voice and no answer. They limped about the altar they had made. At noon Elijah mocked them (goaded or instructed them) saying, 'Cry aloud! Surely, he is a God, either he is meditating or he has wandered away, or he is on a journey; or perhaps he is asleep and must be awakened!' Then they cried aloud, and as was their custom, they cut themselves with swords and lances until the blood gushed out over them. As midday passed, they raved on until the time of offering the oblation, but there was no voice, no answer, and no response.

"Then Elijah said to all the people, 'Come closer to me', and all the people came closer to him. First, he repaired the altar of the Lord that had been thrown down; Elijah took twelve stones, according to the number of tribes of the sons of Jacob, to whom the word of the Lord came, saying, 'Israel shall be your name'; with the stones he built an altar in the name of the Lord. Then he made a trench around the altar, large enough to contain two measures of seed. Next, he put the wood in order, cut the bull in pieces, and laid it on the wood. He said, 'Fill your jars with water and pour it on the burnt offering, and on the wood (perhaps on the stones, since the offering had not been burnt yet, while the wood must not become wet too).' They did this. Then he said, 'Do it a second time,' and they did this a second time. Again, he said, 'Do it a third time', and they did it a third time, so that the water ran all around the altar and filled the trench also with water.

"At the time of the offering of the oblation, the prophet Elijah came near and said, 'O Lord (Yahweh), God of Abraham, Isaac and Israel, 'let it be known today that you are God in Israel, that I am your servant, and that I have done all these things at your bidding (only). Answer me, O Lord, answer me, so that these people may know that you, O Lord, are God, and that you have turned their hearts back !!'

"Then the fire of the Lord fell and consumed the burnt offering, the wood, the stones, and the dust and even licked up the water in the trench. When all the people saw it, they fell on their faces and said, 'The Lord (Yahweh) indeed is God!' Elijah said to them, 'Seize the prophets of Baal: do not let one of them escape.' Then they seized them (they did so in the presence of the King, unless the King had gone away in the middle of the ritual which was aimed at bringing the rain, on some purpose), and Elijah brought them down to the Wadi Kishon and killed them. (The ritual was not over yet, and if he had taken only one minute to kill one prophet, it would have taken him seven and half hours to finish off the four hundred and fifty of them)."

It seems the very objective and the narrative had somehow become altered. The drought was foretold by Elijah. As the drought grew in severity, Elijah was the only ray of hope. Ahab was looking for him everywhere without success, though when the time was opportune, Elijah himself had travelled back to his place and had sent for him. The purpose was to end the drought and stop the suffering of the people. However, from the narrative provided by the scribes, it appears that sole objective of Elijah was to put Baal, whom both the king and the queen paid obeisance, in bad light and to eliminate the prophets of Baal favoured by the queen. The rain would appear to have suddenly become secondary, almost like a non-issue.

The Drought Ends

1K 18:41-46 "Elijah said to Ahab (who had been present all through, thus far), 'Go up, eat and drink, for there is sound of rushing rain.' So, Ahab went up to eat and drink. Elijah went up to the top of Carmel; there he bowed himself down upon the earth, and put his face between his knees. He said to his servant, 'Go up now, look toward the sea'. He went up and looked, and said, 'There is nothing.' Then he said, 'Go again', seven times. At the seventh time he said, 'Looks a little cloud no bigger than a person's hand is rising out of the sea.' Then he (Elijah) said, 'Go say to Ahab, "Harness your chariot and go down before the rain stops you." In a little while the heavens grew black with clouds and wind; there was a heavy rain. Ahab rode off and went to Jezreel. But the hand of the Lord was on Elijah; he girded up his loins and ran in front of Ahab to the entrance of Jezreel."

Needless to say, that as was his wont, Elijah would have disappeared from the public view after his job had been accomplished. Again, nowhere else in the Bible stones are made an object of worship and that exactly twelve stones were picked up to make a proper alter for the ritual Elijah had in mind, made it easy for the scribe(s) to link it with twelve tribes of Israel.

Throughout the entire narratives associated with Elijah, it does not appear that he was a prophet guiding and leading the brotherhood of Jewish priests, though he didn't disown them, since he couldn't have disowned any people, as a true man of God. On the other hand, he did specifically ask for the prophets of Baal to organize the event. The entire proceedings were aimed at bringing in the rains, and the only ritual known anywhere, specifically to meet this particular objective, is called *dwadash rudrabhisheka*, which means a ritual associated with propitiation of Mahesha or Swayambhuva, the God of gods which can manifest and take a form (please see Introduction), in its twelve aspects, using one stone for each of the twelve forms into which it comes to manifest. It is still practiced by the people in India in about twenty of its States, when the rains are delayed, and more often than not with positive result.

The filling of jars three times to bath the stones is a standard practice too, though the liquid content becomes altered for each bath given to the deity worshipped through the medium of a stone. However, the arrangement was being looked after by the prophets of Baal, who had been specifically requisitioned by Elijah. Probably there were three different drums with varying contents, like water, milk and honey, arranged by the prophets of Baal from which the jars were filled. Again, people who worship one particular deity as their principal deity are never barred from propitiating other deities on different occasions. The narrow minded and anti-idolator families of the brotherhood would not know anything of such fine processes and would write anything in the Holy Book entrusted to them to fill in the blanks and to suit their end.

Further, it seems very likely that it was the one hundred and fifty prophets of the brotherhood in hiding who were provided with arms by their families to ambush and kill the four hundred and fifty prophets of Baal, while the King and Prophet had gone abroad to welcome the rain to widen the area of its fall to its maximum. They would still have had their hiding place well secured to go back to when the King returned, and this being well known too that Elijah would be away, shy of taking the bows that were his due (un-interested to mix up with the masses, an uninitiated crowd made up by run of the mill kind of people). Even the sacrifice of two oxen seems doubtful. Probably Elijah had not included a bull sacrifice at all, but on their side the brotherhood may have insisted on sacrificing one bull for themselves, by themselves.

When A Holy Person Feels Sad and Horrified

The families, at that point of time, and possibly right through to the time of Jesus, were made up by gross people, who could not think much far ahead in future. We know of the epithets used by Jesus to describe them, whenever an occasion presented itself. Even the scribes among them appear to have tried to cash-in on whatever they knew about the nature and ways of Elijah; in fact, even of his most beloved disciple Elisha. The scribes seem to go all the way to expose themselves, as they record chapter 1K 19 in the Holy Book. We have seen that Elijah preferred to stay out of public-glare most of the time. It seems, it was true of his most beloved and possibly only disciple Elisha too. The two prophets not only appear to have been treated shabbily in written record, but repeated efforts to misuse their names as a kind of forged rubber stamp for some very black deeds seem to readily become evident to an unbiased reader from their own writings.

If we leave aside the scribes and the so-called brotherhood, the masses held the prophets, and usually also the kings, in high esteem, whereas actions of both kings and the prophets always seem to cause consternation in the leadership of the brotherhood of the day. That was the reason that sheep was available for Jesus, the Christ, to separate from the goats and words like *serpents, brood of vipers, thieves and bandits*, have been used by him. And yet, it cannot be said that brotherhood did not carry a clout of their own amidst the mixed lot of the people, thriving on rumours, and mostly ignorant about what actually went on. These folks could not approach the high prophets, but other members of the brotherhood with a self-worn halo of their own were always close at hand to convey to them the words of Yahweh, their God.

1K 19:1-8 "Ahab told Jezebel everything that Elijah had done, and how he had killed all the prophets with the sword (The king was no fool. Chances are he must have told her what he suspected as actually having happened, and what the political equation was and how the exigency of the hour stood). Then Jezebel sent a messenger to Elijah, saying, 'So may the gods do to me and more also, if I do not make your life like the life of one of them by this time tomorrow (If somebody was writing a cheque to himself, he is free to fill any amount, even if there be no money in the bank. Surprisingly, in the same breath the scribes seem to convey that the queen knew exactly where to find the Prophet to be able to send a message to him. Besides, they do not also mention the action taken by the otherwise ruthless queen to fulfil the punishment promised by her against the prophet)!' Then he (the great Elijah who could appear or disappear at will) was afraid; he got up and fled for his life and came to Beersheba, which belonged to Judah; he left his servant there.

"But he himself went a day's journey into the wilderness, and came and sat down under a solitary broom tree. He asked that he might die, 'It is enough; now, O Lord, take away my life; for I am no better than my ancestors (Getting up in the middle of a great propitiating event where whole of Israel was present, I could get up and butcher 450 people before resuming the ritual) (or that the stigma of killing 450 devout people invited at my instance, should be attached to my name with such ease) (or none of these; he was just shocked to hear of the killings and was extremely sad).'

"Then he lay down under the broom tree and fell asleep. Suddenly an angel touched him and said to him, 'Get up and eat.' He looked, and there at his head was a cake baked on hot stones, and a jar of water. He ate and drank and lay down again. The angel of the Lord came a second time, touched him and said, 'Get up and eat, or the journey will be too much for you (the scribes knew of the long journey ahead, though they forgot to disclose the purpose).' He got up and ate and drank; then he went in the strength of that food forty days and forty nights to Horeb the mount of God. At that place he came to a cave and spent the night there." It seems obvious that he was so aghast to hear the developments and of the killing of the 450 devout people invited by him to conduct the ceremony, that he kept on walking, as if in a trance, as if into timeless wilderness, until his path was blocked by a mountain. True prophets who can give life, can never take life of another. They can be very-very sorry and sad nevertheless, even if they may not think of a severe punitive retribution.

The brotherhood was not through with Jezebel yet, however; nor with the king. They actually had little contact with Elijah. We have seen how afraid Obadiah was when he had an encounter with Elijah, and also how conceited. While Elijah was staying put at Horeb, away from the machinations of the brotherhood, we see back-insertion of some future events, a few to sanctify future misdeeds by the brotherhood on one hand and on the other to cover up their unawareness about existence of Elisha as an advanced disciple of Elijah, who may have been declared by the king as the Prophet, after Elijah had passed away.

1K 19:15-17 "Then the Lord said to him (Elijah), 'Go, return on your way to the wilderness of Damascus; when you arrive, you shall anoint Hazael as king of Aram. Also, you shall anoint Jehu son of Nimshi as king over Israel, and you shall anoint Elisha, son of Shaphat of Abel-meholah, as prophet in your place'. Whoever escapes the sword of Hazael, will be put to death by Jehu; and whoever escapes the sword of Jehu, Elisha shall kill'."

Elijah Ascends to Heaven

2 Kings-2: Elijah and Elisha set out from Gilgal. They first come to Bethel and then to Jericho. Everywhere, they went, the brotherhood of prophets came to meet Elisha to inform him, "Do you know that today the Lord will take your master away from you?' and at each place Elisha replies, 'Yes I know, keep silent'. Also, at each place, Elijah said, 'Elisha, you stay here, for the Lord has sent (only) me to the Jordan,' while Elisha replies, 'As the Lord lives and as you yourself live, I will not leave you!' (Chances are that none of the brotherhood knew about what was on the cards, where they were going and what lay ahead, or even that Elisha was the one who was going to be appointed the Prophet)!

2K 2:7-13 "Fifty men of the company of prophets also went and stood at some distance from them, as they both were standing by the Jordan. Then Elijah took his mantle and rolled it up and struck the water; the water was parted to one side and to the other, and the two of them crossed on dry ground.

"When they had crossed, Elijah said to Elisha, 'Tell me what I may do for you before I am taken from you?' Elisha said, 'Please let me inherit a double share of your spirit.' He responded, 'You have asked a hard thing, yet if you see me as I am being taken from you, it will be granted you; if not, it will not.' As they continued walking and talking, a chariot of fire and horses of fire separated the two of them, and Elijah ascended in a whirlwind into heaven. Elisha kept watching and crying out, 'Father, father! The chariots of Israel and its horsemen!' But when he could no longer see him, he grasped his own clothes and tore them in two pieces. He picked up the mantle of Elijah that had fallen from him, and went back and stood on the bank of the Jordan."

Of course, the fifty of the brotherhood of prophets who had halted some distance away from the river, were not really privy to what really transpired. But to that extent, it is an acceptable privilege of the scribes to fill in the blanks and to complete the narrative.

THE BROTHRHOOD PREVAILS

We have discussed, how the brotherhood of the prophets had become disenchanted with king Solomon and his son and had managed to split the kingdom into two, whereby Judah was left to be ruled by the descendants of king Solomon, while kingdom of Israel was handed over to Jeroboam, who had the backing of a majority of the brotherhood of prophets. We have also seen, how in his own time, even Ahab, the king of Israel, had come to earn extreme displeasure of the brotherhood of prophets by marrying Jezebel, daughter of the king of Sidonians, and who joined his wife in worshipping Baal. For several generations, the brotherhood now disapproved of the ways of both their kings whose loyalty to Yahweh had become divided. It was looking to depose both the kings. However, the masses were not with them. The only way open for the brotherhood, as such, was to have both the kings killed. As for masses, vis-a-vis the written word, the scriptures were written by the scribes working for the brotherhood and only the prophets were able to access the same. Earlier, only they could talk to Yahweh, the God of the Israelites. From here on, however, this norm seems to have been relaxed.

2K 8:25-29 "In the twelfth year of King Joram son of Ahab of Israel, Ahaziah, son of King Jehoram of Judah began to reign. Ahaziah was twenty-two years old when he began to reign; he reigned one year in Jerusalem. His mother's name was Athaliah, a granddaughter of King Omri of Israel. He also walked in the way of the House of Ahab, doing what was evil in the sight of the Lord (displeasing to the brotherhood), as the House of Ahab had done, for he was son-in-law to the house of Ahab.

"He went with Joram son of Ahab to wage war against King Hazael of Aram at Ramoth-gilead, where the Armaeans wounded Joram. King Joram returned to be healed in Jezreel of the wounds that the Armaeans had inflicted on him at Ramah, when he fought against King Hazael of Aram. King Ahaziah, son of Jehoram of Judah went down to see Joram son of Ahab in Jezreel because he was wounded."

Meanwhile, (2K 9:1-3 reads) "Then the prophet Elisha called a member of the company of prophets to him, 'Gird up your loins; take this flask of oil in your hand, and go to Ramoth-gilead. When you arrive, look for Juhu son of Jehoshaphat son of Nimshi; go in and get him to leave his companions, and take him into an inner chamber. Then take the flask of oil, pour it on his head, and say, 'Thus says the Lord the God of Israel: I anoint you king over Israel.' Then open the door and flee, do not linger. (Note: A bit of mix up may have occurred. Probably the scribe who wrote 1K 19:16 which says Yahweh said to Elijah, 'You must anoint Jehu son of Nimshi as king of Israel,' may have retired or died in the meantime and the task had been taken over by another scribe. The current scribe was unaware that the suggested insertion entrusting the task to Elijah in the name of Yahweh had already been made by his predecessor, else he would have made the necessary correction)."

Reaching Jehu, the young man accordingly poured the oil on his head, saying (2K 9:6-10), "Thus says Lord the God of Israel: I anoint you king of Yahweh's people, of Israel. You shall strike down the house of your master Ahab, so that I may avenge on Jezebel the blood of my servants the prophets (probably the one hundred and fifty prophets in the hiding were caught and killed too, later) and the blood of all the servants of the Lord. (And further revealing the resolve of the brotherhood) For the whole house of Ahab shall perish; I will cut off from Ahab every male, bond or free, in Israel. I will make the house of Ahab like the House of Jeroboam son of Nebat and like the house of Baasha son of Ahijah. The dogs shall eat Jezebel in the territory of Jezreel, and no one shall bury her'. Then he opened the door and fled." (The brotherhood of prophets in later times would seem to be taking a lot more freedom as regards the words of Yahweh than the early prophets. In fact, even the mercenaries appointed by them now seem to acquire the power to hear Yahweh, the God of Israel, on a day-to-day basis).

Juhu, the Elect Prepares to Kill

2K 9:14-21 "Thus Jehu son of Jehoshaphat son of Nimshi conspired against Joram. Joram with all Israel had been on guard at Ramoth-gilead against King Hazael of Aram, but King Joram had returned to be healed in Jezreel to recover of the wounds that the Aramaens had inflicted on him when he fought against King Hazael of Aram). So, Jehu said, 'If this is your wish, (and then instructing the senior officers of army that were given in his charge and who were present with him at the time of his anointment) 'let no one slip out of the city to go and tell the news in Jezreel.' Then Jehu mounted his chariot and went to Jezreel, where Joram was lying ill. King Ahaziah of Judah had come down to visit Joram.

"In Jezreel, the sentinel standing on the tower spied the company of Jehu arriving and said, 'I see a company.' Joram said, 'Take a horseman; send him to meet them, and let him say, "Is it peace?" So, the horseman went to meet him; he said, 'Thus says the king, "Is it peace"?' Jehu responded, 'What have you to do with peace? Fall in behind me.' The sentinel reported, saying, 'The messenger reached them, but he is not coming back.' Then he sent out a second horseman, who came to them and said, 'Thus says the king, "Is it peace"?' Jehu answered, 'What have you to do with peace? Fall in behind me.' Again, the sentinel reported, 'He has reached them, but he is not coming back. It looks like the driving of Jehu son of Nimsh, for he drives like a manic.' Joram said, 'Get ready.' And they got his chariot ready. Then King Joram of Israel and King Ahaziah of Judah set out, each in his chariot, and went to meet Jehu; they met him at the property of Naboth the Jezreelite."

Assassination of Both the Kings

2K 9:22-28 "When Joram saw Jehu he asked, 'Is it peace, Jehu?' He answered, 'What peace there can be, so long as the many prostitutions and sorceries of your mother Jezebel continue?' Then Joram reined about and fled, saying to Ahaziah, 'Treason, Ahaziah!' Jehu drew his bow with all his strength and shot Joram between his shoulder, so that the arrow pierced his heart, and he sank in his chariot. Jehu said to his aide Bidkar, 'Lift him out and throw him on the plot of ground belonging to Naboth the Jezreelite, for remember how, when you and I rode side by side behind his father Ahab, how the Lord (Yahweh) uttered this oracle against him: "For the blood of Naboth and the blood of his sons that I saw yesterday, says the Lord, I swear I will repay you on this very plot of ground." Now, therefore, lift him out and throw him on the plot of ground in accordance with the word of the Lord'."

"When King Ahaziah of Judah saw this, he fled in the direction of Beth-haggan. Jehu pursuied him, saying, 'Shoot him also!' And they shot him in his chariot at the ascent of Gur, which is by Ibleam. Then he fled to Megiddo and died there. His officers carried him in a chariot to Jerusalem and buried him in his tomb with his ancestors in the City of David."

Assassination of Queen Mother Jezebel

2K 9:30-34 "When Jehu came to Jezreel, Jezebel heard of it; she painted her eyes and adorned her head and looked out of the window. As Jehu entered the gate, she said, 'Is it peace, Zimri, murderer of your master?' He looked up to the window and said, 'Who is on my side? Who? Two or three eunuchs looked down at him. He said, 'Throw her down'. So, they threw her down; some of her blood spattered on the wall and on the horses, which trampled her. Then he went in and ate and drank."

Jehu made the authorities of Samaria to behead all the other seventy sons of Ahab and to present the head of each son to him on a separate plate as their gift to the new king. Whatever resistance they tried to offer evaporated soon and they had to bow to the wishes of the tyrant to save their own lives and those of their family members. They did behead the sons of Ahab and presented each head on a separate plate to Jehu as demanded by him. Jehu captured all the brothers of Ahaziah also and slaughtered them at the storage-well of Beth Eked. He did not spare a single one, out of the forty-two brothers of Ahaziah also.

The brotherhood of the prophets had their revenge. They had readied the field and set the course for many people like them who were to follow them. Intrigue, murder, beheading, extreme cruelty to women and children, slaughter, massacre—everything in the rule book of the devil was there. The mankind has continued to reap the fruit of the seeds sown some 3,500 years ago. Some six hundred years had passed since then, but the idolators had continued to be the worst sufferers—at the receiving end, and it has been that way since then, at least until now, since now it is spreading further and other people are being beheaded too at the pleasure of the perpetrators, though in the name of God.

Denominations may have changed, but guiding principles have remained the same for many people, for the new kind of carefully crafted phenotype. Intolerance and aggression are no more restricted to permissiveness or authority derived from primitive and obscure religious beliefs any more, new ideologies have come into existence. These may have begun in the name of people, with declared objectives of freeing them from oppression and misrule, but these are turning into dictatorships with lifetime liens not only in favour of individuals but individual families as well. Naked aggression, territory grabbing, bullying of smaller, weaker or befooled neighbours; luring island nations, turning them into rented out territories for strategic maritime operations; all the tools of the devil are employed by brazen faced dictators assuming titles of presidents, general secretaries and the supreme commanders of people's republics.

The situation needs to be rectified. The mankind needs to survive, especially the young ones. Of the seven million people who have fled Ukraine till date, close to a half were kids. Their parents expected that all of them would grow as normal persons. However, now many among them may grow with 'revenge' as the principal 'word' inscribed into their system to guide them in their life, as they grow. Houses may have been destroyed, one or both parents may have or may get killed, mother-land or it's parts, may have been annexed, economic hardships caused and abhorrent decisions may also come to be imposed by people with murder in mind and written on their countenance. Luckily for the mankind, less than a third of the humanity follows the communist ideology at this point of time.

Chapter 4

BEGINNING OF THE END

The Indian Sub-continent was once an island located at the western end of the Indo-Australian plate. By about eighty million years ago (Ma), pushed by the convection currents generated in the inner mantle, the Indo-Australian tectonic plate had begun to move northward. India was approximately 6400 km south of the Eurasian plate at that time, and separating the two was the Tethys Ocean.

As India approached Asia, around 40 Ma, the Tethys Sea continued to shrink and a better part of its seabed slowly pushed upwards. It disappeared completely under the Eurasian plate around 20 Ma and sediments rising from its seabed formed a mountain range, which would be the precursor of the Tibetan plateau and the Himalayas, as these are known today. An often-cited fact used to illustrate this process is that the summit of Mount Everest is made of marine limestone which may have come from this ancient sea.

It is a peculiarity of the Himalayan formation that the end of the Tibetan plateau is situated at a distance of more than 300 km from the Himalayas on one hand, while on the other, the Earth's crust in this region is almost 75 km thick as against an average global crust thickness of 40 km. Tibet is often called the "Roof of the World" as this plateau is the largest and highest area ever to exist in the Earth's history, with an average elevation exceeding 5000 meters. It was able to gain its present height by about 8 Ma.

On one hand, the Tibetan plateau continued to gain in height on the side of the Asian plate, while on the other the Himalayas proper, the middle range and the Himalayan foothills came to form on the side of the Sub-continent. The Himalayan range runs west-northwest to east-southeast in an arc which is 2,400 kilometers long with its width varying from 400 kilometers in the west to 150 kilometers in the east. It is home to the planet's highest peaks, including Mount Everest which at 8,848 meters is the highest of all. The Range includes over a hundred mountains which exceed 7,200 meters in elevation. The youngest and newest chain of mountains built by Nature is the Himalayas.

THE SEAT OF THE HOLIEST OF THE HOLY

Being the roof of the world, and accompanied by the highest of the peaks, there should be little surprise that Tibet and the adjoining regions of the Himalayas should have been a favourite with the ascetics, mendicants, and others in search of spiritual enlightenment. Nature itself, in a way, has created this ideal spot, which is actually and naturally like a holy roof of the world. It is removed from the evil of down-under. Basal impurities, like evil thoughts and tendencies, are slow to emerge and to evolve at this place. The Masters too have whole-heartedly accepted it and have patronized it.

The holiness associated with a place, and the spiritual power naturally exuded by a place does not, however, arise out of a name or merely a geographical position, but by the long and continued presence of the holy people, who remain in close touch with the divine. The Himalayas and the Tibetan plateau have remained associated with Great Masters (Siddhas), Great Bhairavies (Women Siddhas), Great Lamas, and the other divinities for more than seven thousand years without any break.

Having been blessed by continuous presence of some very great souls right since the prehistoric times, spiritual powers can arise easily and naturally at this pious land to make it an ideal place for rise of Siddha-lands and for setting up of Siddha ashrams (These very special kinds of places are explained in detail in *Jesus Christ and the Spirit of Truth*). The place was sparsely populated in the prehistoric times and Mount Kailash, situated in this very region, is traditionally revered as being the abode of Aadinath

Shankara of the Hindus, right since those prehistoric days—going back much beyond the 7,000 years' mark.

Two of the world's greatest religions have also come to be born and to prosper under the backdrop of the Himalayas and Tibet. From the earliest of times, this roof of the world was indisputably considered to be the seat of Sanatan Dharma—of Nature's own religion (or the way Nature likes the things to work) that may extend into the eternity. Descending from here only, Sage Agastya (*Jesus Christ and the Spirit of Truth*) had first chosen the Java Island in Indonesia as his abode, before turning back to settle down in South India.

Buddhism may have entered Tibet as early as the 2nd century after Christ, and there have been repeated efforts—some even with gaps of several centuries—to gather texts from India and to translate them and imbibe them—by the kings, Lamas (like Marpa, the Translator), and other teachers in Tibet. Thus, apart from being the favourite abode of the siddhas since prehistoric times, naturally and of its own, Tibet has also emerged as the supreme seat of the Buddhist religion over the last 1,200 years. Especially the Lhasa town and the Potala Palace are accorded a similar status by the Buddhists as is accorded to Vatican City by the Christians. Even today, the Tibetans look upon the Dalai Lama with similar reverence as the Christian world looks upon the Pope.

We can see that a great injustice has been perpetrated on the people of Tibet. And yet, even though the political situation is unfavourable to them in the present time, the Buddhist monks and the active practitioners of Buddhism have retained the same thought process and life style of positive values and non-violence, as displayed by them over the past 1200 years. Even today, millions of Buddhist monks and other followers of the Dalai Lama pray day and night to the God Almighty to forgive them for any offence or oversight on their part committed in the past, that may have led to what they consider to be an ultimate deprivation, and to return their land to them so that they may be able to lead their lives in their own ways once again.

For sure, a grave wrong was done. Without any context, Tibet was invaded and occupied. There was a time when the ruling clans to the south of the Himalayas were called the Kurus and the land further north was called the land of the Uttar Kurus in the Aryan scriptures. The people on both sides travelled freely to either territory. The idea of encroaching each other's land was beyond imagination for either of the two people. On the other side, the ruling families in Tibet often entered into matrimonial alliances with the ruling families in China and there was little apprehension of any invasion from that end also. Fact is, these peace-loving people, serving as a buffer state between two huge civilizations, never felt the need to maintain any armed forces to defend their borders.

It is well-known that just by killing the city guards and the guards of the Potala Palace of the Tibetan religious and administrative head, the People's Liberation Army of China had gained victory on the pious land and had declared it as part of its own country. In the whole of human history, it is an unparalleled instance of extreme injustice, that went totally unopposed. It was the easiest of the walk-ins by an invading army in the known history, when nobody else anywhere in the world even batted an eyelid, as if it was an un-event. It was like the incident narrated by Jesus in the parable of the 'Good Samaritan', the only different being that there was no Samaritan in this case, so that the injured lay on the road dying and the people nonchalantly passed by.

The Tibetans were like poor hapless sheep who never thought of securing their borders or building a sheepfold for themselves, as Jesus had thought about at one time. Only the followers of Jesus were in a position to help, but they never considered this particular neighbour as an equal—as worth loving or bothering about. We do make mistakes, however. And, it was a historic blunder, of course, to allow this change in geography to be precipitated in an artificial manner in blatant violation of every human value.

It is a situation of great shame and discomfort for the mankind as a whole that today the Dalai Lama should be forced to live in exile on a different soil. However, it is still possible and very much desirable to set this blunder and historical injustice right. Else, it should be assumed that the western world following Jesus, the Christ, is still not ready for the Second Coming promised by him. They are not ready to understand the Spirit of Truth even if it was to be revealed to them and even if the signs outlined by Jesus should all be present. There is no purpose in knowing God's Truth, if one lacks the courage to stand for it, fearing and worrying about some economic disadvantage or a personal discomfort. Besides, it is not suggested that a military expedition should be launched. All that is needed at this stage is to pronounce the mischief and take a stand, and then firming it up more and more in the days ahead.

The world, in a way, has shrunken to a small size now—a kind of hodgepodge, in which people believing in different religions, harbouring different values and following different political systems have moved much closer to each other. It has turned into a heterogeneous mix, where people are linked to each other in a variety of complex ways. In the interest of communication, trade, and exchange of industrial outputs, often a policy of appeasement is pursued by the nations. And yet, willingly or unwillingly, knowingly or unknowingly, we have already moved into a very dangerous zone, that may lead to undoing of the human race itself.

The stake of the people on the right side of the scale is bigger, and naturally so. The world has already seen through the havoc, destruction and spoilage brought about by the two world wars, and they want to avoid a third one at all costs—even by going to the limit of all reasonable tolerance. But haven't they playing their hand wrong? In place of buying time for themselves, have not they been buying all the time for those with most ulterior motives and with least care for the fate of the humanity as a whole? Why the other side should also have displayed same restraint, once it was ready? We can see that there been spillages already, leading to the calamity of a nature never seen before. And now we see that Ukraine has been invaded and other countries are being threatened of dire consequences.

Aren't we forgetting the warning given by Jesus? Hadn't he said (Matthew 24:6), "You will hear of wars and *rumours* of wars; see that you are not alarmed, for this is something that must happen, for the end will not be yet?" The message given by Christ is clear. We are already hearing the sound of bombs and missiles raining on some forty towns of Ukraine for over four months now, killing people and reducing a lot of good work to rubble. We are hearing *rumours* (or threats) about use of nuclear weapons capable of destroying the whole of Europe in a couple of hours.

Jesus, however, had not stopped at this point, as this was something that was due on one or the other of these days anyway, but has urged the mankind to not to become so alarmed as to altogether cow down, *as the end will not be yet, or to become so provoked as to jump headlong into the fray. They probably need to be proactive and more and more pre-emptive at the same time.*

An Ideology of Terror and Havoc

The philosophy of Karl Marx did appear to hold a high promise when it first appeared. And it may have high achievements to its credit as well, for the time when it had come to surface. But those times are behind us now, and possibly forever. The main objective of communism was to organise the farmers and the common workers to uproot the unscrupulous ruling clans which were exploiting the masses of ordinary people. Raising of arms was permitted too.

However, as far as the knowledge of the author goes, there was no proposal for expansionism, especially by overthrowing of any just and benevolent regime that had the full approval of its people. The people of Tibet had not chosen the way of Karl Marx—they had little use for it. Rather it was the Marxist leaders of China who had invaded and subjugated the people of Tibet against their wishes and to their great consternation. If it was in accordance with the communist ideology, then, for sure, it was the worst face of that ideology. Seen in such context, it is the worst thought process and worst ideology; a hawk ideology, waiting for an opportunity to pounce on its prey. It may be straightway inimical to all humanity!

It was not a case of uprooting the rule of an unjust ruler, but of uprooting a people and uprooting a ruler that was revered by one and all, that was selected by a universally accepted transparent procedure and that was most popular. It was merely an event of invasion and occupancy of a peace-loving country by another nation which called itself a communist country and falsely claimed that it was committed to serve the interest of the commoners. Originally, the ideology was not proposed to create new super-tsars with ambitions of their own. That is a later development, and could be beyond the wildest dreams of Marx himself.

The communist ideology remains only in name in present day China, or in any other country having been formed after overthrowing the then existing regime, in fact, following the principles of Karl Marx. It had served its purpose already and its place has been taken by a new breed of leaders harbouring high personal ambitions unmatched by the tsars and emperors of yore. In fact, a breed of wily dictators is coming to evolve, not to speak of the rise of dictator families and the menace posed by their trigger-happy heirs as well, or by the dictators turning senile with age.

This is a very dangerous situation for the mankind. In democracies of a common or normal kind, the head of state can be changed every four or five years. In the communist world we are able to witness rise of super-dictators with lifetime liens, in control of large war machineries equipped with huge arsenals, but little respect for any democratic values. They have already entered the arena, and now they are ready to invade countries and to expand. Nations (the people) have become irrelevant in all such systems; persons controlling such countries and their regimes can now begin to hold the world to a ransom.

We see precisely such a situation developing in Eastern Europe. After the unwieldy colossal USSR had become sick and had to be dismantled to provide for the long-delayed glasnost or reforms, a number of East European countries were able to walk out of the yoke of communism, opting for a democratic framework of political structure and identity. Within the Russian state, however, though constitutional role of the Communist party was technically removed, the only real change was a division in finer aspects of the ideology and there are two communist parties now in place of one. The communist ideology and its rule have remained, though arguments can be aired and discussion can take place now to the extent the people at the helm are willing to allow or accept.

The strategic alliance working in the name of NATO had served its purpose, after the second world-war was over. However, threat perception of a different kind had begun to emerge from the Communist block for the world at large and, especially, for the comparatively much smaller countries of Western Europe. As a result, even after the break-up of the USSR, for strategic reasons the alliance had not broken up. With Russia having emerged as a super-power again, and piling up more nuclear weapons than all the European countries and the USA combined, the grave suspicion harboured by the developed countries of the West were coming true and NATO too has come to stay. None of the NATO countries can possibly think of extending its borders, but they do seem to want to keep an option in hand to intervene if unhealthy developments take place. Some of the European countries coming out of the former USSR as independent democratic countries have also joined the defence umbrella offered by NATO, and their foresight seems to have proved correct, as those who couldn't or who vacillated are under grave threat already.

The Russian army had invaded Ukraine a few years ago to occupy and subsequently annex the Crimean Peninsula with comparative ease. On the 24th of February this year, in 2022 AD, it invaded Ukraine again, hoping to be able to annex more areas, before taking over the whole of Ukraine in time. However, there are no presidents for life in Ukraine and the new President, Zelensky, was a hard nut to break. Both the invading Russians and the world media were hoping that Kiev will fall within days and it will be a miracle if it could survive a whole week. However, a strong President, ready to give his hundred percent for the defence of his country and the brave Ukraine soldiers, have proven all such prophesies of a near walk-over wrong.

The Russian invasion has entered its nineteenth week already as we write these lines. Over twenty-six thousand Russian soldiers are dead already, leaving aside those that are reported missing. If we exclude the civilians, the toll on the Ukrainian side may be smaller in comparison. In the civilized world of today, the invading army is always at a disadvantage in all such situations. The invading soldiers are sent by a leader to fight and risk their lives not to defend their country but to invade another. The defending army, should it be made up of brave patriots, willing to spend the last drop of their blood fruitfully in the defence of their motherland, on the other hand, stands on a different footing. Unlike the invading army-men not overtly keen to waste their lives, these people have a purpose, and they can fill steel in their heart if they are on the right side of the dividing line of nationalists versus the others and have a firm resolve.

It seems surprising that twelve of the generals have also been killed along with over twenty-six thousand soldiers of Russia. As a ratio of soldiers versus the generals, that seems six to eight times too many. However, but for this on the field improvisation by the generals in the early stages of the Russian invasion, the figures of casualty could have easily doubled. The fighters in frontal ranks during the first month were all young recruits, mostly students, and the rifles they carried were of the 1940s vintage series that failed to work when most needed. The king may have wanted to save his best for the bigger battles he must have in mind. The morale of the young army men was low and in place of keeping to the safe position of the near-tail, the generals must have chosen to take positions at the front.

Perhaps it was over confidence or bad planning, or both. In the early stages of invasion, the news channels kept showing thirty-three kilometre or even longer column of armoured vehicles and tanks marching towards the Ukraine capital. Bombings of cities and towns and the long column of army with its war machinery moving Kiev-ward were a bluff that failed to work. As a result, the plan for young recruits and students gaining first-hand experience in real war situation also went awry. It turned into a nightmare instead. Now hired mercenaries have been introduced in a very large number and perhaps no death record of these people needs to be maintained.

A similar situation had arisen at Doklam on the borders of India a few months earlier, where the Indian soldiers defending their country were able to kill over forty Chinese soldiers with bare hands, losing only half the number in comparison to the invading Chinese. In fact, that is the normal ratio everywhere between the defending army and the invaders, in the post Moghuls scenario—the Tibet being an exception. Further, one disadvantage the invading soldiers obeying their leader face, is death in ignominy, often into hurriedly dug mass graves, since the invading army must conceal the number of deaths for weeks and months, if not for ever. The brave of the defending country, on the other hand, are given a heroic send-off with national anthem and flag, et al.

Introduction of the mercenaries and the brutal force of the Chechnyan fighters under its leader Ramzan Kadyrov holds a frightening prospect for the Ukrainians and the mankind as a whole. In the town of Bucha three hundred civilians with their hands tied behind their backs and shot from point blank range were found from one spot only, and an equal number from other locations. Unfortunately, over thirty thousand civilians including many children have died in Russian bombings of Ukraine. This, of course, is a common curse of invasion anywhere. Yet, luckily every second house in Ukraine has an underground bunker which had been built during the Second World War. Otherwise, the civilian casualties would have multiplied some ten or fifteen times, for sure.

In the reckoning of the author, the young in Russia and China too have a right to be saved and preserved for the morrow and it is a sacrilege to sacrifice them to fill colours in the ambitions of their leaders. As stated, the very system is faulty, and things seem to have reached a stage, where only life-time rulers are likely to emerge now, even if there should be a change in hands.

Vigyan Mitra

In People's Name but Not in Their Interest

It beats all imagination. why the God fearing, decent and highly amenable people of Tibet should have been invaded and burdened with the self-defeating ideology of Karl Marx? It was an ad-hoc ideology for a limited purpose and for a given objective only—it was not a philosophy or even a great policy in the long term. Why the people of Tibet need to go and work in the factories of the Chinese rich? Why should they learn to wield sophisticated weaponry and why should they endanger their lives on borders that do not belong to them or that did not exist before?

Is this fair at all? For sure, it is a highly unwelcome and uncomfortable situation for the people of Tibet. Similar may be the case with the Ukrainian citizens, with nearly a third of them being made up by Russians and about a fourth of the remaining having relatives in Russian mainland. Russian soldiers invading Ukraine to kill people identical to them or to kill their own relatives is ghastly. It may be a war-game none except their leader probably wanted to play. Further, 'not everyone' even among the small number of separatists owing allegiance to Russia, would have wanted towns to be devastated and people to be killed.

The Tibetans are not Chinese; nor do they speak the Chinese language. The slogan coined by the Chinese leaders of one people one country, does not apply to the Tibetans at all. Further, the slogans can be a means employed to win an election or to motivate a people, but not to annex territories, or to bully the mankind as a whole. Nature itself, in a way, had created this holy land of the Lamas as a neutral territory between two large countries. It could have exchanges on both sides, while acting as a buffer state, leaving the two great people on its either side to evolve their respective cultures keeping independent of each other. The common goodwill due and extended to a holy people by both sides, was the reason the Tibetans never felt the need to maintain an army of their own. Else, it would have been impossible for the People's Republic of China to over-run Tibet and occupy the same without a major blood-shed on both sides. It was a trust betrayed, and it seems to precisely indicate a state of affairs, where Jesus himself should have wondered (Luke 18:8) "*And yet, when the Son of Man comes, will he find any faith on earth?*"

Given the backdrop, and after occupying this holy country by force when least expected, how the common people of China can continue to call themselves as followers of Buddha and as a non-violent and peace-loving people, a reputation they enjoyed in the past. In fact, it is more likely that the residents of mainland China, except the rich who needed cheaper labour, themselves may not have been interested at all in enlarging and extending their borders in this manner. In the name of people, the leaders of the country seem to be making use of the People's Army to meet their own ambitious goals only.

Without any valid reason, young people of China are now being deployed to far away borders in such difficult terrains where it is difficult to survive even in the absence of a war. Often, a great reluctance is seen on the part of the young men deputed on such missions. In fact, many of them can be seen shedding tears out of fear and crying in public. In the civilian parlance, even causing a single death calls for a punishment by the law of the land. In a communist country too, shouldn't the people's courts have a say in such matters where young lives are involved?

This being the case and such being the situation, opposition in the public is natural. To counter the same and make the people compliant, on one hand, similar harsh methods as were prevalent some five or six decades ago are now back. On the Tibetan side, likewise, every family is being advised that if they want to remain alive, at least one person has to be spared by them for the Chinese army. What kind of state policy and what kind of communism is this, it is hard to understand? And how can such an army be called the People's Liberation Army? Isn't it turning itself into their leader's Occupation Army instead, now?

On the sides of it all, the citizens of China are now looked upon with a degree of suspicion all over the world. Be it a job in an industrial unit or a technology company, an educational institution or issuance of a visa or renewal thereof, the general attitude of the people on the other side now is to resist or to block. Likewise, the techniques that are now being employed to suppress the growing dissatisfaction among the people, are proving to be counter-productive and are increasing the prevailing dis-satisfaction instead. In a way, it falls in the same category as change of religion of a person or a people through coercive means.

People, in fact, have begun to ponder whether at all they are obliged to remain tied up to the present leadership and to being controlled by it any-more, or at all. The situation in Russia is not much different, with dissenting voices being sent to jail within the country and assets of its citizens being seized or blocked in all parts of the world. Even more surprising than the death of the generals, in fact, is the mysterious death of at least five billionaires in Russia since its Ukrainian invasion commenced. They all made money for themselves and for their country, running into hundreds of billions of dollars, and were on the approved list—all forming a part of what is known as Oligark. They probably over-estimated their opinions as part of the Oligark, offering advice when it was not asked for, since they all may have voiced their uneasiness as far as the invasion in Europe was concerned. The prospect faced by many of the generals in the army may seem as bleak in fact, as a majority of them may be opposed to the idea of first use of the nuclear weapons by their country.

WRONG-WARD: IN WRONG HANDS

God has not been banned, but that may be only a matter of time, if the affairs of the world continue to drift, as at present—in a kind of free fall, and with no one in charge. At least in some parts of the world, God has already been made to look like an outcast. Its role has been kind of taken over by the prophets of modern science. The world, according to them, can arise from nothing as an accident, on its own, and it does not need a God or a creator—much less a purpose or some objective. Haven't they more or less solved all problems of matter and life already, they seem to suggest? Isn't it them who have rid the human thought of superstition and brought the light of scientific knowledge into their lives? Aren't they around already! Why ask for a God—they had begun to sound offended at one time? Why worry about good or evil, or an after-life—they even now seem incredulous?

God could now be treated as unnecessary baggage—a nuisance that one must try to erase from the human memory at the earliest opportunity. And such considerations as an afterlife, goodness or evil, a reward or punishment in the hands of God also went out of fashion with many people, in the post Relativity and post Quantum Theory scenario of the world. A new kind of thinking, with new kinds of political systems based on the proposals of Karl Marx was quick to emerge. It brought in its wake a radical change in the way people thought, and it also opened up the way for dictatorships and lifetime control of a new kind to emerge on the scene.

The systems have the power to galvanize people for their good, for sure. However, if they become too big, they store that much more power to dominate and to harm the people. Whatever the system, and whatever the original objective, some people are clever and they can manoeuvre. In the end, all such systems must pass into the wrong hands—even to families with their own aspirations. Such dictatorships or families can never bring anything good to mankind as a whole and, in the long run, not even to the people under their care or control. Corruption, extortions and exterminations become a fact of life under such regimes.

The workers and labourers uniting and forming unions is quite okay on the merit side of the communist ideology, but the use of might in their name to decimate and destroy people, countries, or even nations, is outright deplorable and totally unethical. An essential fall-out on the side-lines of the communist ideology is rise of a 'left' even among the developed countries. For sure, it may not be the same as communism, but more of a confusion—only a fall-out on its side-lines. It is true as well, at the same time, however, that people may have been forming local communist parties in other democratic countries that covertly become affiliated to or begin to owe allegiance to the communist regimes in Russia or China. Naturally, they remain in correspondence with such principals, working in sync with them and possibly also deriving financial and other support from them. There may be many places in the world, where such systems do now exist, and they do seem to carry at least some potential to try sabotage the right and the constructive.

It may be noteworthy, that to begin with, what even Adolf Hitler did, was to form a Workers' Party with a very restricted following of less than a dozen people, which first converted itself into a Socialist Party and which gained fame and renown later as the Nazi Party.

Science has managed to keep the Church out. However, the bulk of research funding has now moved over to business and industry, which do not care about God or the good. Now a very large chunk of the science fraternity must promote consumerism of all kinds and try to keep the people from talking about God, Jesus, or goodness. One does not know whether one should feel proud about the human achievement or sad. Things do not seem to be moving in the right direction for the Homo-sapiens—for the wellbeing and survival of the 'Son' of man. Things do seem to be passing into wrong hands and moving wrong-ward.

The Right Side of the Scale

The books named by us are as much about the Holy Trinity of the Christian faith as about the Holy Triad of the ancient Indians. These are as much about the wisdom of the ancient masters of India, as about that which Jesus Christ had tried to convey to his apostles. Among other things, they both speak of the same Kingdom of Heaven and the Son of Man. However, whereas keeping in mind the limited understanding of his disciples of those days, Jesus merely makes a reference to a common foundation for both, the ancient rishis of India have also provided a beautiful explanation for this 'foundation' which is in full conformity with the findings of the modern science. This secret of Nature, hiding at the most basic level of all manifestation, is easy to grasp for the fairly evolved human generations of the day now, especially for those who are genuinely curious and have an open mind.

It is only into the Homo-sapiens, the Son of Man, that all the elements that make the world (the macrocosm) are present and are working, as in him the Nature has evolved a complete microcosm too. It is into him that both Shiva and Shakti, the Father and the Holy Spirit have come to manifest to their true potential. It is only into him that besides the relative observer, which is restricted by space, time, and the means of observation at his disposal—the absolute observer side also has its quarters that can be accessed. To access the sublime level of the absolute observer side, however, mere knowledge about the ultimate 'truth' is not enough. The mass of the subtle baggage of good and bad thoughts carried by a person must be reduced first for the awareness to begin to rise to the higher levels, and then it must be left behind altogether. Only then it can cross the doorway to the 'observer-of-the-whole' side.

The humans have two levels of mind, and also of the brain, and have two kinds of tendencies. We have a mammalian brain with animalistic tendencies and to that extent, we are the best animal around that Nature could have produced. However, we are also blessed with a functioning intellectual sheath. We also have it in us to rise above the animal instinct, and animal behaviour. So, we also have human tendencies that are different from those of the animalistic kind, while these may still be latent for some of us and may have managed to come to the fore for many others. That is the reason that we live in a human scenario which has become so badly mixed-up at this point of time.

Naturally, the bulk of the mass that we carry into our subtle body which is substantially impure, giving rise to the evil in us, and which obstructs or restricts our rising to the higher levels of awareness, is contributed by the animal side in us. Another substantial part of the impurity into humans which can have an appreciable mass, is an insatiable urge for endless enjoyment of the objects of the five sensing capabilities that we possess, and an endless craving for consumerism of one kind or another.

There are times, however, when virtue is on the rise, and there are times when it is on the decline: When the devil's hand begins to show itself. Presently, the negative attributes of the devil have been able to bring matters to a stage when by logic and legal means people can set God aside. In practice though, a majority of the people have not set God and its fear aside, only the clever ones and those with evil propensity, taking recourse to the legal technicality, have done so. However, even these handful of leaders in science, religion or philosophies have managed to serve the purpose of the devil sufficiently enough, and aplenty. The global cultural mix could begin to corrupt with proposals of low ethics and no-holds barred stratagems, and some four generations since acceptance of the self-defeating ideology of Karl Marx is a long enough time for the anarchy to spread throughout the globe.

Despite the precarious scenario in the present, however, the things need not be as bleak for the Son of Man, as these appear—if care is taken and in time. First, the knowledge of the realm of the Father, of the abstract, was revealed to the mankind before consumerism could arise to block and blot everything out. And now the knowledge of the realm of matter has been more or less laid bare for it by the cosmic forces at work. The two are not mutually contradictory, however, even if some people may think so.

The Son of Man is in a position to pursue one or the other, or both—the relative interaction with the world, as well as, observing and interaction with the whole. As pointed out by Jesus Christ, this faculty has been with the human progeny from the day the foundation of the world was laid. However, now it is in a position to understand the same. The son of man need not remain ignorant of the huge mansion of its Father in its wholeness which is shared by it, and of the laws of its Nature anymore, i.e., unless he so wants and makes its choice—Let's say, between 'open', 'show later' or 'do not show again'.

As suggested, all that modern science could discover has more or less been discovered. If the intellectual in a son of man was waiting for the science to be over—before it could begin to take stock, and begin to think about the real nature of its own self and of the world—then that time has already come. Nothing spectacular is expected to take place in physics for many centuries and that is hardly going to make much difference anyway when it happens—like the discovery of the Higgs' boson—called the God's particle by the physicists—a few years ago, that was not more than a whimper, failing to make any new bells to toll.

An Endangered Species

The day of the Son of Man may have already arrived. The Homo-sapiens can be said to have fully evolved now—to its true potential, and ready to really take off. During his last round of talks with his disciples, Jesus had spoken of the future and had mentioned 'kingdom of Heaven', which we have discussed in detail in both the books mentioned by us, and also the 'Son of Man', that we are discussing now. For the rightful Son of Man, Jesus had pointed out, 'Then the King will say to those on his right hand, 'Come you who are blessed by my Father, inherit the kingdom prepared for you since the foundation of the world'." (Matthew 25:34)

Jesus had mentioned this situation as the next important event for his followers, which is known as the Second Coming, or the coming of the era of the Son of Man. The movement, he had hinted, will begin in the East. According to Matthew 24:26-28, he had said, "So, if they say to you 'Look, he is in the wilderness,' do not go out. If they say, 'Look, he is in the inner rooms,' do not believe it. For as the lightning comes from the east and flashes as far as the west, so will be the coming of the Son of Man. Wherever the corpse is, that is where the eagles will gather (where there is genuine curiosity backed by a desire to learn, it is there that the spirit of truth shall be welcomed).

"But about that day and hour", Jesus had said (Matthew 24:36), "nobody knows, neither the angels of heaven nor the Son, but only the Father." Jesus had given three signs, however, besides the wars and rumours of war, nation against nation, kingdoms against kingdom, and famines and earthquakes, and had urged his followers to stay awake, so that they may remain alert and may not hesitate to take firm action when the need arose. The first sign Jesus mentions is, "And many false prophets will arise and lead many astray. And because of the increase of lawlessness, the love of many will grow cold. But the one who endures to the end will be saved. And this good news of the kingdom will be proclaimed throughout the world, as a testimony to all the nations, and then the end will come (Matthew 24: 11-14)."

The immediate context mentioned by Jesus was east and, among plenty of other examples, we do see prophets—the funny characters, mostly scions of one failed political family or other, who are false—lacking in wisdom of any kind whatsoever, and yet trying to deceive the people. They keep vying with each other in defining 'everything of value in the east' afresh—kind of believing that if they keep munching the words into their mouths long enough, these would turn into pearls of wisdom on their own—and trying to pull people away from God, from Truth and from the godly (Besides, we can see prophets from across the border crying themselves hoarse, instigating their kind to destroy Hindus). As a second sign, he speaks of the days of great distress, of a worldwide calamity of an unprecedented nature, and we do see a similar situation at hand—caused probably by an unfortunate leak at a wrong hour and wrong place (The rumor when the virus spread, was that after a vaccine was developed it may have surfaced in Taiwan first), and then followed up by an aggression backed with the rattling of nuclear sabres. The days of great distress now include a calamity of two kinds existing side by side, like twin fruits sharing a common seed, and a single stone that has begun to roll adding to its momentum (Daniel).

And, as his third sign, Jesus speaks of an importunate widow to whom justice was finally delivered after great delay. "(Luke 18: 6-8) And the

Lord said, 'You notice what the unjust judge has to say (choosing political expediency to deny the justice)? Now, will not God see justice done to his elect if they keep calling on him day and night even though he still delays to help them? I promise you he will see justice done to them, and done speedily. *But when the Son of Man comes, will he find any faith on earth?*'" Frankly, faith in people's words, or the motives they can harbour, now does not exist anymore. About half the mankind plainly seems to have moved to a side that no one would want to trust even for giving the correct time of the day.

We do see that the 1985 judgement of the Supreme Court of India, which too—like each of the succeeding levels of courts, over a period of seven years, upheld the initial judgment of the lower-most court that favoured the unfairly divorced lady, Shah Bano, at the end of this long chain, had been reversed by a superior judge, in charge of the country at that time, through the might of legislation. We also see the rise of commitment to Justice and Truth coming to prevail in the end and the judgement of the Supreme Court being reinstated (in the most recent times), by a counter legislation, after a delay of another 33 years. The importunate woman too has become a widow in the meantime, while justice could be done speedily enough, since she is still alive, to verbatim match the prophecy.

That the woman had to suffer for some forty years may have to do with the karmic forces at work. However, she did carve a history and still lives to prove the efficacy of the power of foresight of Jesus Christ. The change of hands from wrong and the partisan to the right and universally benevolent powers in this land of the rishis, known for its wisdom, is there for all to see. Millions of women on this chunk of the globe have moved out of centuries of injustice and a dark bleak prospect for ever. It is significant that Jesus too had changed the wording and had replaced the single woman with 'if they keep calling on him' and 'justice done to them'.

We can see that the signs mentioned by Jesus Christ seem to have presented themselves already, and a situation as foreseen by him now actually exists. There seems to be a real need for the mankind to take a prudent and long-term guard. The human survival is all about securing its most precious, the Son of Man, who can start afresh if the need arises. Nations of the world need to heed Jesus and take appropriate actions before it may be too late. Leaders of the men, in their graceful esteems, need to take time off as well to read Jesus and to make an effort to try to understand the God's plan, and also the Truth—as best as they can. They may take a leaf from how Jesus would have acted in such a situation, however. Provided, of course, if they wish to show courage and the needed resolve.

Let's help Nature! Let's help God! Let's defeat the devil! Let's change the gears! Let's help the Son of Man to SURVIVE. Let's DIVIDE in a major way with good or near good on one side and evil and near evil on the other. Let's create a sheepfold, hard to breach, so that the Son of Man does not lose; so that the evil mongers are defeated, while the Son of Man can WIN!! If the economies can survive the Covid, these can survive the gas shortage and other such inconvenience as well. To survive in the long run, the order of the world needs to be changed, and for once the cost must be paid. The benefits, if the other prophesies are to be believed too, may last the whole millennium.

Chapter 5

A MESSAGE ACROSS
TWO MILLENNIUMS

This book, now in in the hands of our readers, itself should be a sign that the time, the situations, and the people, even the opportunity—have all changed now. The edicts to kill, to strike first blow, to punish at the hint, assumption, or allegation of blasphemy or apostasy have all become mostly infructuous now. Times have changed and the humanity is maturing. Purging and reform is the need of the hour to save and preserve humanity in the mankind.

It was time that the heads of the religions should come together and must issue fresh edicts specifically withdrawing the old and the infructuous ones that target idol-worshippers or any other particular communities or people or which confer special punitive powers on one or more of their followers as against any other person. This may save the mankind from being obliterated altogether and it may help people to come together to be able to work for a still higher evolution of mankind.

Mankind has matured in a major way, even if not as a whole. It was the time that religious beliefs were replaced by true knowledge about the reality, and about the omnipresent and omniscient God; When the mankind can leave behind the clumsy baggage of the past and can learn to travel light. Clumsy baggage not only slows the journey of a people, it also obstructs the traffic for others.

There are only two broad sides to Nature—a right side, and a left side which we can also call the wrong side (Matthew 25:32-33). It should be possible to so divide the road for the traffics in a way that everyone can travel at its own pace, without coming in the way of the other. At some point in time, the lanes may merge and everyone may be able to unload the extra baggage—no longer of any use—and to catch up. Mankind may begin to breathe as a single organism then, free from lack of mutual trust, and from any sense of insecurity from another of their kind, forever. And then, there will be neither fear nor guilt to hinder the Homo-sapiens, and even the sky may keep raising the limit! However, a broad divide—as once instigated by Jesus, and as foreseen by him as a likely event in the future—may be necessary beforehand, as a measure of ultimate prudence on the part of the leaders of the world, especially those who have a stake in survival of the Homo-sapiens.

Matthew 25:31-35 "When the Son of Man (the Homo-sapiens as a petitioner—as a species wanting to survive and seeking to be saved) comes in his glory and all the angels with him, then he will sit on the throne of his glory. All nations will be gathered before him and he will separate people one from another as a shepherd separates sheep from the goats, and he will put the sheep at his right hand and the goats at his left. Then the King (The Judge, not the plaintiff) will say to those at his right hand, 'Come, you who are blessed by my Father, inherit the kingdom prepared for you from the foundation of the world, for I was hungry and you gave me food, I was thirsty and you gave me something to drink, I was a stranger and you welcomed me'."

Matthew 25:41-43 "Then he will say to those on his left hand, 'You who are accursed, depart from me into the eternal fire prepared for the devil and his angels, for I was hungry and you gave me no food, I was thirsty and you gave me nothing to drink, I was a stranger and you did not welcome me'." Matthew 25:46 "And these will go away into eternal punishment, but the righteous into eternal life."

The last journey of Jesus Christ begins with his final words to his disciples that he will not be able to repeat, as he will be betrayed. And it was then, that he had broached up the subjects of the Kingdom of Heaven and the 'Son of Man'. About the time of its coming Matthew 24:32-36 reads: From the fig tree learn its lesson: as soon as its branch becomes tender and puts forth its leaves, you know the summer is near. *So, also when you see all these things: you know that he is near, at the very gates.* Truly I tell you, this generation will not pass away, until all these things have taken place.

Heaven and earth will pass away, but my words will not pass away. *But about that day and hour, no one knows, neither the angels of heaven, nor the Son, but only the Father."*

It took two thousand years for the science of consciousness to take a concrete shape. Modern Science too, in a way, took its own two thousand years from the days of Archimedes to those of Dalton, Thompson, Niels Bohr, Rutherford, Einstein, Heisenberg and the others. And now that physics and other sciences have evolved fully and have stabilized, the day of the Son of Man can be said to have fully and finally arrived as well. Knowledge about Consciousness and Matter can be linked now to construct a single narrative with a beginning, a middle and an 'end'. The Son is both matter and spirit, and now he is in a position to understand this. Jesus did not know 'the time' then, but he had mentioned three signs and had said *"So with you, when you see all these things: know that he is near, right at the gates."*

THE SIGNS ON THE WALL

All the signs which Jesus had outlined, seem to have arrived and seem to be present already at this moment. And now that they stand reminded, all our learned readers should already have witnessed the first sign that Jesus had mentioned; *a calamity of a nature never seen before.* The immediate source of this calamity lies in Asia, in Wuhan in China, as we all know; into the East, in the global context.

The Introduction part of this book is based on Maha Artha Manjari, authored by Gorakshnath (Maheshwaranand), a Great Master. It is also looked upon in the scholastic circles as the second part of Bhagwat Gita, the holiest book of the idol worshipping Hindu; as its technical side, in fact. In a way, it also carries into itself the technical key to the New Testament; since the technical aspects do not change with denomination. The whole of the technicality, as explained in the Introduction to this Postlude, remains associated with the Holy Triad of the Hindus as well as the Holy Trinity of the Christians.

Our books, *Matter, Life and Spirit Demystified* and *Jesus Christ and the Spirit of Truth*, begin to explain the Father, the Holy Spirit and the Son, and then either of the two books (the second one, for most part, reproduces only the third-section of the first) moves towards rise of the Son of Man and the procedures and options following which an aspiring Son of man can gain parity with the Father.

Jesus had said that a number of false prophets will arise who will try to deceive and misguide the people in different ways. Besides a few mentioned earlier, in India, we already have two of them, each with a multi-million following and acres upon acres of farm lands and praying facilities of his own, who are serving jail sentences for the rape of minor girls; both living examples of deception. We are also at the same time able to hear perpetual curses and war cries of two other prophets, inimical to Hindus and cajoling people to do worst things to them, from across the border.

These two are visible in every format of media, spewing poison and curses, and exhorting their followers to launch attacks of terror and to kill people. They have been sending suicide bombers, suicide squads and explosives-laden vehicles to smash into guard convoys, besides providing training to the terrorists on Jihad duties against the Hindus in India. Both these prophets are already on all the black lists that exist, and especially of the United Nations. It is surprising that the Human Rights people in the US, who want to punish India for everything it does, never heard about them (at least until very recently, and yet mostly as events unrelated to them). The UNO, however, is already without any teeth now and there are lobbies which are able to influence almost all aspects of its functioning.

An Importunate Widow

The incident of the importunate widow is referred by Luke at the beginning of chapter 18 as a continuum after discussing the topics of 'the coming of the kingdom of God' and 'the Day of the Son of Man' in chapter 17, and he considered it to be a related topic, as the Son of man was likely to find little faith when he arrived.

A democratic country's political head making a mockery of justice by over-riding Supreme Court through legislation for political gain does highlight why people must not repose blind-folded trust or faith. Yet the word 'faith' chosen by Jesus also shows the context of the times he was speaking about. We are able to see clear signs for a growing deficit of trust between the people and the regimes today. Even without a specific covenant, processes of disengagements have been initiated by the leaders and the countries.

Luke 18:2-8 "He said, "In a certain city' there was a judge who neither feared God nor had respect for people. In that city there was a widow who kept coming to him and saying, 'Grant me justice against my accuser!' For a while he refused, but later he said to himself, 'Though I have no fear of God and no respect for any one, yet because this widow keeps bothering me, I will grant her justice so that she may not wear me out by continually coming'.

"And the Lord said, 'Listen to what the unjust judge says. And will not God grant justice to his chosen ones who cry to him day and night? Will he delay long in helping them? I tell you he will quickly grant justice to them. *And yet, when the Son of Man comes, will he find any faith on earth'?*"

We have discussed the case in more detail in the previous chapter, drawing attention of the readers to the fact that Jesus has replaced 'widow' by the words, 'elect of God who keep calling on him' and about 'justice to them'. A single widow did not keep calling him for justice but all like her did, and the justice was finally done to all of them as well, but it resulted not from a change of heart of the judge but from changes brought in by the Nature and the history, and was greatly delayed. The context for all Jesus mentioned of the revelation about the Son of Man, its arrival, the false prophets, the calamity, and the importunate widow, is the East, while those who are asked to remain alert for the signs and to take a position are located in the West.

The signs that Jesus mentioned are there for all of us to see. These were meaningless when these were spoken about; the stage was not set then. Neither him, nor any of the angels, knew about the timing of these events, Jesus had said, when giving these signs, but he had highlighted East.

An Unholy Nexus of Very Evil Portents

Three things appear on the scenario on 11th of December, 2019. First, the Muslim organizations in India, take control of an important arterial road linking two major sections of the National Capital Region to express their opposition to the amendment in the Citizenship Act to allow grant of citizenship to the minorities facing persecution in the three neighbouring countries.

The diminishing number of non-Muslim minorities in the three neighbouring Muslim countries and their persecution by the majority population of these countries, whether aided or abetted by the changing regimes in these countries or not, was a constant source of concern for the governments in India. To remedy the situation, a new law was passed in the Parliament which allows the Govt. of India to grant citizenship to members of Hindu, Christian, Jains, Buddhist and other minorities entering the country from three neighbouring Muslim countries seeking an asylum on account of their persecution there.

It was made abundantly clear that it will not and could not affect the citizenship status of any Muslim in India, but the Muslim leaders, as usual, put their unreasonable face and the coercive foot forward. They claimed same facility for people of their Faith from these countries wanting to come to India. And there is no way to reason against such non-reason.

Besides even a prophet from the Deccan who is himself a legal expert came to hold the stage and to exhort people, in place of explaining to the supposedly illiterate people the reasonableness and open bona fides of the long overdue provision. Taking the mike in hands, his brother and the second most important functionary of his political party, not merely exhorted the illiterate mass but also brought in the mathematics of 'fifteen' being more or less sufficient to neutralize 'the hundred' if need be. All he asked for was, that the police force everywhere in the country should be stilled or removed for just fifteen minutes, implying that 15 crore (150 million) Muslim will be able to wipe out 100 crore (a billion) Hindus within these fifteen minutes. The Moghuls have gone, but the memories of the past can still water the mouth of some people in India.

How the leading ladies and the others involved in this new incarnation of a holy 'opposition' were reimbursed for their time or attendance is not known, but all the common ladies were paid about eight dollars per day to sit at the site of the blockade. The money was distributed to queues forming every day in several localities to their relatives staying back home. Even mothers with babies at breast could not resist the lure, or their family did not, and would persuade them. At least two suckling babies of three and four months were killed due to cold (Incidentally, in Matthew 24:19

women with babies at the breast are mentioned, and in 24:20 winter is also mentioned).

The other thing that was present on that very date were some six thousand Muslims, owing allegiance to Tablighi Jamaat, who had gathered in the capital at a large facility created for discussion and exchanges on matters of their faith. And these included many foreigners with petrodollars and other currencies. (Last year, Saudi Arabia took the initiative to ban Tablighi Jamaat, the Islamist proselytizing movement. Since then, several other Islamic countries have followed suit). The third thing, though it is difficult to pinpoint the date, it can be a day plus or minus, but more likely the 11th itself, that coincided with this blockade, was the accident at a Chinese genetic research lab, which caused the Corona virus to spill out and spread.

The leakage at Wuhan is said to have been conveyed by the office of the World Health Organization in China based on its internal resources to its Headquarters, who then sought information on these cases, which China provided only on 3rd of January. We can look upon this coincidence as the punitive mechanism of the Nature simultaneously activating itself so that one virus arises to kill another. Prophet Daniel of the Bible appears to have hinted as such.

Top scientists in India had estimated that the ancestor of the novel coronavirus strain from Wuhan was in circulation by December 11, 2019. Using a scientific technique called "time to most recent common ancestor", scientists estimated the viral strain circulating in India in March-April, 2020 had originated between Nov. 26 and Dec. 25, the median being December 11.

A Nation is Stalked, But No Shot is Fired

The Devil's workshop was working overtime and so were the minds of its apostles at several places in India and abroad. It was a stage contrived and created to serve as a lead platform, where a mass of paid humanity had been placed into a very vulnerable situation that could be used as a sacrificial bait. Riots could be instigated by inflammatory speeches, that included mathematics, and the political elements in the country are also known to use paid hoodlums to convert even a single heated discussion into a riot. If a wrong move by the government or one of its personnel did not blow the fuse between the communities, paid gangs would do the same if one has dollars to spare.

The country's capital remained divided in two parts for three and a half months. Some fifty million people were directly affected with no end of their misery in sight. The Government of the country, however, displayed maturity of its leadership and exemplary restraint. The sheep belonged to it, not to the people claiming to be its leaders with their calculators from within the country or outside. In any non-Hindu majority country, anywhere in the world, force would have been used. Tiananmen Square is still fresh in human memory, where thirty thousand people were killed in a single day, many of them crushed under the wheels of army tanks. Here, in India, no force was used. The sheep belonged to the nation and it had to take care of its sheep. It kept reasoning and explaining and it kept its cool.

As for the leaders, the prophets and the priests on the job, Jesus has effectively described them and what they usually aim at, at more than one place. These may easily include leaders arriving into the political arena riding on the back of some saint-like person decrying the politics in general, but highly respected by a large mass of people, and also those who can understand the law but in place of explaining the same, choose instead to mislead one part of the humanity and deliver unwelcome threats to another. In fact, anyone making a plaything of the ethics, gaining sympathy and donations through foul play, is unlikely to deliver anything good for the mankind in general, ever and at all. It is for the people, however, to see that such leaders lacking in principles should fade out with time to make room for the visionaries and builders.

Unfortunately, however, for both the organizers, the prophets and the other vested interests, a stone untouched by any hand began to roll. The virus leaked; it was Nature's magic at work now, for a change; and the magic of the prophets failed. After a time, the sport became spoiled on its own; the actors were made to pack up, not by the government, but by a virus itself; of a different strain. Besides, the paid humanity, the thieves, bandits, serpents and the broods of vipers—all had to pack-up and go home too.

A Stone Untouched by Any Hand

In the hills, however, as we walk or drive, we are more used to coming across a stone that is not touched by any hand and yet it begins to roll. Unknown and unseen hand of the Nature came to wind up what the government had failed to do in three months and a half. Local angels, were the first to be withdrawn by their party headed by some very crafty leaders, impure in heart. (One of them, a king-pin, sort of, was in jail until recently but may have managed to come out now, probably on bail. Among other things, he had amassed truckloads of bricks and other missiles at the roofs, backed by improvised catapults at many places). Then the prophets and priests from afar vanished too; and then the elite. On the day the security personnel moved in, they sent the twenty or so destitute that had remained and that had nowhere else to go, to the shelter centres.

A fact the people overlook, is that Muslims in India cannot be safer and more secured. They can leave the pasts of other people behind and can begin to live their own lives with their sons and daughters in confidence and dignity, as due to them as a citizen of this great country. They can grow beyond the murky waters of the neighbourhood and try to gain into the much broader area and its limelight. They need not follow the Hindu procedures, but may select co-operation over collision, so that evolution of the Son of Man is not hampered.

They should think of reforms and think big, not small; think of light and not darkness; and they should share it with the world. They must not allow others to disturb the cooperation and spirit of next-door neighbourhood that prevails and which the outsiders and the vested interests within keep trying to disturb. They must not upset their lives for the sake of non-issues, non-matters; anything bye-gone.

India, as a country was divided when the British left. Two chunks of large territories were given away to be governed by the Muslims according to the Islamic Law. Yet a large number of Muslims stayed back. They do not derive their lineage from the Mughals and they all also accept that their religion does not allow a place for prayers to be built by destroying one of some other Faith. By their own law, the prayer offered at such a place is not acceptable to God; it is not in order.

The Moghuls, on the other hand, rejoiced on destroying Hindu temples and, more particularly, those that were the most revered. Whereas Muslim Faith does not really permit prayer at such places, only one of about half a dozen such disputes have been resolved in most recent times amicably (by order of the highest court), where the Temple at the birth place of Lord Rama of the Hindus was returned to them and virgin land on an alternate site has been provided to the Muslim community to build a proper mosque in conformity with their Faith.

It was the Moghuls who were at fault, not the community as a whole. The community is under no obligation to defend a wrong done by one of its branches known as the Moghuls. At least thirty thousand Hindu temples were destroyed by the Moghuls, from Babar to Akbar to Shahjahan to Aurangzeb, out of which thousands were converted into hybrid kinds of mosques. Among these, like the birth place of Rama, there are several other places of great reverence for the Hindus, with rooms below the floors locked, concealing evidence that Hindu places of worship have been converted into mosques. The Moghuls are now gone a long time ago and there should be little point in owning and clinging to the acts of great injustice perpetrated by them on the people of this country. It was high time that, to promote kinship among the two sets of people, similar solutions as for the birth place of Rama must be found for the few remaining places of great reverence for the Hindus as well in a spirit of co-operation.

It is easy to proffer advice and to preach, however, and it may be too much to expect the hearts and minds of the people to change overnight. For sure, our two people can live as good neighbours, without attempting a marriage that need not be; a marriage that is not ordained.

It is worth citing the opinion of Dr B. R. Ambedkar, who had adopted Buddhism by choice, on this issue. He was the wisest and most impartial person around when India was being handed over its freedom by the British and people of India are unanimous in calling him as the Father of Indian Constitution. Whereas the other people of importance at that time, like, Jinnah, Gandhi, Nehru, and Patel may have said different things about the need for a partition, Ambedkar was forthright in saying, "This (*the partition*) is necessary to save the 'Hindus'."

From the point of view of the ground reality, it may be over-simplification to speak of a shared DNA, since a normal genotype can always be overcome by a dominating phenotype that is stronger. Leaders of the Muslim Indians who oppose any proposals of equity, based on a common DNA, do have a valid point, for sure. The freedom of a people to stick to their given phenotype also perhaps needs to be acknowledged. In his book, "*Thoughts on Pakistan, or the Partition of India*", Dr Ambedkar has written, "The brotherhood among the Muslims is restricted only to themselves; for those outside it, it only harbours hate and enmity. Further, the only allegiance they owe is to their religion and not to the country in which they may be living. ...In other words, the Islamic Religion does not allow its truthful followers from accepting India as their motherland and the Hindu as their near kins."

There may be more to lose and little to gain by attempting a marriage that need not be, must not be, and that does not seem to have been ordained. The idol worshippers have managed to survive barely by a width of their hair and, now, they must be allowed to preserve their values, without being obliged to experiment with a new kind of hodgepodge. Verbal assurances mean nothing in today's scenario. Jesus too has hinted, "it may be difficult to find 'any' faith on the earth" at this point of time. Since lives are precious at both sides, it may be far better to promote co-living as good neighbours, and there the matter should end, period.

Neighbours: Not Couples

You need to trust your spouse and your family, but you do not need to trust your neighbour to live with him. In fact, you can have more than one neighbours and while one of them can steal your apples or a chicken, the other one can poison your dog or may be wrongly eyeing a female of your house, or your very house. And yet, changes can take place with time and your neighbourhood can turn into a happy place of love, co-operation and mutual trust.

However, you take guard when it is needed; as much as should be possible. Many nations are faced with problems of lack of trust now, against regimes, against people, against ideologies; and they are blocking people and organizations and taking guards. It is really a big sheepfold, India; and it is a place of great importance for the natural and the catholic way of thinking. Changes have taken place to threaten this important part of the world. It is a Hindu country with a large Muslim population and it shares border with three other Muslim nations; one of them hostile in the extreme. It follows a thought process typical of the ancient Semitic way of thinking, which Jesus absolutely disapproved; thinking violence and revenge, and planning murder and terror.

With its arrogant leaders and its lack of principles, aided by its self-imposed desperations and bad company, it may be already leading itself on a path of self-destruction. The unholy nexus formed by it with another expansionist country may have already begun to propel it on a suicidal course, towards turning itself into the first rented out country in the world. To be honest, the author wonders for whom Daniel 11:37-39 may have been written, and would like to hope it should be just a warning.

It reads, "Headless of his father's gods, headless of the god whom women love, headless of any god whatever, he will consider himself greatest of all. Instead of them, he will honour the god of fortresses (the general of its army!), will honour a god unknown to his ancestors with gold and silver, precious stones and valuable presents. He will use people of an alien god to defend the fortresses; he will confer great honour on those whom he acknowledges, by giving wide authority and by parcelling the country out for rent."

Daniel could not have named a country that did not exist, but he has mentioned a god whom women love. In south Asia, while most of the gods of the world have a representation, nobody can make a mistake in identifying the god whom the women love. There can be a hidden reason for mentioning him, in particular; because he is also regarded as a World Teacher, a second reference point available to anyone in these lands who does not want to follow the advice of his father's gods. All through the Gita, this god whom the women love, teaches only one thing and that is to try to discriminate between right and the wrong action; more particularly, if one was about to burn its bridges or to take a headlong plunge.

WHY PEOPLES' REPUBLICS NEED TO EXPAND?

And yet, all the evil cannot be blamed on the religions alone. Non-religion or atheism can do much worse. It can stream-roll a country of God-loving and God-fearing people and make its king flee for his life. Such aggression must be reversed and the protocol must be reinstated, as a living example of the humanity coming to mature. It is like a neighbouring country overtaking the Vatican, and insisting on its right of a trespassing hunter to keep its 'prey', or of a victor to keep its loot. This is not only a matter for the heads of states to address, but also for the holy ones. The people in the Republic did not possibly want to own Tibet, the regime continuing in their name and on their behalf, nevertheless, did.

Efforts of nations or regimes to liquidate minorities like Rohingyas in Myanmar or the Uighurs in the Chinese province of Xinjiang must be not only condemned universally but also resisted and opposed. The need to bring legislation to grant asylum to minorities being persecuted by nations or regimes is a highly deplorable state of affairs, as well. The opposition to it at the home front by the leaders of the community carrying out such persecution should appear to be even more glaring and an eye opener.

The falling population ratio of the minority in an area, regime, or country must occupy the top slot in the list of Human Rights organizations. The presence of concentration camps for manual labour and as guinea pigs for genetic research or medical use must be looked upon as outright inhuman. The people in such nations must be advised to dismantle not only such hateful activity but also such regimes.

SURVIVAL OF THE HOMO-SAPIENS

Every living thing in the world has been equipped by the Nature with a 'self', possessing a survival instinct of its own. Species have vied with each other to survive. Those which were better suited, kind of the fittest, according to Charles Darwin, survived; others became extinct. Nature tries to preserve merit or value and to discard what is ill suited, or which is no more suitable.

It is Nature which takes the decisions, in fact, and it takes the path of natural selection. Species have no part to play (*Matter, Life and Spirit Demystified*). Things change with the rise of man, however, since he is made as a microcosm and a free agent by Nature itself. It needs to make its own effort to survive and to preserve. And what it needs to preserve most, as its first priority, is merit and best value; its own sons and daughters.

All this is natural instinct—both as a community instinct and as the individuals' survival instinct. In fact, it is the question of survival of the humanity itself as a whole, and of giving best security to the most precious and deserving Sons of Man; the more fit and the more competent, who can take the ship ahead and not sink the same. If there are wars on the horizons and catastrophes, the best of the mankind, the most meritorious and the most deserving sons and daughters of the Man, must be preserved to make a new beginning, if such a need should arise. It is not selfish at all, and it does not mean that one must become oblivious to the humanity at large.

And yet, the atmosphere that prevails, does seem to raise questions of security, in the face of rapidly decreasing lack of trust and confidence between the nations and the regimes. Threats of different kinds are being posed, even being conveyed. Confrontations are taking place. Nuclear weapons enough to destroy the whole Earth several times over, are being rattled, by three or four countries, and until recently even by the one almost rented out. The threat to the survival of the mankind is not imaginary; it is real. And even Jesus has asked the people to remain alert. Tough decisions may have to be taken. Nations need to take note and need to prepare. They must not hesitate to initiate all the surgical steps as may be necessary to remedy the situation once and for all; whatever the cost. And there need be no going back, ever, from here onwards.

The Threats Faced by The Son of Man

Three different kinds of threats to the survival of the mankind seem to be present; more particularly to the survival of the civil and true humanity. The first and foremost, of course, is expansionist designs of one or more countries or regimes. It creates such disturbance all around that it needs to be nipped for all times, if the mankind is to survive. The Son of Man not only needs to survive, but to ready itself for a quantum jump now. All baggage that is troublesome, hindering and unwelcome must be left behind; entirely dumped, totally boycotted and absolutely restricted or fenced out.

Tough days do seem to be already on. And tough decisions may have to be taken. Nature's wheel seems to have begun to move too, already. A stone that had begun to roll, may not have stopped yet (Daniel 2:40-45). And, it may not be a mere coincidence as well, that there are strong leaders in the arena and on the scene, who can begin to write a new history for the mankind, like Mr. Modi, the prime minister of India and Mr. Zelensky, the President of Ukraine. Even the United States has begun to move towards less belligerency and deeper diplomacy.

A second big threat is from the terror outfits who think they have the sanction of their religion to do what they have been doing and trying to do for many centuries now. And, of course, it would be a hypocrisy to say that there is no mistrust and only an avoidable mental phobia or imagination that should not be and which is more the fault of the affected than those who perpetrate—be it the decades old Islamophobia or a new word recently coined by the Russian Foreign Minister viz. *Russophobia*.

The third serious threat to the mankind is from the atheist way of thinking. Persons can choose to be atheists; it is a part of their freedom. Countries should not be atheist countries, however. All kinds of human rights violations and other violations of the Nature's laws are likely to sneak into the system and even affect its people, if a dictator or his party must get priority over God. A regime known for its atheist line of thinking does not evoke confidence or trust. If someone was to say that a virus was deliberately developed by an essentially atheist regime, at least half of the people in the world would believe, and many among the rest would tend not to disbelieve.

The peoples' republics, it can be said, do not seem to be able to invoke a great amount of faith in general. That precisely is the way, the phobias develop. How the power was gained by a party or a leader, becomes a history in time. But the inability or unwillingness to understand right from the wrong gives rise to wrong actions and to what is popularly called, a deep mistrust, leading in time to one-phobia or another. If some people have the right to perpetrate, those on the receiving end have an even better right to feel apprehensive and to initiate all the action they deem proper.

One big disadvantage the people under such a regime working in their name may need to cope with is the ever-growing mistrust in the Free World, and in general. Religion-wise the people of China may have enjoyed a very high rank at one time, but with atheism injected into their thought process and behaviour pattern, others may not judge them on their religion anymore but by their regime. How can they claim the benefit of being a follower of Buddha when the very King of the Buddhists, the Dalai Lama, is required to live in exile and the very demography of Tibet, his constituency, is being altered with laborious zeal by their near-atheist people's regime? Indigenous people are being packed off as labour to business provinces in China, and people from mainland are being settled there.

Nations have become accustomed to follow policies of appeasement in dealing with the diverse mix of humanity with different faiths and political systems. Perhaps a few firm decisions, howsoever tough, may have to be taken now to user in a change in the paradigm; to give mankind the break it deserves! Shouldn't a single surgical or sustained operation be preferred to address the several threats in one go, over the half-hearted and ineffective measures attempted thus far? Sometimes a set of sanctions by other countries may succeed in hindering or partially restraining some unwelcome activity, when other things are normal. In the present state of affairs, however, a total boycott of unhealthy thought and reasoning process seems necessary to segregate the people—in the language of Jesus, to segregate the sheep from the goat, or to shut the door on the face of the goat.

Should Quarantining of a New Kind Take-Over?

When all the nations will be assembled, according to Jesus, and supposing that such an assembly may somehow be triggered as well by the most recent invasion of a small democracy by a giant super-power, holding the whole world to a kind of ransom, the Jesus narrative may show the path, to the effect "he will separate people one from another as the shepherd separates sheep from the goats. He will place the sheep on the right side and the goats on his left. Then the King will say to those on his right hand, 'Come, you whom my Father has blessed, take as your heritage the Kingdom prepared for you since the foundation of the world. ...Then he will say to those on his left hand, 'Go away from me, with your curse upon you, to the eternal fire prepared for the devil and his angels."

It is here that the difficulty will arise for the nations, for the people who want to offer their 'sons'—a world guarded from evil eyes, evil noises and evil contact and letting them grow, so that they can move from one pasture to another with freedom. The nations cannot send the people or the goats on the left anywhere, much less to the eternal fire. The only thing they can do is to leave the goats on the left where they were and the other things as they were, and build their own wall of freedom around their sheepfold. It can be a sheepfold with no iron curtains; just doors that they may try to guard with an ever-increasing efficiency. The Nature may have let a stone to roll in such a way that not only the problems are highlighted and so jacked-up that these may be seen, but a remedy is also suggested at the same time.

Would the nations consider an advanced quarantining system in some form—a state-of-the-art kind of a system in effect? People have already become accustomed to it. Would they choose to divide as well, as Jesus once did, to preserve goodness, putting aside the evil to pursue its own course without being able to come in the path of advancement of the good; to preserve it for the morrow? We see countries were quarantined, cities and villages were quarantined, within a city the areas were quarantined and within an apartment house the flats and families may still be quarantined, and people are still able to live. There are zones of different colours, all of which are able to move in their own lanes towards the green, and to a zone-less regime—at their own pace; in their own time.

The mankind needs to guard its sons and daughters not only against unholy people and regimes, but also against the active and sleeper cells fuelled by either of these doctrines. It is such elements, agents or sympathizers, and who can manoeuvre to occupy chairs and positions of vantage to spy, to steal and to sabotage, or even brain-wash the unawares, which constitute the threat from within for a country with democratic values.

Eventually, possibly, ways may be found to address the privacy concerns of the people; and every person, every big or small group, may come to be rated in an autonomic system in the new world. Every branch of quarantining can have its own parameters to be decided by the brotherhood of nations, if they should come together as envisaged by Jesus and the other prophets.

Strictly regulated sales, purchases, investments, ownerships, and exchange of people, screened and reduced interaction, and other measurements for disengagement can be initiated by a club of nations that may be near colourless or white. If necessary, people at the opposite ends of the divide may be allowed to auction their products at a common and transparent platform, with only as much interaction as should be absolutely necessary. Again, eventually, it should be possible to rate individuals on a scale of country, regime, faith, ideology, affiliations, and even record of fraud, violence, crime and other violation against the standard whiteness. Privacy cannot be allowed to take precedence over survival, when the times are as difficult as now, and yet there can be an option to walk over to the other side of the divide.

The word 'nations' used by Christ means the people; it may or may not be the same thing as the regimes. People choose regimes, and in today's reality, there may be regimes that have chosen the people to rule over. And again, while a single regime may be shared by more than one 'people', scores of separate regimes may prefer to be considered as one 'people'.

Therefore, the word 'nations' used by Jesus would possibly include both people and the regimes, while it need not include all the people and all the regimes. The wise of different people and the regimes, that may share a common concern, could come together and even constitute or select an authority for a white, colourless world, as hinted at by Jesus, the Christ, and by God through Daniel—the Prophet. Like a deity can become a legal person in India, Homo-sapiens, the Son of Man, may also be accorded a legal status by the nations with a right of its own, as a species, to evolve in ambiance and to survive.

THE COVENANTS

It is the God who holds all the powers, and these go in two directions. Initially, any covenants imposed by the prophets or agreed by human brotherhoods were based on the simplest of all covenants: trust in God and fear against any wrongdoing. Later, the people began to confuse God's powers with a 'God' which does not resist or even interfere. They began to inject their personal preferences. The fear of God was gone, the covenants became diluted and the evil began to creep in.

"My covenant with him (Levi) was a covenant of life and well-being, which I gave him; this called for reverence, and he revered me and stood in awe of my name (was God-fearing) (Malachi 2:5)." Incidentally, the two hundred and fifty prophets who were feeling uneasy with the way the things were going and who were sent down alive to the Sheol, and with their families and properties as well, were all Levites too.

It was the priests in particular whom Jesus blamed for much of the evil that lay scattered around and which had made people heartless, losing track of God's natural laws. People had lost track of the laws of life and peace, and of respect returned for the favours received. Respect for God was replaced by people with faith in personal cleverness and human design, enough to put all the words in the mouth of God as they deemed fit.

Jesus had provided a kind of neutral-white base or a platform into its sheepfold for the sheep to move about in a familiar environment. Nature, we have seen (*Matter, Life and Spirit Demystified* or *Jesus Christ and the Spirit of Truth*), likes to evolve properties of mind, and even the properties of matter, from a zero-plus kind of a neutral state. Likewise, it also allows a person to begin to write it's every new life with a clean, neutralized slate.

In the same way, there can be covenants of a positive zero or neutral state from which the journey of a person, a nation, or a regime could begin. The higher side is the side of virtue and is the right side. It is on that side, that the Son of Man needs to evolve. The lower side is the side of evil and sin, which is harmful and injurious for the Son of Man. So, there are two kinds of covenants; those that must be observed and those which need to be firmly prohibited and must definitely be shunned.

The No Negative State

Zero level positive covenants are like uniform civil code, human, animal, and plant rights, positive food protocol and positive belief systems favouring nature's law of preservation and growth, and so on, which, in a way, follow directly from nature. These fall within the jurisdiction of the religions, which should be the first in the list of the covenant-making body, should and whenever one may come to be formed.

The belief systems failing to qualify but offering to approach the white state must definitely and reliably expunge all hate, revenge, or punishment against any people on the ground of race or religion. And a season and a date for purging a system, faith, or group can be agreed, without letting anyone out of the hooks. The date may come first with a declaration, and the season may conclude with the return of the date, to establish confirmed compliance with the avowed declaration. And there can be periodical meetings and data verification. Words like 'heathen', 'kafir', 'witch' 'jihad', 'kill', or 'stone to death' must be expunged by public declaration and wide display of such expunction. Regimes, systems, or ideologies teaching that God doesn't exist and cannot punish must be made totally unwelcome by the holy ones.

A CONSTRUCTIVE INVITE

As for the atheist way of thinking preferred by the science fraternity, the author would like to invite them to try to disprove the predictions made by the Theory of Manifestation advanced by the ancient rishis of India and elaborated in our books, which clearly show that consciousness is eternal but matter is not; that it holds primacy over the matter and that all the common sciences like physics, chemistry and biology derive their properties and potency from the manifest consciousness only. Neither logic, nor any new discovery in physics, chemistry or biology should ever be able to disprove these claims. Besides, it needs to be understood that logic cannot stand in the absence of a given base. It is something that can be experienced under certain fixed and given conditions, and can also be argued about in relative terms only, citing one set of facts and comparing them to some other relative scenario, that may actually exist or could be proposed. Consciousness, on the other hand, can stand alone, even when there is nothing to see or to talk about.

Albert Einstein, Max Planck, Werner Heisenberg, David Bohm, Erwin Schrodinger, and many others had favoured primacy of the consciousness, a hundred years or so ago, as soon as the basic physics had become known and understood. Its acceptance can, of course, be delayed some more. But, would that serve any purpose, really? or at all? And would such acceptance and recognition really take anything away from what the modern science has discovered or achieved, or any of the perks, privileges, and power the men of science enjoy today? It is obvious, that it will not!

The only bone of contention on the 'sciences' side happens to be: Whether consciousness must arise out of neurons and the nerve-connections made of matter that go into making of a brain? or it could be the other way round! It should seem more logical that to equip itself better for even grosser relative interactions, where distances and velocities were required to be measured—first tentatively, for a quick brown fox to jump over a lazy dog; and then more precisely for a supersonic missile carrying nuclear armament fired by Kremlin to hit a specific soft spot in the USA, the manifesting Mind may have decided to bring in the neurons and the nerve cells as well. The studies undertaken and the experiments made by Eugene Marais from South Africa would seem to suggest as such, for sure (unlucky for Marais, looked upon by many as the direct spiritual heir to Aristotle and Durkheim, that his research was used by someone in Europe to appropriate the Noble Prize that was his due and, unable to come out of that shock, he first became sick and then died, while the guy in Europe made merry and possible lived for many long and 'blessed' years).

Courtesy Lyall Watson, parts of the research of Eugene Marais have been included by us under 'Samvit Interpreted', the 11th and 3rd chapters respectively, in our two books named before. We can also perhaps cite Wilder Penfield—whose work could not have been stolen even if someone may have wanted to—who was able to live the full span of his life, and who is widely considered to be the father of modern neurosurgery.

Penfield too, for many years, believed that there was no soul or an independent consciousness in human beings. Yet, towards the end of his trail blazing career of around fifty-years, he too had felt the need to change this erroneous belief—a product of deep relativity built into the very fabric of the manifest world (please read *Jesus Christ and the Spirit of Truth*). He no longer believed that the neurons of the brain could explain all mental activity among the humans.

The words of the Rishis of India and Jesus are not hollow. These were not designed to mislead the humanity, but to bring light into the lives of all human progeny. When there is no brain, instincts can still work. That is the mechanism relied upon by nature at the more basic levels before it would begin to evolve a brain, first a most rudimentary one and then with increasing doses of sophistication added to it. Especially, instinct is the only mechanism that can work at the particulate levels, to enable an electron to know another particle as a proton or electron, etc., and to even collapse the wave function altogether, if someone tried to instal a hidden camera (literally, in the changing room of the Nature). Further, even after a most sophisticated brain has been evolved by Nature, there can be things that must keep out of the range of dry logic, and which can still be felt through the medium of higher instinct, that we may call as 'intuition'.

We know that Newton had tried to wind up the last stages of his research rather quickly, and once he was through, he was in a hurry to give up science in his pursuit of the light of God. Albert Einstein was forthright too in saying that 'science' was like a lame person in the absence of religion (or its lack of knowledge about the spirit). These two stalwarts, the two 'gravity' persons, represent what is known as the classical side in physics. The quantum stalwarts in the pre-WWII world too, were not much behind either, and they neither lacked in logic, nor in intuition.

Max Planck was a simple person. So, he had simply said: "*I regard consciousness as fundamental. I regard matter as a derivative of consciousness. We cannot get behind consciousness. Everything that we talk about, everything that we regard as existing, postulates consciousness.*"

Werner Heisenberg was a little more specific, however. He stated, "Consciousness may be an essential aspect of the universe and *we may be blocked from the further understanding of material phenomenon* if we insist on excluding it".

Elaborating on his refrain, he had said further, "The electron does not have any properties independent of the observer's mind. *In atomic physics, the sharp Cartesian division between mind and matter, between observer and observed, can no longer be maintained and we can never speak about nature without at the same time speaking about ourselves.*"

On his part, Erwin Schrodinger, who created the Quantum Wave Mechanics, and while he liked to call himself an atheist, was not way behind too, and had said, "*Attempts to resolve this dualism was also made in the West, but the attempt was always carried out on the material plane and it failed. This was no good. If we decide to have only one sphere, it has to be the psychic one since it exists anyway.*"

These were some of the people who actually made science. In a way, they all had played key roles in laying the foundation for modern science; and they were men of discretion, not of superstition. The quantum people, in particular, were able to sense the need for a change in paradigm straightaway. And, through our aforementioned books, as we reveal the so far (more or less) hidden Spirit of Truth before the evolved intellect of the humankind, we also make a pitch for a two-way change in the paradigm. For sure, we need to change the paradigm on both sides, on the side of science on one hand and, likewise, also on the religion side. We invite the honest and the unbiased intellectuals, especially on the science side first, to come forward and make an honest assessment to begin with.

It was Stephen Hawkins who wrote in one of his books (*The Grand Design*), "Because there is a law like gravity, the universe can and will create itself from nothing. ...Spontaneous creation is the reason there is something rather than nothing, why the universe exists, why we exist..." It was like a shot in the dark when it was written. In the light of the 'Science of Consciousness', which uses the term 'manifestation' in place of the phrase 'spontaneous creation' used by Prof. Hawkins, it is no longer a shot in the dark, but a whole theory. As the norms for acceptance of a new theory go, it provides an answer to some of the questions still hanging in the air, like how the polarized electric charges come to arise and why there need be a colour index, why there are precisely three families of quarks and electrons, why there are exactly three quarks into every nucleon, and why there should be just three sub-atomic particles which go into the making of an atom, besides, of course, why there should be just three forces (Gravity, Electro-weak and Strong Nuclear Force), and why we need to understand each of the three levels of this vibratory existence to actually fathom the world we live into. As for the predictions a theory needs to make for gaining the acceptance, this ancient Theory of Manifestation, of the Indian rishis, does predict wave-particle duality, exclusion principle and the uncertainty relation, among other things (e.g., it also explains the survival instinct, that becomes more visible into anything that lives).

Unless we deliberately try to obstruct our intellect, it should be easy to understand that, as explained in our books, like everything else (including the man), the whole of the physics also rests on these simple bricks laid by Nature in the very realm of foundation of the world itself. On the other hand, the only prediction of modern science in this context that "consciousness can only arise out of a nerves-based neural network", has been proved totally and utterly wrong and lacking a reasonable basis. And this has been done again and again.

As such, we invite the men of sciences from all over the world! The world has arrived on a cross road! It is high time that leaving aside their personal preferences or the likes and dislikes, for once, the science fraternity must collectively apply their minds to judge whether a change in paradigm should be postponed any further?

A Theft in the House of Truth

Directly or indirectly, a setback has been caused by Amazon India, and Cloudtail which is another big name in that country, hampering our effort to promote the knowledge about the reality. The Hindi rendering of our book 'Jesus Christ and the Spirit of Truth', published under the name, 'Vishwa Guru Bharat Ke Teen Mahavigyan' and priced at US $ 12.5 was pirated, and it was sold at $ 3.5 apiece by Amazon.in between about mid-February and mid-May, and at half our set price in the e-book segment too. In fact, one of our associates was able to buy a pirated copy also under an Amazon Invoice and Delivery Order, that she is keeping with her as a souvenir.

It should appear highly sacrilegious that all this was going on behind our back, even before our official launch of the book in Uttarakhand in India on the 16th of April this year by a battery of saints, led by the 132 years old legendary sage Parmanada Puri before a gathering of close to a thousand persons. In recent weeks, however, the Amazon.in advertisement has disappeared, though sales in the e-book section and the book stalls may be continuing. For the information of our readers, sage Parmananda Puri had obtained his masters in surgery from Oxford in England in the year 1919. He had carried out surgical operations lasting seven to eight hours and had worked as Chief Medical Officer for two different states for about eleven years before renouncing the world, to become a renunciant.

Honestly, the author has no issues with Amazon India, Cloudtail, or any other people contributing in this laudable effort. For sure, money earned by promoting the words of God, Jesus or the rishis must bring in auspiciousness all-around, and even the grey market can brighten up since light in itself is always pure. However, hadn't Jesus himself warned (Luke 18:8), *"And yet, when the Son of Man comes, will he find any faith on earth?"* It is a fact that whether in India, or elsewhere, people are just not interested to know and understand the *Truth*; they would rather cling to whatever ideas they may happen to have. Should Cloudtail still be eager to spread the Good News? perhaps, it must consider to print, or even buy, copies of our principal book 'Matter, Life and Spirit Demystified' for free distribution to its employees, associates and other friends, as well, and as it may deem proper!

MUST THE RELIGIONS HAVE A BASE?

It has been proffered that besides in science, our books propose a change in the paradigm on the side of the religious beliefs system as well. Recently, a brotherly suggestion was received by the author from a really intelligent person, also intelligently devout, that people associate God only with someone whom they can worship and to whom they can pray. More than dry logic, the popular God seems to favour faith. For sure, this faith is a great solace providing factor for the masses. For its effectiveness, it does not need to appear to depend on logic all the way (even if it may still be doing so). Besides, it hides into itself a little trick that can put even a lay person in a kind of direct contact with the 'supreme thing' and with the ultimate levers that control the various things or issues in a human world.

It sounds to reason that for a majority of the people, it may be difficult to associate God with logic itself and even less with science. 'Science' for most people is the domain of a few intellectual elites, profanely erudite and handling businesses which they believe, in all fairness, should lie outside the scope of God. As for the common people, while they may no longer be that amenable to the idea of the God making man from his arms, woman from his thighs, the teacher from his forehead and the warrior from his chest, or from the dust and ribs of another, and so on, they may still find it difficult to comprehend him as the very principle of 'intelligence' that could itself come to manifest as the world.

From the practical point of view, therefore, it may be in order to divide the two functions that the God may be obliged to discharge to meet the expectations of a common but truly faithful—one related with creation of the world and the other with its day to day running. For sure, there would be the masses who can pray and confess to a benevolent God. Likewise, however, there can be a section of the scholarly people as well, that may be as determined to know about the how's and why's of this world as a whole, as the science fraternity may be keen to learn about matter and life; but without being biased or partisan like the latter, and without having to cope with any peer pressure to keep 'God' out of it all.

A division of this nature, in fact, already seems to exist and prevail in every social set up of the wise homo-sapiens. It is not surprising that a majority of the people should be interested only in products of the religions, like prayer and the seeking of boons of one kind or another, or forgiveness against any mistakes that may have been made by them; whereas the number of people seeking to understand the how's and why's should be much smaller. And yet, it is the extent of knowledge about such how's and why's or about the structural and functional details of the world we live in, that may or may not have gone in the body of a religion, that shapes and determines the social behaviour of its adherents for its effectiveness—both within the community, and also with the outside world.

It is not unlikely that some of the people should easily end up by constructing a strategy in the name of a religion. The religion, for them, would become more of a means then, rather than a goal. Had the knowledge about the spiritual and more sublime realms been more common? such mistaken beliefs or ad-hoc measures may not probably have come into existence, and had there been friendly interaction with the other communities? any anomalies could have been easily rectified too, after an exchange of notes.

The change in paradigm on the religious side, in fact, needs to address this structural aspect associated with the human world, and the world in general, that goes into making of the different religions. By consensus or persuasion, the basics about the nature of Truth need to be made a common public knowledge, in a similar manner as the knowledge about science, with little or no room for arbitrariness of any kind. A universally agreed definition of the human reality must govern the most basic aspects that need to be complied with by each religion—in the manner similar to a uniform civil code that may need to be applied for all the men and women in all the societies of the civilized human world.

It is easy to see that the most common refrain has remained the same for all religions: Every religion believes that both the world and the man have been made or created by a God, called by whatever name. This belief is instinctively placed into human mind by Nature. Hence, there is little or no mix-up of any kind, as far as this aspect is concerned. The other instinctive inputs that follow naturally are: equality, justice and purity of thought. Differences began to arise among the people, however, from this very next step itself, especially where knowledge was in the lacking or could be disputed, and it was convenient for a strategy that could outsmart the others, to come to evolve and to take over.

The three earliest known civilizations were believed to have arisen in India, Mesopotamia and the Egypt. It was here that cultural activity had commenced and notions about a creator and his role had begun to take a form. In time, however, people began to branch out and also began to move to populate some other lands—in search of new pastures. Most of these people possessed little reliable knowledge about how the world and the people may have come to arise. Accordingly, they were also hardly in a position to understand as to what God, the creator, actually wanted or expected of them.

We see such fundamental ideas, that in the beginning there was 'word', which was the thought of God, and that 'man was made by God in his own image', were retained in Judaism. However, since its followers lacked even a fair understanding about these sublime concepts, these were assumed to be more like some high sounding and fanciful ideas that could be copy pasted to begin a nice preamble. In still later denominations these would be replaced with mere fanciful thought constructs of a pre-emptive and strategic nature. There is the Truth, and there is Illusion—a 'huge relativity' cleverly planted by God, to enable a diverse multiplicity to arise. Together these two prevail, in how the God becomes manifest—there is the truth, and there is the deep illusion as well.

According to their temperament, people made their choices to move towards God, which is the Truth, or away from it. In most practical terms, for some of the people, it was like Maya or the devil taking over, veiling the truth and giving rise to an illusion, or to what is false, untrue and outright deceptive.

We can see that weird assumptions and weird logic began to fill in the space both in Judaism, and in the more astute later denomination deriving therefrom, from the very start. Such notions like better than thou, holier than thou, superior than thou, mightier than thou and such claims as being a people more favoured by God than any other, came to arise to become the order of the day and to provide some people with kind of a handle to invade, plunder, rape and kill innocent people.

The notions about equality, justice and purity of thought may have been retained at the preamble stage in the new and emerging religions, as well. People were able to judge, however, that that they could not only tamper with the written word or twist the same to suit their need of the hour, but could also put words in the mouth of God as often as they should be pleased to do so. Equity, justice and fair play were included in each of the umpteen sects of the later denominations also, though only as show-case ideas, and merely to nip any arguments in bud itself—without ever being put into practice. These were the very notions, in fact, that were to become highly compromised in the hands of such later and newer people, where even common clerics would be bold and confident enough to issue injunctions about anything and everything, like blind people leading the blind. In consequence, the whole religious scenario has become dismal and highly vitiated, with people vying with each other to destroy everything of value among the humans, and to push the world over the precipice.

The Case of the Idol Worshipper

We have seen that the more understanding and more tolerant idol worshipper has been at the receiving end for some 3,500 years now. 'Tolerance' is not born out of one's DNA, but is evolved out of one's way of living, learning and interacting with the others. It is not a genotypical shortcoming, but an acquired phenotypical virtue, even if it could work to its owners' disadvantage, when the neighbourhood is hostile. Among the three neighbouring countries of India, even today there may be millions of well evolved phenotypical homo-sapiens who will not bat an eyelid if there was an opportunity at hand to snuff out one or more of Hindu lives, should it be safe enough, since it is approved under this or that law or sub-law of their faith, or can be made to appear as such.

Again, one must not eat one's cake and try to have it too. Either a mosque must be built on an unencumbered and plain piece of land properly acquired, for the prayer to be acceptable, which is the position up-front for the Muslim faith; or it can be made on the ruins of a Hindu temple after destroying it as well, without affecting the worth of the prayer that can be offered on the site, which seems to be the position at the back-end of the Faith flashed in broad daylight with a sense of delight. One wall of the Gyan Wapi Mosque at Varanasi deliberately retained in its lower portion 'a part of' the original temple wall, 'at a spot' visible from the road so that people should know that the Hindus were subjugated by the Moghuls, to derive a long-term sadistic satisfaction.

The Moghuls are gone and the scattering of the power of the Hindus is now over as well. It was time that the confusion in the minds of the adherents of this dominant religion and the other people making up its neighbourhood at hundreds of locations in India and some of the neighbouring countries, about the sanctity of a mosque was sorted out, for the ground reality to be understood by one and all and for the life for them to move on in place of being stranded eternally at the same confused spot.

In the 'introduction' part of this postlude, we have tried to summarise the Theory of Manifestation put forward by ancient Indian masters. The theory has been described in detail in our book *Jesus Christ and the Spirit of Truth*. It has been explained that only '*Sat*' (the Truth), which always exists, can manifest as Swayambhuv or the 'Son'. And it must manifest like a coin with two faces—one face of the 'manifest' Son represents 'Father' (or *Chit*)—the mind or the experiencing side, while the other face represents 'Spirit' (energy), that can be known or experienced. This manifesting 'Truth' has a 'self', but no specific form, since it can assume any from depending on what item—a particle, a thing, or an aggregate—it wishes to manifest as.

As a sign of presence of the 'self', it is called a Shiva 'Lingam'. In Sanskrit language, 'lingam' means a 'sign' only which does indicate a presence, but no specific form. To assume a from, the egg or the seed into anything begins to show two asymmetries as it begins to grow—one in the head-tail direction and the other indicating a growth on the sides. Accordingly, since most ancient times, Swayambhuva or the Param Shiva, in symbolic terms, is worshipped by the Indians as a somewhat elongated and rounded stone which is otherwise formless, indicating the 'self' and its potentiality to manifest as any and everything of this world, besides the world as a whole.

Out of the over sixty thousand temples of the hapless Hindus destroyed by the Muslim invaders, about half were destroyed by the Moghuls. Though some of these temples were left in ruins, for being too big or of little consequence, most of these were converted into make-shift hybrid mosque. by the invading Moghuls. And these included the great Vishweshwara Temple of Varanasi with its famous Gyan Vapi 'well', whose sacred water is still known to titillate the wisdom bud and to confer purity of thought. If the narratives provided by Nicolai Alexandrovitch Notovitch of Crimea, based on the first and second century Buddhist writings, or those provided by Dowling in his Aquarian Gospel, should be correct, then as a young scholar Jesus too had visited Varanasi in search for wisdom and had stayed there for several years. For sure, he must have visited the great temple as well and drops of the holy water may have been sprinkled on him too.

It is a pity that during a fully video-graphed survey recently conducted by a team of officials, under the Court orders, the ancient Shiva-lingam of this famous temple of the Hindus, highly revered by them for thousands of years, was found hidden under the surface water of a tank used by the Muslim faithful for washing their feet, hands, etc. and for rinsing their mouth. They have been ridding themselves of the impurities on their bodies, dumping it over the head of the most revered symbol of the majority people in these lands, before they could offer their prayers to their own God. After discovery of the idol, bearing visible marks of an effort to tamper with it, the washing hall has been sealed by the Court and alternative arrangements have been made for washing of feet, and rinsing of mouth etc. for the Muslim faithful wishing to offer prayers at the make-shift mosque.

Surprisingly, the community has lodged a petition with the Court that its rights were being violated, that the survey undertaken by the government agency under the Court order must be nullified, and that they must be allowed to wash their feet and mouth etc. at the same place and in the same manner as before without any change in the status quo. How the author wishes that followers of other religions—right or wrong—could begin to show a similar commitment to the cause of their community as well? So much, for the anguish of the hawks who have been deprived of their opportunity to insult their neighbour, and so much for the avowed wish of the sooth-saying arm of the same people of living in peace like good neighbours! To him it sounds more like the duplicity displayed by a political set-up where one spokesperson would placate and a score of others must go all out for a frontal attack!

It is not surprising, however, that voices in support of the Muslim brotherhood are now being raised not only by the neighbouring Muslim countries, but several other kingdoms as well. Again, it is even less surprising that bolder and more vocal among the people supporting the deliberate insult to the idol of the principal Hindu Godhead, must compare the holiest of holy 'lingam' to the male sex organ. People do derive grosser ecstasies with grosser thoughts, and that may constitute all the cricket and all the fun for them!

Out of the seven levels or chakras within the human structure, to which the human consciousness can rise, according to the experts in fine structural aspects that go into making of a man (*Jesus Christ and the Spirit of Truth*), the consciousness of the people with average intellect (and this may include most of the present day Hindus as well), can seldom rise beyond the two lowest levels of the chakras, the lowest of which is concerned with procreation, and the next in order with other enjoyments of the gross senses only.

Even if the 'spirit of truth' was served on a platter to the people with such gross intellect, they will still be unable to comprehend the same. It may be too much for them to bear or to understand, and could pass over their heads even if it was to be repeated to them a hundred times. Again, a teacher himself confined to the two lowermost levels in the human structure even if authorised to issue injunctions, can hardly be in a position to teach anything that is of any real worth to anyone, except for the gross gratification of the beneficiary and of the teacher himself.

Do We Really Need to Protect God?

If we wish to usher in a change in the paradigm, or a healthy reform in religious beliefs, we need to make people really aware about the nature of Truth, both vis-à-vis scientific findings and matured philosophical reasoning. It may perhaps be possible to make wise people from different religions to sit together, even if it should call for some fair degree of persuasion at the initial stage. These wise from all over the world should be requested to proffer proposals backed by logic, as to how the world may arise—by the hands of God, of its own, or in some other mysterious way, and then move further and try to arrive on a common basis for constructive religious beliefs; to enable the new millennium to move on the right track—to bring peace, happiness, and prosperity to one and all.

An extensive and thread-bare discussion must take place, and the wise people from every religion may be invited on the pattern of a World Parliament of Religions, like the one held at Chicago in 1893. It is not really necessary that a consensus may be reached in one or two sittings. The conference may continue for as many days as deemed proper, but a fresh beginning can, nevertheless, be made. And then it may be followed up about once a year or with such gaps as may be agreed upon.

We know that the Big Bang Theory of creation was proposed by Georges Lemaitre, a Belgian cosmologist, who was a Catholic priest. Preferably some priests and other scholars with knowledge of physics, in particular, must be included in the deliberations of the Council. An effort should be made to move towards a logical hypothesis about existence of God, as well as the rise of the world and humanity; and based on a firm footing, different people should decide on the ways of prayer and worship they will prefer to adopt for their own branch of the humanity, keeping the principle of peaceful co-existence among the different people in mind.

A rational narrative that can withstand reason and logical scrutiny, and which can apply to the whole of the universe and the whole of mankind, besides conforming to scientific findings and scientific reasoning, must be agreed upon and be frozen like a universal civil code, sort of, leaving little scope for a private agreement or a personal law for any persuasive violation of one son or daughter of man, or another.

We have mentioned the case of the importunate widow earlier. In

India, now a Muslim husband can no longer divorce one of his wives by merely uttering the word 'divorce' three times in quick succession. Now it will need at least two months for one to rid himself of his wife, since interval of a month is now necessary between two such utterings. There is one other side to a wife's ordeal, however—a nightmare like procedure that many self-respecting women may refuse to follow, rather than accepting a husband's offer to mend a broken marriage.

The religious injunction of 'halala' has been dropped by a majority of the Muslim countries now. In India and its neighbourhood, however, it is still prevalent. If, under the fit of a rage or incited by some misinformation, motivated or otherwise, provided by some relative or another person, a husband has uttered the words 'I divorce thee' three times and, after realizing his mistake, he wants the wife to return to her children or to the safety of her husband's house, the procedure of 'halala' is required to be complied with. The personal Law provides that the wife thus divorced should first marry some other person and that marriage must also be consummated, before her former husband can remarry her. The one-night marriage is only a token formality, like a mindless procedure, however, since other than a 'tiff' or other exchange of a similar nature, nothing may have changed between the couple in real terms. To overcome the unwanted consequence of a thoughtless religious injunction, should the wife become pregnant during the prescribed procedure, the first preference for the person to give effect to the religious compliance is the father-in-law of the women, so that should she become pregnant, and if a child should be on the way, it may be pure in blood and faith; the second preference, for the same reason is a priest, and so on. For sure, the father-in-law may be more loyal to his son and daughter-in-law than to the religious prescription. Yet, such debasement of a woman's honour must be stopped for ever. Among other things, a universally uniform civil code must be insisted upon by all the people on the right side of a merit based human world.

It must be clearly understood by one and all that goodliness is godliness. It is God, whom we pray to protect all his children! He does not need our protection. Prophets and books are also holy because they relate to God, and so may be case with idols of God. Neither of these too, need human protection, even if the God may have made 'man' in his own image. Prophet Daniel had predicted total cleansing and purging for the mankind, which many people will accept, and it is to them, in particular, that this ode for a change in the paradigm is addressed; so that the falsehood may be overcome, and righteousness may prevail.

The rule of the land must be benign and intelligent, and if that should be so or nearly so, every faithful must consider law of the land as the first divine injunction and any injunctions of religion as secondary. Blasphemy must be universally disapproved, but it must not be a punishable offense except in rarest of rare cases, where a deliberate hurt is intended or some other grave civil transgression is committed. And yet, only the state should initiate an action. No individual can be permitted to assume the role of a judge, or an executioner. If ever, a division as suggested by Jesus (and by the other holy ones through prophet Daniel) comes into effect—to create a white unblemished lane and a good number of other lanes, those who wish to delay joining the mainstream should find them on the lanes more and more farther from the colourless regime of the evolving Son of Man.

AND NOW ABOUT THE GOD OF PHYSICS

Earlier, we have stated that the only bone of contention on the 'sciences' side vis-a-vis the findings of the rishis, happens to be that according to modern science, consciousness must arise out of neurons and the nerve-connections made of particulate matter only, which has been proved totally and utterly wrong and lacking a reasonable basis. And this has been done and is being done again and again. This, in a way, is over-simplification of certain basic issues, but since a number of stalwarts of physics have also insisted on primacy of consciousness over matter, rather than trying to open up the whole of the Pandora's box, we had restricted our argument thus far to this most basic misconception built into our scientific understanding of the day only.

We have mentioned Prof. Hawkins, who had said, "Because there is a law like gravity, the universe can and will create itself from nothing. ...Spontaneous creation is the reason there is something rather than nothing, why the universe exists, why we exist..." Of course, the great physicist, who had to turn himself into a make-shift philosopher also by his own admission, was speaking only about one aspect of the wholeness, as to how the world could arise.

Save for the names mentioned by us, like Newton, Planck, Einstein, Heisenberg, et al, modern science, led by the physics fraternity, has a great faith in things already given to them by the Nature to play around with. This enables them to repose their faith in a God who must act in an autonomic fashion but in a random unpredictable way, since he lacks a neural framework and hence also intelligence of any kind. If there is a whole, as such, it is only accidental in the fraternity's view, and by examining the parts, it is entitled to exchange notes and to predict this accidental whole as well. With an autonomically active God of Physics of their own, Modern science is also opposed to the idea of any intelligent cause at the back of the universe, as such, or to objectivity of any kind being involved at any stage.

Life, the Modern Science seems to suggest, could be a chance happening, which may not have happened at all if due weightage was given to the laws of probability. There was a better than even chance that after getting created, the world of stars, galaxies and chemical elements could have gone on for ever without appearance of life forms. Man, and intelligence are also considered by it as another chance happening resulting from random mutation of chemical elements of biologically active substances. But for a number of lucky breaks, the universe with all its stars and galaxies, could have been a failed enterprise, which could have gone on and on for billions or trillions of years, unknown to anyone and without serving any ostensible purpose—an uncalled-for exercise in futility by an unintelligent and autonomically active principal! Luckily, all these are mere conjectures and not actual findings. And the conjectures can always be opposed or contested, and even replaced by facts that can be ascertained.

The faith of the science fraternity in things already given by this unintelligent and autonomically active God of Physics would seem pathetic, to say the least, to any unbiased and unencumbered wise man, a homo-sapiens worth the name. For sure, the electric charge, the colour charge, the wave particle duality, the exclusion principle, the uncertainty relation, the three sub-atomic particles and the three kinds of forces, can all be given, if the physicists were allowed to go back and create an autonomic yet unintelligent God of their own, to suit the specifications they spell out.

Yet, even a pencil, with or without an eraser attached to it, needs an address to be, a place where it can go and come to exist. The world, in comparison, is somewhat larger, and with specifications of its own. And, still it needs an address too to build itself, even if spontaneously and entirely unassisted! A basic question would still arise, where? O, where? The autonomic God of Physics! Where?

The answer that would readily come to the mind of an indignant physicist would be, 'in space'! In empty space, of course! Waiting for the world to arise of its own in a spontaneous manner and to contain the same! For sure, the space need not be empty! It can be filled with vacuum energy, with pairs of particles and anti-particles coming to arise and annihilating each other at intervals too short to measure for the time being; waiting for even better tapes and clocks to come into use! Yet, the question of an address is not really addressed; still left in the lurch, hanging precariously at a place unknown to anyone! Perhaps, it would be more specific if we can say the address for the empty space lay in the top drawer of a particular person's bedside table or to be plucked out of a tree growing in his garden! And yet, we shall only be going around in circles. The question would only stand modified, as to where do the bedside table or the tree from which the space can be taken or plucked-out lie? the address that may hold up the table, or the garden!

When nothing exists, and a world is to be made to arise by the God of Physics, he has a problem at hand! First of all, he needs to ascertain his own address and then that for the world he can make to arise in a spontaneous manner. The physicists are apt to suggest that both space and the energy came to arise from a singularity of immense mass and density and both space and matter began to expand. However, the basic question still remains, where did the singularity rest and held by what or whom? It may be understandable, should it be proffered that the contents of the singularity may once contract and once expand in a cyclic order. And yet, the broad question shall remain, how the singularity came to arise in the first place and, above all, where? It is known that the space which can hold stars and galaxies is not really empty, but is a home for vacuum energy with a negative pressure. We need to understand which total void, held by what or whom? can hold and support the singularity first, and the space with vacuum energy, besides billions of galaxies and trillions of stars later!

To the question, how life came to arise so quickly after the formation of the Earth, we are, likewise, told that it probably evolved elsewhere and may have arrived on the Earth astride some meteorite. For sure, it is not incumbent upon our brothers taking care of the science side, after its separation from philosophy a few centuries ago, to necessarily have a fool-proof answer to explain how life may have come to arise. It is only that they would rather set aside things they are not that comfortable with, but must keep insisting on non-existence of an intelligent principal or any intelligent design.

All life, we are aware, is made of cells which have a DNA that are huge molecules, made of millions or billions of atoms, and comprising of a number of genes. The DNA works like a manual of life for a particular organism. Most of the tasks inside the cells are, however, carried out by the proteins. A Protein is itself a complex and huge molecule. It is assembled by stringing amino-acids together in a particular order, which is unique for each type of protein. There is a set of twenty amino acids chosen by the Nature to make life on Earth. The amino-acid molecules are themselves made of Hydrogen and Nitrogen atoms.

For every position in a long chain leading to a protein, one amino acid out of the twenty comes to get installed, while a chain leading to a particular protein can easily involve from a few hundred to more than a thousand of such steps. We shall be deceiving ourselves if we were to harbour a belief that all the blocks of amino-acids could come to be placed one upon the other in the correct sequence in the chain, forming a protein, by an accident or through a process of trial and error over a long period of time.

Further, not just one or two, but a hundred thousand different types of proteins may be needed for an intelligent life form like us, during its life cycle. "By all laws of probabilities—proteins should not exist. It is stunningly improbable to produce a single protein by random events", writes Bill Bryson, in his famous book 'A Short History of Nearly Everything'.

"The chances of a 1,055-sequence molecule like collagen spontaneously self-assembling are", he points out, "frankly, nil. It just isn't going to happen. To grasp what a long shot its existence is, visualize a standard Las Vegas slot machine but broadened greatly to accommodate 1,055 spinning wheels instead of the usual three or four, and with twenty symbols on each wheel (one for each amino acid). How long would you have to pull the handle before all 1,055 symbols came up in the right order? Effectively forever! Even if you reduced the number of spinning wheels to 200, which is actually a more typical number of amino acids for a protein, the odds against all 200 coming up in a prescribed sequence are 1 followed by 260 zeros. That in itself is a larger number than all the atoms in the universe."

The only way for the protein molecules to come into existence, as such, is to do so inside a living cell. However, in-spite of all the knowledge at our command, how the first living cell came to arise, and whether it arose here on Earth or somewhere else in the universe, remains anybody's guess.

Again, like the notion that consciousness must arise only from neural framework, the assumption that only somewhat evolved life can have intelligence is equally erroneous. True that particulate matter would seem to be greatly restricted and almost (not fully) predictable in its behaviour. Yet, all that is there about us, or even the particles of matter, is not fully known or understood yet. Even these basic blocks of matter need an amount of intelligence to make the world work in the way it is known to work. We do not think we actually need to bring in more details in our support of the Theory of Manifestation in this postlude, since the matter stands explained in proper detail in our main book *Matter, Life and Spirit Demystified*. It may, however, be in order to remind that where necessary, the world of particles is also capable to collapse one or the other of its functions (Appendix-1).

Root Nature: United Common Force

All the 36 elements (*tattva*) which constitute the world according to the Agama are a transformation of *Para Shakti*, which is the 'nature' of *Param Shiva*, also known as '*Mool Prakriti*' or the 'root nature'. It is also referred to as *Adya Shakti*, or the original force, by the Shakta branch of the Tantra scriptures. It is called root nature because, as explained in the Introductory essay to this book, roots of both the principles, mutually opposed and yet inter-dependent, can be held by it in their state of equilibrium, or their *yaamal* state, from where they can manifest in their respective directions. They are both infinite and between them they can make a finite world to arise by holding and supporting each other to any degree or extent.

We have explained that from time to time and in in a cyclic order, the world arises from the eternal principle of existence 'Sat' (*Truth*), which is 'the spirit or essence'—the real substance, or 'the final and unlimited potency to be', and then it can be reabsorbed by it. This 'Truth' is the property of just 'Being'. When nothing else exists, eternal awareness still exists in a state of total self-contentment, and is called Nishkal Brahma, since it has no other attributes in this state.

When it is awake or manifest, the attributes of awareness (*Chit*) and contentment (*Ananda*) of the 'supreme consciousness' come into prominence as well. The rishis then call it *Sat-Chit-Ananda* Brahma, or *Sakal Param Shiva*. When nothing else exists, this principle of existence is said to be in sleep mode, like a tortoise that has withdrawn its head and limbs into itself. During its sleep, the world with all its constituents including space and the time remains withdrawn—held and hidden by this principle, in a merged state—like the hidden potential of its unseen qualities.

Shiva is the static element that represents pure awareness, but *Shakti*, its dynamic counterpart, can only manifest with *Shiva* as its support. It cannot stand on its own. In symbolic terms, in the tantric lore, it is represented as a female figure in motion with one of its feet resting on the chest of an inert *Shiva*, who is represented by a male figure lying motionless on its back. The universe is the body of this primal force that is always on the move and it uses the static and unqualified awareness of Shiva for its address, or as a support for it, or a ground for itself, to stand upon. In Eastern India, Mother Nature is widely worshipped in this form as *Mahakaali*, the consort of *Mahakaal*, the Great-Time, which is also called the Great Void (in which even a thought cannot arise, much less the particle-antiparticle pairs). In this void, the wish of God arises as a vibration with a sound of its own.

All objects of the world including physical space, according to Agama, are vibratory by nature as all are projected by *Para* Shakti on the canvas of *praan*, the primary vibration, which remains active and effective in all the energy realms and dimensions. *Praan*, it has been stated (*Jesus Christ and the Spirit of Truth*), is the vibrating creative energy at the cosmic level, arising out of the union of *Shiva* and *Shakti*, the first two elements, and it can carry both negative and positive components. From 'one eternal reality' these two diverge as this reality's own mind and heart pair, giving rise to an internal space, called *Chidakasha*, into the as yet unmanifest eternal awareness. In the manifest realm, the two reunite to form a seed of the world and of every entity into it. All manifestation, as a matter of fact, happens within this primary field *Chidakasha*, and hence no other address is required outside the consciousness of God.

All the subsequent elements of the Agama, down to air, water, and the earth, arise from this creative energy, *praan*. In its general form, the *pranic* vibration remains simple. Down the line, however, the vibration becomes more and more complex depending on the particle or the object which it needs to create or to manifest. We already know that the latest string theory, which is the principal candidate for being called the 'The Theory of Everything', tries to visualize the fundamental particles of matter as entities with their own unique vibrations that extend to (not just three but) ten dimensions, besides 'time' the eleventh dimension. As far as the Theory of Manifestation is concerned, the primal cosmic vibration of *praan* continues as long as the world lasts, and so does the sound of this vibration which has been called 'word' by the Old Testament.

The Teacher Universal

The field of historical linguistics began, first as an idea, in 1786, when Sir William Jones, a British scholar living in India and studying Sanskrit, a language spoken and written in ancient India, noticed similarities between Sanskrit and classical Greek, Latin, and some more of the recent European languages. "He declared that it was of a wonderful structure, more perfect than Greek, more copious than Latin", writes John Keay in compiling 'a History of India', ...yet bearing to both of them a stronger affinity, both in the roots of verbs and the forms of grammar, than can possibly have been produced by accident; so strong, indeed, that no philologer could examine them all without believing them to have sprung from some common source, which perhaps no longer exists."

The Aryans were seen as a great people with great missions by some very renowned historians of the 19th century. They were even referred to as *'the rulers of the history'* by Sir Friedrich Max Muller, the German Professor of Sanskrit and as *'the master race'* by some others. This was, of course, a later development. Early in his career, Max Mueller was employed by the British to play down ancient Indian culture. Among other things, he translated the most ancient scripture of the mankind, Rigveda, in a kind of demeaning way. Later, when he began to translate the Upanashidas, he began to mature as a thinker and as a gentle and sober person that he really was.

Lord Macaulay, on the other hand, was more of an executive policy maker and a determined executioner. Early in the 19th century, he had decided that all the memories of the great Indian culture had to be erased from the minds of the common Indian people to serve the purpose of the British in an adequate manner, and he came up with a policy of education for India that was effectively able to serve this end. Max Mueller was roped in for this purpose too at one time, but wisdom began to prevail with him as he began to mature.

Soon after the knowledge of Upanishad came to prevail, around 3,000 years ago, besides as Father of all, the scholars and mendicants had begun to see God as the most effective principal teacher of the mankind as well. In the 8th century, the great reformer of the Vedic School, Shankaracharya had strung in a Guru Stotram. We reproduce a few verses for the benefit of our readers to help them understand and try to visualize their own reality, and also the reality of the world we live in.

Verses from Guru Stotram:

Brahmanandam, param sukhdam, kevalam, gyanmurtim,
He is (*I am*) of the nature of eternal and unbroken bliss; it is great joy to try to perceive him (one's own self'); he (that) alone exists, and he exists as the principle of awareness without any other body.

Dwandwateetam, gagansadrisham, tattvamasyadilakshyam,
There is no room for any duality in him, who is like an expanding field

of awareness, and which is hinted about by the teachers in the know with such statements, as 'you and that 'Father' are one'.

Ekam, nityam, vimalam, achalam, sarvadhi sakshibhutam,

He is one without a second, eternal, spotless, unmoving, and a mere witness of every manifest event, without participating in the event in any manner. He is the observer of the whole, who remains at absolute rest.

Bhavateetam, trigunrahitam, sadgurum tam namaami.

We bow to that supreme teacher who forms a part of our being, who is beyond all thought, and which remains unaffected by any of the three properties of attraction, repulsion and interaction.

Chaitanyam, shaswatam, shantam, vyomateetam, niranjanm, Naad, vindu, kalateetam, sadgurum tam namami.

He is conscious and aware, eternal and ever at peace (free from thought, without any agitation), beyond the space and is self-effulgent.

We bow to that supreme teacher into our own being, which remains beyond the three spheres of causal impulse (word), mental awareness (thought) and gross action (kala, or action) (kala is kamkala, the interaction between the two dimensions of the powers of two different kinds).

Om namh Shivay gurway, satchidanand murtaye,
Nisprapanchay, shantay, niralambay, tejase.

We bow to that supreme teacher in our being, who is Shiva (pure), who is only in the nature of existence, awareness and bliss (and is otherwise bodiless), who remains un-involved in any affair, undisturbed, and who shines of its own without the need for any outside address or support (yet it can provide an address and support to a world of multiplicity, as a lay person can support the objects seen by him/her in a dream).

Readers who can, must put faith in the Biblical statement, 'God has made Man in his own image', and when they are calm in mind and alone, they may try to visualize the qualities ascribed to the Teacher Universal, that apply to them as well, in a like manner, to be able to understand the Reality, or their very own 'Truth'.

Chapter 6

PROPHET DANIEL AND HIS VISIONS

The ruins of Nebuchadnezzar's Babylon are spread over two thousand acres, forming the largest archaeological sites in the Middle East. He enlarged the royal palace, built and repaired temples, built a bridge over the Euphrates, and constructed a grand processional boulevard and gateway lavishly decorated with glazed brick. The 15 miles by 15 miles city was surrounded by a 350 feet high wall, which was 87 feet wide. They could race 6 chariots abroad on the wall and there were 250 towers on the main wall. The Euphrates River flowed through parts of the palace grounds with drawbridges. The hanging gardens of Babylon were at one time counted among seven wonders of the world. Nebuchadnezzar also possibly built the world's first museum.

Daniel was a prophet of Semitic roots trained by the Babylonians. When the Semitic people attacked the idol worshipping Dravid or the Aryans, they killed all men, women and children, except the virgin girls. The booty carried back by Nebuchadnezzar included no women however, virgin or otherwise, but it did include four early teen agers from the prophet families selected by the king himself as the "King's scholars". The king arranged for their study and learning. He kept a personal 'eye' and kept himself in the know. This, however, does not mean that the King was all goodness rolled into one.

The scribes of the Holy Book do try to paint him as a cruel king. In an act of blind arrogance, along with the young scholars, the king also carried with him the sacred utensils used in worship in the temple at Jerusalem. While a part of him still showed glimpses of his ancient roots, he was highly vindictive and as whimsical as the kings and dictators are known to turn into, invariably, at some point.

All the four children learnt and excelled, but Daniel was most intelligent among them. He had also come to gain a gift of interpreting every kind of a dream and vision; besides he was open to the idea of a common Father who was not partisan and for whom all humanity was one. He received the honours due to a learned man in the King's court. At one time, he was appointed by the king as the governor of the whole province of Babylon and also the head of all Babylonian sages.

The history of Babylonia started near the end of the year 2000 B.C. and it came to an end in 539 B.C. Babylonian system of mathematics was a sexagesimal numerical system. They were good at astronomical observation and calculation too. They believed there were 360 days in a year and this formed the basis of their numerical system. From this we derive the modern-day usage of 60 seconds a minute and 60 minutes an hour, besides 360 degrees in a circle. They also developed a system for writing numbers using symbols for singles, tens and hundreds. According to some expert opinions, the origins of Western astronomy can be found in Mesopotamia. The Babylonians believed in fixed position of stars and were able to make great contribution to development of astronomy in the 7th and 8th centuries B.C. and all Western efforts in the exact sciences, according to some of the historians, may be the descendants in direct line from the work of the late Babylonian astronomers.

A significant increase in the quality and frequency of Babylonian observations appeared during the reign of Nabonassar (747-734 B.C.). The systematic records of ominous phenomenon in Babylonian astronomical diaries that began at this time allowed for the discovery of a repeating 18-year Saros cycle of lunar eclipses, for example. The Greco-Egyptian astronomer Ptolemy later used Nabonassar's reign to fix the beginning of an era, since he felt that the earliest usable observations began at this time.

THE VISIONS ABOUT THE END

The New Jerusalem Bible, mentioned by the author, begins the Book of Daniel with an introduction and states: "The first six chapters describe the life of Daniel, a Jewish sage, at the brilliant court of Babylon under Nebuchadnezzar (605-562 B.C.) and his successors... The next six chapters contain allegorical visions given to Daniel which guarantee the collapse of the persecution and a glorious future for the people of God. The vivid imagery of these chapters uses coded symbolic terms to convey a secret, the message of comfort for the future. The message of a future kingdom, founded by God and ruled by the Son of Man, stretches far beyond its immediate purpose of strengthening the Jews under persecution."

However, it may be a wrong assumption on the part of several Biblical experts who tend to hold a general view that the whole of the first six chapters of the Book deal with life of Daniel only and do not contain any message for the future. By his own admission, Daniel was instructed (D 12:4) "But you, Daniel, keep the words secret and the book sealed until the time of the End," and was advised (D 12:13), "But you go your way and rest; you shall rise for your reward at the end of the days." This seems to indicate that at the right time the message concealed by him will become understood and will help the children of Israel to choose the right path and to escape the God's curse of destruction for their country (Malachi 4:6).

The word 'end', used by Daniel, and in the gospels, seems to create different images in the mind of the readers and the scholars, often contradictory in nature. It is easy to see that the end of the world and the setting up of an everlasting kingdom, founded by God and ruled by the Son of Man, are kind of spoken in the same breath. To understand these properly, and to reconcile the apparent contradiction, these need to be examined in the light of other available details and pointers. Especially, we need to keep in mind that coded symbolic terms have been used by the prophet to convey a secret good news.

For one thing, the author would like to suggest that Daniel was under no obligation to not to hide a part of his secret in chapters 2 and 4 of his book. Secondly, the secret news was to serve as a comfort for the future, and such a 'good and great news' cannot be the end of the world. Jesus too has spoken about one flock and one shepherd some six hundred years later {John 10:16 *"I have other sheep that do not belong to this fold. I must bring them also, and they will listen to my voice (too). So, there will be (only) one flock, one shepherd (following a common nature's religion)"*}. And, in a covert manner, both have also mentioned that the rule shall pass to the institution, the 'Son of Man', as well.

Both Jesus and the Prophet speak of a time that was to come and they both seem to attach a kind of urgency to it as well. And, if now was the time, then Nature too may have pressed its fast forward button already. Half of the four million people who had fled Ukraine during the early weeks of its invasion by Russia were kids. We see future of two million kids hanging with thin threads, so that half of them will carry scars for their whole lives and many will harbour hatred and revenge too, whereas over five hundred among those who could not be shifted are dead already.

"Go your way, Daniel! he said (D 12 9:10), "For the words are to remain secret and sealed until the time of the End. *Many shall be purified, cleansed, and refined*; but the wicked shall continue to act wickedly. None of the wicked shall understand, but those who are wise shall understand (and will begin to act, to part ways, to shun their evil company and boycott them as best they can, and to build a sheepfold hard to breach, *'since wars are something that must happen'*, Jesus had said, *'but the wicked will never understand'*).

We are able to see that the 'end of the world' may not be the right interpretation for the arrival of the 'end', though wars are spoken about by Jesus, and a great war is indicated by Daniel too, when that time comes. Perhaps, we can recall two other exigencies concerned with the event. For the 'Son of Man' aspect in the context, the direction is indisputably indicated as the East, from where the spirit of truth must come in and become known. For the direct 'beneficiary' aspect in the context of the good news, however, which happens to be the Jewish progeny, the word 'end' could carry a different hint, that should be in conformity with the rest and that may also act as a reprieve and harbinger of some glad tidings for the avowed beneficiary, and those may include the Ukrainian President too at this point of time.

In the light of the prevailing exigencies associated with the 'event' and the 'moment', if we visit the very last two paragraphs of the old Bible, Malachi 4:5-6, we find, "See, I will send you the prophet Elijah before the great and terrible day of the Lord comes. He will turn the hearts of parents to their children and the hearts of children to their parents, so that I will not come and strike the land with a curse (of destruction)."

One way of looking at these concluding paragraphs of the old people's Testament, the Parent Testament, will be a likely abolition or merging of several separate religions and the two branches, represented by two testaments, coming to reunite as one, both subscribing to a new universal covenant that aims at protecting the 'right to inherit the world' for the 'Son of Man', in general—for the true human progeny to finally arrive! What a universal covenant must look like is also, in a way, already indicated by the Prophet: i.e., full cleansing of all ill-will and fear, *total purging, and absolute whiteness* free from all colours or any bias.

Dream of King Nebuchadnezzar

Daniel was not a prophet then, but he was on way to become one, when one day the King had a very unusual dream. Nebuchadnezzar thought his vision held portend of some great importance. He invited the learned and the wise to interpret the dream for him; but none was able to do so and the king was very angry. To save the lives of Babylonian sages and the brother priests, Daniel, who had been maintaining a low profile so long, then decided to come forward. He prayed through the night and presented himself in the king's court the next morning.

Daniel 2:26-29 "The king said to Daniel whose name was Belteshazzar, 'Are you able to tell me the dream that I have seen and Its interpretation?' Daniel answered the king, '...but there is a God in heaven who reveals mysteries and he has disclosed to King Nebuchadnezzar what will happen at the end of days. Your dream and the visions of your head as you lay in bed were these. To you, O king, as you lay in bed, came thoughts of what would be hereafter, and the 'Reveal-er of Mysteries' disclosed to you what is to be'."

Daniel 2:31-36 "You were looking, O king, and there appeared a great statute. That statute was huge, its brilliance extraordinary; it was standing before you, and its appearance was frightening. The head of that statue was of fine gold, its chest and arms of silver, its midsection and thighs of bronze, its legs of iron its feet partly of iron and partly of clay. As you looked on, a stone was cut out, not by human hands, and it struck the statue on its feet of iron and clay and broke them in pieces. Then, the iron, the clay, the bronze, the silver, and the gold were all broken in pieces and became like the chaff of the summer threshing-floors, and the wind carried them away, so that not a trace of them could be found. But the stone that struck the statue became a great mountain and filled the whole earth. That was the dream; now we will tell the king its interpretation.

Daniel 2:37-45 "You, O king, the king of kings to whom—to whom the God of heaven has given the kingdom, the power, the might, and the glory, into whose hand he has given human beings wherever they live, the wild animals of the field, and the birds of the air and whom he has established as ruler over them all—you are the head of gold. After you shall arise another kingdom inferior to yours and yet a third kingdom of bronze, which shall rule over the whole earth. And there shall be a fourth kingdom, strong as iron; just as iron that crushes and smashes everything, it shall crush and scatter all these. As you saw the feet and toes partly of potter's clay and partly of iron, it shall be a divided kingdom, but some of the strength of iron shall be in it, as you saw the iron mixed with clay. As the toes of the feet were part iron and part clay, so the kingdom shall be partly strong and partly brittle.

"'As you saw the iron mixed with clay, so will they mix with one another in marriage, but they will not hold together, just as iron does not mix with clay. And in the days of those kings the God of heaven will set up a kingdom that shall never be destroyed, nor shall this kingdom be left to another people. It shall crush all these and bring them to an end, and shall stand forever.

"'Just as you saw that a stone was cut from the mountain not by hands and that it crushed the iron, the bronze, the clay, the silver and the gold. The Great God has informed the king what shall be hereafter. The dream is certain, the interpretation trustworthy'."

Here, we may try to look at the things from the point of view of the Prophet, who has been made privy to a huge secret, but he is also instructed to conceal it until the day of a final reckoning, while its timing was known neither to the angels in the heaven nor to any Son of Man. The best way for the Prophet, to both conveying and hiding the very important message at the same time, would be to begin early and to stretch it to the end, changing sequences and inserting such detail that my confuse or distract, without having much implication from the angle of the main narrative. And that is what the Prophet seems to have manged to achieve.

Again, it is Nebuchadnezzar, the king with a dream, that brings Prophet Daniel into the limelight with the very idea of a prophesy, since his own people who could have divined such things were unable to interpret for him, what he had seen. Daniel, on his part, brings in the people, the kingdoms and the emerging world arena which will evolve further, at the earliest opportunity in his book. He speaks of races and the kings, and he brings in Gold, Silver, Bronze, Iron and Clay to identify the different people that were concerned with the long-term narrative, its beginning and its end. It begins with the fate in store for Nebuchadnezzar and ends with the stone that rolls and grows into a great mountain, filling the whole world, and a kingdom that will not pass into the hands of another race.

The king himself, possibly, represents the ancient Indian mix of Aryan and the Dravid, and has been identified by the Prophet with gold. The prophet, likewise, should represent the silver people, the first set of people in the Abrahamic lineage. And both were faced with the prospect of persecution in their own ways, and both in need of a deliverance at a distant date. Further, in both cases, though there were many differences present, but not possibly without the prospect of a shared ending at a distant date, when the deliverance finally arrived, and when there could be only one flock and one shepherd.

The sons of Abraham had first separated from the people of Brahmavart (formerly Ilavart and then Aryavart and later Bharat) to go their own way and then a major branch had taken off to give rise to Christianity, though in the end each of these people seem to be destined to unite in a firm bond again. That the very trigger that set the timing of this book, President Zelensky finding himself in sudden distress (on account of a war of aggression on Ukraine), should be a silver man, may be more than just a coincidence.

A Stump to Roots Connection

King Nebuchadnezzar saw a dream that he discussed with others. At last Daniel came before him. (Daniel 4:9-18) The king said "O Belteshazzar, chief of the magicians, I know that you are endowed with a spirit of the holy gods and that no mystery is too difficult for you. Hear the dream I saw, and tell me its interpretation. Upon my bed this is what I saw: There was a tree at the centre of the earth, and its height was great. The tree grew great and strong, its top reached to heaven, and it was visible to the ends of the whole earth. Its foliage was beautiful, its fruit abundant; in it provided food for all.

"The animals of the field found shade under it, the birds of air nested in its branches, and from it all living beings were fed. I continued looking, in the visions of my head as I lay in bed, and there was a holy watcher coming down from heaven. He cried aloud and said, 'Cut down the tree and chop off its branches, strip off its foliage and scatter its fruit. Let the animals flee from beneath it and the birds from its branches. But leave the stump and roots in the ground, with a band of iron and bronze, in the tender grass of the field.

"'Let him be bathed with the dew of the heavens and let its lot be with the animals in the grass of the earth. Let its mind be changed from that of a human, and let the mind of an animal be given to him. And let seven times pass over him! The sentence is rendered by the decree of the watchers, the decision is given by order of the holy ones, in order that all who live may know that the 'Most High' is sovereign over the kingdom of mortals; he gives it to whom he will and sets over it the lowliest of human beings.' This is the dream that I, King Nebuchadnezzar, saw. Now you, Belteshazzar, declare the interpretation."

Here again, a camouflage may have been created by the Prophet. A holy watcher coming down from the heaven to pronounce a judgement: this seems to hold much too larger portends than a temporary setback to the king that is mentioned further down in this chapter. It should seem outright possible that this vision was related to the king not as a person but as a people; as a branch of the people which constituted a large tree with its trunk and roots lying outside the domain of the king, and seemingly in the middle of the earth for him.

As the prophet begins to explain the meaning of what he had witnessed to the king, first he tells him (D 4:20-22), "The tree that you saw, which grew great and strong so that that its top reached to heaven and was visible to the whole earth (not confined to a spot of 1,000 hectares, extending to about 15 miles in either direction), whose foliage was beautiful and its fruit abundant, and which provided food for all, under which animals of the field lived, and in whose branches the birds of air had nests—it is you, O king! You have grown great and strong. Your greatness has increased and reaches to heaven, and your sovereignty to the ends of the earth (15 by 15 miles)." (As stated, there can be a trick at work here. The prophet is describing Nebuchadnezzar as a tree of which he is a branch too, but the king is satisfied that he himself was being described and was the tree itself).

And then, Daniel verbatim repeats what the holy watcher had ordered in his dream (D 4:23-24), "Cut the tree down and destroy it, but leave its stump and roots in the ground, with a band of iron and bronze, in the grass of the field; and let him be bathed with the dew of heaven and let his lot be with the animals of the field, until seven times pass over it—this is the interpretation, O king, and it is a decree of the Most High that has come upon my lord, the king." However, when Daniel gives his interpretation of the dream for the king, he excludes the future and includes only those parts in the prophecy which were related to his present and which he was himself going to experience. The prophet makes no reference to the king being bound with the hoops of two different metals.

(D 4:25-27) "You shall be driven away from human society and your dwelling shall be with the wild animals. You shall be made to eat grass like oxen, you shall be bathed with the dew of heaven, and seven times shall pass over you, until you have learned that the 'Most High' has sovereignty over the kingdom of mortals and gives it to whom he will. As it was commanded to leave the stump and roots of the tree, your kingdom shall be re-established for you from the time that you learn that Heaven is sovereign'. Therefore, O king, may my counsel be acceptable to you: my advice: *atone for your sins with righteousness and your iniquities with mercy to the oppressed, so that your prosperity may be prolonged.*"

A further very interesting development is reported by the scribes, after twelve months from the day of the king's last dream. On that evening, the king was strolling on the roof of his royal palace in Babylon, full of gratefulness about what he had received in the hands of God (and possibly also of remorse for the way he had led his life and also possibly thinking about the advice Daniel had given while interpreting the dram for him; *to atone for his sins with righteousness and his iniquities with mercy to the oppressed*).

Daniel 4:31-33 "While the words (of gratefulness) were still in the king's mouth, a voice came down from heaven: 'O King Nebuchadnezzar, to you it is declared: The kingdom is taken from you. You shall be driven away from human society, and your dwelling shall be with the animals of the field. You shall be made to eat grass like oxen, and seven times shall pass over you, until you have learned that the Most High has sovereignty over the kingdom of mortals and gives it to whom he will.' Immediately the sentence was fulfilled against Nebuchadnezzar. He was driven away from human society, he ate grass like oxen, and his body was bathed with the dew of heaven, until his hair grew as long as eagles' feathers and his nails became like birds' claws."

The king may have heard a voice from the heaven, though it was unlikely that anyone should be around to eves-drop, especially any scribes from the opposite camp, to be able to verbatim describe it. It was also unlikely that out of such a good mood in which he had found himself, overnight he would have turned into a dangerous lunatic, to be driven out by his sons, wives and ministers, in the morning itself. And, of course, the willy king may have left for the forest the following morning, deciding to undergo a particular penance, within the sight of everyone. Only his close family and ministers will know the real reason. Kings going out for a penance do not declare to their subjects that they had done great wrongs and so a penance was called for.

Possibly the king may have sent back most of his close attendants as well, and possibly, his kingdom was distributing alms and clothes to the poor. The task of a scribe is never easy. Narratives are required to be completed even when reliable information may be unavailable. In such cases, the scribe needs to use his judgement, according to a situation, and according to the side on which he stands.

The voice from the heaven verbatim repeats what Daniel had said by way of interpretation (D 4:25-26). It should not be surprising that the narrative, possibly a back-insertion, seems to only pick-up what was visible to a man on the street. It says, "Nebuchadnezzar was driven (or went away) from human society and ate grass as oxen do (avoided eating meat of animals), he was drenched by the dew of the heaven, his hair grew like an eagle's feathers and his nails became like a bird's talons (he avoided using the services of a barber-cum-manicurist during the period of his penance)."

Some of the strange customs of the idolators could be interpreted by the scribes as they should be pleased. In any case, bands or iron and bronze are not mentioned by the voice of heaven or in the narrative of its being fulfilled.

On his part the king neither makes a mention of the voice from heaven or of the prophecy made by it after he returns. On the other hand, his counsellors and noblemen acclaim him (for having completed a penance heroically? Or for overcoming his confusion and gaining his objective?)! "When the period was over (Daniel 34-36), I, Nebuchadnezzar, lifted my eyes to heaven ...my reason returned to me ...and my majesty and splendour were restored to me for the glory of my kingdom. My counsellors and my lords sought me out, I was re-established over my kingdom, and still more greatness was added to me. I blessed the Most-High and praised and honoured the one who lives for ever."

Now, let us once again return to the main vision or the dream that was seen by the King, that he had discussed with Daniel and that included many other details. This was the second dream or the second vision seen by Nebuchadnezzar and there is no ground for presuming that it was unrelated to the first. While the people were identified with metals and clay the two discussing the first dream were the first two metals in the analogy followed by Daniel—gold and silver, the comparatively softer ones, that were destined for much suppression and persecution in the days ahead. And we are talking about people, not about families of the brotherhood of prophets and the scribes, whom Jesus was accustomed to call 'thieves and bandits', among other things. Now in this second dream, we find that bronze and iron too (that did not exist then) join the prophet's narrative, that must move finally to the principal event in the history of the future mankind, and which has been mentioned in the first vision itself, and where the clay comes in as well.

The holy man shouts, 'Cut down the tree and chop off its branches, strip off its foliage and scatter its fruit. Let the animals flee from beneath it and the birds from its branches. But leave the stump and roots in the ground, with a band of iron and bronze, in the tender grass of the field. Babylon was not the tree really but a major branch that was ordained to be lopped off, and soon. And like the gentile Nebuchadnezzar, all other branches of the great tree which could be seen from the very ends of the earth, and which at one time was seen as the World Teacher by some people, and later also as a country full of gold by a different set of people, were lopped off as well with the passage of time, both of Aryan and the Dravid descents, differentiated on account of the languages they spoke.

All the gold and other earthy valuables were looted, like all the feathers of the golden peacock being pulled out one by one—only the stump was graciously left in its place of origin, and then it was first bound by hoops of iron, the Lodi and Mughals et al, for five hundred years, and later also joined by hoops of bronze for its two hundred that was allotted to it by the 'Father'. And the stump was turned into a slave. 'Let its mind be changed from that of a human, and let the mind of an animal be given to him (bound, and obliged to obey its master)', the holy man had decreed. The seven times or the seven centuries (or seven hundreds) have passed; also, the cusp period of seven tens is behind the 'Gold' people; yet even today there are people around who have not come out of their reverie and believe that if the police force was removed for only fifteen minutes, they may be able to chop off a billion people.

It is a matter of record, that when the present Govt. of India came into power for the first time in 2014, its significance could not have escaped from being noticed by the thinking intellectuals—true to their profession and otherwise unbiased. The first editorial of Washington Post, following this event, said something to the effect that 'for the first time in independent India an 'Indian' government has been formed'. The process of transfer of power had now been completed. The shattering of the power of the holy people (Daniel 12) can be said to have come to an end at this point of time. As for significance of this need of the hour event, at the end of just eight years since then, our readers have the present book in their hands. And this, by the way, is only a postlude to our main book, *Matter, Life and Spirit Demystified*.

Again, within the first six months of the fresh term, of what Washington Post has acknowledged as "the first 'Indian' government of an independent India", the show of strength of the muscles of brute force, to suggest a fifteen-minute wipe out of a billion, is a matter of record too. For sure, it smacks of a policy, and the occasion was enactment of new Law that empower the government to grant citizenship to Hindus and other minorities that may cross over from the three neighbouring Muslim countries to avoid persecution in the hands of the majority people, the Muslim. Now, we see an elaboration, as 'people' who wish to convert the 'brother' prophet's promised muscle into a reality, would hardly be found in lacking within the precincts of this stern 'phenotypical' aspect into the Homo-sapiens, coming forward. It represents a 'no holds barred' aggregation that seems dedicated to contain any people that may be righteous, or close to the realm of Truth.

We are not talking about a religion at all! should anyone from a religion, who is personally unaligned to any brutish proposals, imagine an infringement, and feel personally indignant? A mere five or seven in a thousand, who apart from their religion, also represent a typically stern phenotype among the humans, do not really represent their religion. In fact, they display lots and lots of what their own religion prohibits and often also proscribes. Such phenotype is found among other religions also, and also among groups of people aggregating on considerations other than of a religious nature. This typical instinct, in fact, predates the very religions. Being selfish, aggressive and working in defiance of all norms of the righteous, is not a new human-trait.

The focus of its onslaught at the moment may lie in this part of the world, but on principles its target is righteousness itself. We now hear of slogans like 'direct jehad in 2023', and '*gajwa*' or total cleansing of the land of India by 2047. Throats are being slit and the act is being video-graphed. Men are entering schools or medicine shops and after asking the name and faith of the principal or the owner, or of the fruit-seller on the road, they are being shot in the head at point blank range. Such plans and executions are very disquieting, for sure. Total cleaning of a country (to begin with) of the righteousness is not really a welcome idea. The son of man everywhere must be under threat. He does need to take a note, as the world and its humanity continue to move along the upward arrow of time.

The animals fleeing its shelter possibly indicates that many people will convert to the domineering and coercive religions of the iron people, lending strength to the new shelter they hoped to build for themselves, after finishing off all other faiths through killing or conversion. The true Sons of Man, however, remained. Brahmin priests were raised above the ground by holding the tuft of their hair by tall mercenaries in the employ of the invading Mughals, as the others waited to chop their heads off. Yet, only the weak in mind converted. Two young sons of the Sikh Guru, aged seven and nine years, were plastered alive into the walls, but they would not covert. Even during the cusp period, hundreds of thousands of Pundits were made to flee from Kashmir Valley, where daughters were raped before the eyes of parents and wives before the eyes of husbands, but they refused to convert.

The birds deserting its branches likewise, possibly indicates many borderline people taking up to Christianity. Only after undergoing a slavery of seven hundred years (besides a hang-over period of seventy), the holy people of these lands, who had resisted conversion to a strange faith through coercion or allurement, could be set free and were given back a human heart.

The Most-High rules on human sovereignty. A majority of the idol worshippers had become corrupt in thought and deed. Many of them had forgotten the covenants of their original religion that was the eternal religion and that was into their roots. The idol was to be used as a prop to worship God, it could not have taken the place of God. Token worship or display of worship mean nothing to God and does not make one virtuous. Insulting God of another is unforgivable offence in the hands of God too (though power to punish is never relegated by Him).

Use of the vessels from the Temple at Jerusalem by the successors of Nebuchadnezzar, their wives, noble men, and the women singing for them to drink wine out of them (Daniel 5:23) was a horrendous offence against God, a direct upfront act of contempt, and a proof of living in extremely sinful ways. This branch of the great tree had chosen a sadistic and suicidal path for itself. A correction had become due for sure then, as it seems to have become due in the present, though in a reverse order.

Mention of Four Beasts, Four People

In the first year of Belshazzar, king of Babylon, who succeeded Nebuchadnezzar, Daniel had a dream and vision that passed through his head as he lay in bed. He wrote it down, and this is how the narrative begins. Daniel said (Daniel 7:2-8), "I, Daniel, saw in my vision by night the four winds of heaven stirring up the great sea and four great beasts came up out of the sea, different from one another. The first was like a lion and had eagle's wings. Then as I watched, its wings were plucked off, and it was lifted off the ground and made to stand on two feet like a human being, and a human mind was given to it.

"Another beast appeared, a second one, that looked like a bear. It was raised up on one side, had three tusks in its mouth among its teeth, and was told, 'Arise, devour many bodies!' After this, as I watched, another appeared, like a leopard. The beast had four wings of a bird on its back and four heads, and dominion was given to it.

"After this I saw in the visions by night a fourth beast, terrifying and dreadful and exceedingly strong. It had great iron teeth and was devouring, breaking in pieces, and stamping what was left with its feet. It was different from all other beasts that preceded it, and it had ten horns. I was considering the horns when another horn appeared, a little one, that came up among them. Three of the original horns were plucked up from before it. There were eyes like human eyes in this horn and a mouth speaking arrogantly."

Later, same narrative has been linked to the Son of Man by the prophet, in the chain of visions he had that night. We are perhaps hearing him describe the people here, and not the nations, if the vision really portrayed the scenario corresponding to the event, and assuming that the event is taking place now.

The first people linked to lion and the eagle perhaps are the oldest of the cultures; of Hindus who associate lion with the mother aspect that creates, and eagle with the father aspect. The lion is set on the ground standing like a human being with a human heart in their emblem. They had developed too lofty ideals too soon; the realities of the world taught them to keep to the ground and to begin to think contemporary, like a man, not like a Mahatma. They have been wiped out from everywhere else. At their place, they were given the heart of a beast for seven times or seven hundred years. At the moment, however, they are once again able to think like a nation with a human heart. They can defend themselves now; and even today they are not interested in attacking any man or a country. The crushing of the power of these holy people is now over.

The second beast is, of course, the second people; a very great people, the people of China and we are not talking regimes or histories, but the 'people' here. There were times when Masters of India will stay in China for many decades; they were welcome by the local wise people. They too had been taught to treat their guests with care and honour. The emperors would be good and bad, but the people of China were allowed to eat quantities of flesh and of all kinds, and to outnumber all others. Their symbol is dragon. Dragons are shown rearing on one side and have three tongues (against the two of the common python), between their teeth.

The third beast was like a leopard and with four bird's wings on its flank; it had four heads and it was granted dominion. Authority in the catholic world in all practical terms is shared by France, Britain, Germany and the United States. And yet, we are not talking about these four nations, but the people, who extend to Australia, Canada, Italy and several other places as well, but authority in a way is naturally vested on the four and decisions agreed upon between them are honoured by all the others as well.

Next in his visions of the night the prophet is shown the fourth beast. This too had a past and a present. That it was different from previous beasts and had been born with ten horns, it had great iron teeth and was devouring, breaking in pieces, and stamping what was left with its feet. Nobody should undermine a scribe; Jesus didn't. They could slip in things, sometimes even for a personal back slapping in the private and at others as an expressed personal disapproval, unknown to the Prophet and the Priest approving the text (For example, they have tried to create a hint that Juhu may have eaten the flesh of Jezebel, as he ate and drank after killing the queen mother, and they had to insert a curse about the dogs doing it to the queen). And now we are discussing the people that remained; for Daniel the fourth beast; which he has discussed in much greater detail, as the second part of his dream and as if these were the main people he wanted to mention, in relation with the key event and its time.

Reference is also made by the prophet to the *noise made by the boastings of the horn*, using the word 'horn' in the sense of an identity and qualifying it with 'noise' made by it. Thus, in a way, all the four important people are covered by the prophet's dream, leading up to the present.

Reference to Son of Man

In Chapter 14, *The Kingdom of Heaven*, in our main book, under the heading '*Resurrection and Sri Yukteswar*', under sub-heading, '*Usual and Lower Sections of the Astral World*', a statement of the great Master has been quoted, "Among fallen dark angels or prophets, expelled from various astral worlds, friction and wars take place with *pranic bombs* or *mental mantric vibratory rays*." Here, in the Bible too, the angel who reveals to Daniel the future events, also speaks of a prince Michael who is helpful to the cause of the Jewish people and also of the princes in the astral world who actively try to work against them and in favour of the people cognized as of Persia and of Javan. In Chapter 12, he again tells Daniel that their prince Michael will arise when the days of the great distress arrive, to set the stage for the Son of Man to arrive.

Daniel 7:9-14 "As I was watched, thrones were set in place and an ancient one took his throne; his clothing was white as snow and the hair of his head like pure wool; his throne was fiery flames, and its wheels were burning fire... A thousand served on him, and ten thousand times ten thousand stood attending him. The court sat in judgement and the books were opened. I watched then because of the noise of the arrogant words that the horn was speaking. And as I watched, the beast was put to death, and its body destroyed and given over to be burned with fire (whether it was a Person, a Faith or an Ideology that was put to death, only the time will tell, as the event would seem to lie in the future). As for the rest of the beasts (there were four in all) their dominion was taken away, but their lives were prolonged for a season and a time.

"As I watched in the night visions, I saw one like a human being (a son of man in some versions) coming with the clouds of heaven. And he came to the Ancient One and was presented before him. To him was given dominion and glory and kingship, that all peoples, nations and languages should serve him. His dominion is an everlasting dominion that shall not pass away, and his kingship is one that shall never be destroyed."

MENTION OF FOUR KINGDOMS

Talking of the four people, the author is reminded about the dream of King Nebuchadnezzar, in which the four kingdoms are discussed. In the present context, we can presume rule of a king, a prophet or religious head, and a democratically elected rule as the three conventional kingdoms. Now we see single party systems, which always must resolve into dictatorial regimes, a fourth kind of kingdom in a way. In the same context, the prophet also provides a hint of a likely universal regime of colourless godliness rising, which will last forever.

Daniel 2:40-45 "And there will be a fourth kingdom, strong as iron; just as iron crushes and smashes everything, it shall crush and shatter all these. As you saw the feet and toes partly of potter's clay and partly or iron, it shall be a divided kingdom, but some of the strength of iron shall be in it, as you saw the iron mixed with clay, so will they mix with each other in marriage, but they will not hold together, just as iron does not mix with clay. And in the days of those kings, the God of heaven will set up a kingdom that will never be destroyed, nor shall this kingdom be left to another people. it shall crush all these kingdoms and bring them to an end, and it shall stand forever, just as you saw that a stone was cut from the mountain not by hands and that it crushed the iron, the bronze, the clay, the sliver, and the gold. The Great God has informed the king what shall be hereafter. The dream is certain and its interpretation trustworthy."

In the end, after the stone that rolled comes to a halt, growing to the size of a mountain, we see a threesome left behind—two separated feet of iron and clay, that remain inter-mixed with a sense of uneasiness, and a universal transparent system purged of all evil, that will last forever without ever passing into the hands of another race (a new sheepfold that may begin as a separate lane, but in time other lanes may merge in it—like one flock and one shepherd.)

The Ram and Goat Vision

In the third year of rule of the son of Nebuchadnezzar, Daniel saw a vision, in which he finds himself at Susa the capital, in the province of Eam, standing by the Ulai Gate. Daniel 8:3-14 "I looked up and saw a ram standing beside the gate. It had two horns. Both horns were long, but one was longer than the other, and the longer one came up second. I saw the ram charging westwards and northwards and southward. All beasts were powerless to withstand it, and no one could rescue from its power; it did as it pleased and became strong.

"As I was watching, a male goat appeared from the west, coming across the face of the world earth without touching the ground. The goat had a horn between its eyes. It came toward the ram with the two horns that I had seen standing beside the gate, and it ran at it with savage force. I saw it approaching the ram. It was enraged against it and struck the ram, breaking its two horns. The ram did not have power to withstand it; it threw the ram down to the ground and trampled upon it, and there was no one who could rescue the ram from its power (Possibly invasion of India by the British at a time when the hold of the Moghul empire had somewhat weakened, is being alluded to). Then the male goat grew exceedingly great, but at the height of its power the great horn was broken, and in its place, there came up four prominent horns toward the four winds of heaven.

"Out of one of them came another horn, a little one, which grew exceedingly great towards south, towards the east and towards the beautiful land. It grew as high as the host of heaven. It threw down to earth some of the host and some of the stars and trampled on them. Even against the prince of the host it acted arrogantly; it took the regular burnt offering away from him and overthrew the place of his sanctuary. Because of wickedness, the host was given over to it together with the regular burnt offering; it cast truth to the ground and kept prospering in what it did.

"Then I heard a holy one speaking and another holy one said to the one who spoke, 'For how long is this vision concerning the regular burnt offering, the transgression that makes desolate, and the giving over of the sanctuary and host to be trampled?' And he answered him, 'For two thousand three hundred evenings and mornings; then the sanctuary will be restored to its rightful state'." From 1st Sept, 1939 to 2nd Sept, 1945, the official dates of World War II add up to 2,194 evenings and mornings; easily a very fair estimate, given that other associated events are also spoken about. The reference to four, and the small one, which should be Germany, is hard to mistake.

What Angel Gabriel Told the Prophet?

Gabriel then touched Daniel. 'Come, I shall tell you what is going to happen when the Retribution is over, about the final times.' Daniel 8:20-26 "As for the ram that you saw with the two horns, these are the kings of Media and of Persia (the idol worshipper and the other; the Moghuls). The male goat is the king of Greece, and the great horn between its eyes is the first king. As for the horn that was broken, in place of which four others arose, four kingdoms shall arise from his nation but not with his power.

"At the end of their rule, when the transgressions have reached their full measure, a king of bold countenance will arise, skilled in intrigue. He shall grow strong in power, shall cause fearful destruction, and shall succeed in what he does. He shall destroy the powerful and the people of the holy ones. By his cunning he shall make deceit prosper under his hand, and in his own mind he shall be great (Possibly, there will be two kings, an iron king and a clay king, trying to create a poor mix and working in mutual collaboration). Without warning he shall destroy many and shall even rise against the prince of princes (the USA). But he shall be broken and not by human hands (possibly a stone untouched by hand will begin to roll and do the king or the pair of kings in! Being deposed by its own people?). The vision of the evenings and the mornings that has been told is true. As for you, seal up the vision, for it refers to many days from now."

BEFORE THE CHRIST

There is a note on the web about the Book of Daniel by Ed Knorr—based largely on work by Dr Rob Lindsted and Dr Chuck Missler, which provides very useful details, and more particularly, about Chapter 11 in the book. This chapter substantially discusses the pre-Christ scenario in its first 35 verses. And these were prophesied much in advance too.

Daniel 11:2-4 "Now I will announce the truth to you. Three more kings shall rise in Persia. The fourth shall be far richer than all of them, and when he has become strong through his riches, he shall stir up all against the kingdoms of Greece. Then a warrior king shall arise who shall rule with great dominion and take action as he pleases. And while still rising in power, his kingdom shall be broken and divided toward the four winds of heaven, but not to his posterity nor according to the dominion with which he ruled, for his kingdom shall be uprooted and go to others besides these."

The four kings, according to Ed Knorr, were likely: Cambyses, Artaxerxes, Darius, and Xerxes. Of them, the last was so rich that it encouraged Alexander the Great, of Greece to conquer them. Alexander, however, died in his thirties without a qualified heir to succeed him. His son Hercules died before he did and son Alexander, who didn't want to rule, was also killed. His kingdom was divided into four parts. Verses 5-21 of this chapter give the story of the four generals who got possession of Alexander's kingdom. Of these Ptolemy got Egypt (including Cyrene, Arabia, and Petraea), and Seleucus got Syria and lands to the East all the way to India. The King of South mentioned in the text always refers to Egypt, and the King of the North always refers to Syria.

After the death of his mother Cleopatra, Ptolemy IV, Philopater, received bad advice about Antiochus Epiphanes, the clever and manipulative younger brother of his late mother, who had gained control over the kingdom of Syria. Antiochus defeated him, and took him under his protection. In a second campaign against Egypt, Antiochus failed to take Alexandria. The Roman ships of Chittim came against him. Antiochus was humiliated, notes Ed Knorr. The Jewish people had heard that he had been defeated and were celebrating even as Epiphanes returns back through Israel. He was angry with the Jews, and took out his frustrations on them. One of the three references to installing of the *appalling abomination* by Daniel relates to this event.

Daniel 11:30-32 "For the ships of Kittim shall come againt him, and he shall lose heart and withdraw. He shall be enraged and take action against the holy covenant. He shall turn back and come to an understanding with those who forsake the holy covenant. Forces sent by him shall occupy and profane the temple and fortress. They shall abolish the regular burnt offering and set up the desolating sacrilege. He shall flatter with smooth words those who violate the covenant, but the people who are loyal to their God will stand firm and take action."

Referring to the above verses 31 and 32, the note reads, "History records that Antiochus Epiphanes brought a pig into the temple, slaughtered it on the altar (which he dedicated to the pagan god Zeus

Olympus), and caused the daily sacrifices to God to cease. The Israelites refused to enter the temple after this. This series of events resulted in an 'abomination of desolation' in 168 B.C. This is a type of future Antichrist, who will also set up an abomination of desolation, referred to by both the prophet Daniel and our Lord Jesus Christ. Note that all this was told 300-400 years in advance!"

The Jewish Feast of Hanukkah celebrates, inter-alia, the rebellion of the armies of Judas Maccabeus against the Syrian army, whereby the Maccabean family captured the Temple Mount and cleansed the sanctuary in 165 B.C. However, the words 'appalling abomination' used by Jesus have been mentioned by him with reference to a future event. "While every detail up to this point in Daniel can be confirmed through history," says Rob Lindsted, "verses 36-45 in Daniel 11 go beyond just Antiochus Epiphanes. In particular there is a high likelihood of future fulfilment under Antichrist."

Verse 36 describes the Antichrist, "The king will do as he pleases, growing more and more arrogant, considering himself greater than all the gods; he will utter incredible blasphemies against the God of gods, and he will thrive until the wrath reaches bursting point; for what has been decreed will certainly be fulfilled."

Verses 40-45: "At the time of the end, the king of the south shall attack him. But the king of the north shall rush upon him like a whirlwind, with chariots and horsemen and many ships. He shall advance against countries and pass through like a flood. He shall come into the beautiful land, and tens of thousands shall fall victim, but Edom and Moab and the main part of the Ammonites shall escape from his power. He shall stretch out his hand against the countries, and the land of Egypt shall not escape. He shall gain control of the treasures of gold and of silver and all the riches of Egypt, and the Libyans and the Cushites shall follow in his train. But reports from the East and the North shall alarm him, and he shall go out with great fury to bring ruin and complete destruction to many. He will pitch the palatial tents between the sea and the beautiful holy mountain. Yet he shall come to his end, with no one to help him."

Ed Knorr writes with references to verses 40+, "He will prosper for a time. The King of South and the King of the North will push against him. Many countries will be overthrown, but for some reason, not Jordan (i.e., Edom, Moab, and the children of Ammon). This may give the Jews a place to flee to, in the latter days. Tidings out of the East, from across Euphrates: Some authors think this may involve China but that need not be the case. Tidings out of the North: possibly Russia."

The Crucifixion

As the Chapter 9 in the Book begins, written about 539-538 B.C. according to Ed Knorr, we find Daniel studying the scriptures, counting over the number of years—as revealed by Yahweh to the prophet Jeremiah—that were to pass before the desolation of Jerusalem would come to an end, namely seventy years. And the count of seventy, which apparently started in 606 B.C., was coming to an end.

Daniel finds himself full of anguish and remorse for the days spent by the Jewish people in ways full of sin, wickedness, and non-observance of the covenants, and by way of a prayer on their behalf for forgiveness, confession and supplication, he embarks on a three-week propitiation of the divine powers.

Daniel 9:20-23 "While I was speaking and was praying and confessing my sins and the sin of my people Israel, and presenting my supplication before the Lord my God on behalf of the holy mountain of my God, while I was speaking in prayer, the man Gabriel, whom I had seen before in a vision, came to me in swift flight at the time of the evening sacrifice. He came, and said to me, 'Daniel, I have now come out to give you wisdom and understanding. At the beginning of your supplications a word went out, and I have come to declare it, for you are greatly beloved. So, consider the word and understand the vision'."

A word was uttered by the holy ones, or a prophecy was made, when Daniel had commenced his pleading and propitiation, and on its completion, Gabriel had come to speak to him, not in a vision but in the evening when he was fully awake, and to convey that word to him.

Daniel 9:24-26 "Seventy weeks are decreed for your people and your holy city: to finish the transgression, to put an end to sin, and to atone for iniquity, to bring in everlasting righteousness, to seal both vision and prophet, and to anoint a most holy place. Know, therefore, and understand:

From the time there went out this message: From the time that the word went out to restore and rebuild Jerusalem', until the time of an Anointed Prince, there shall be seven weeks, and for sixty-two weeks it shall be built again with streets and moat, but in a troubled time. After the sixty-two weeks an anointed one shall but cut off and shall have nothing, the troops of the prince who is to come shall destroy the city and the sanctuary. Its end shall come with a flood, and to the end there will be war. Desolations are decreed."

Each week constitutes a 7-year period of time, according to an extant Jewish system of calculation. We can see that there is a 'word', about an ultimate event, 'the anointing of a holy place or the *holy of holies*. In the elaboration part of this word or the statement, we can see that an Anointed Prince, an Anointed One, is also mentioned to distinguish him from the anointing of the *holy of holies*.

From the time the message went out to rebuild Jerusalem: Ed Knorr tries to explain, King Artaxerexes issued the decree to rebuild the walls and the streets of Jerusalem. According to Sir Robert Andersen's calculations, and by reverse engineering our Gregorian calendar, this decree was issued on March 14, 445 B.C. Of the words, 'seven weeks and sixty-two weeks', a period of seven weeks or 49 years possibly refers to the complete restoration of Jerusalem, and the next 62 weeks may refer to the time from that point on until the coming of the Messiah.

And 'after the sixty-two weeks an Anointed One put to death' or cut off and executed, in Daniel 9:26, points to the event of crucifixion, according to the Biblical experts. The prophecy was already available in the Book of Daniel, and it was easy for the scribes and priests to calculate the time of arrival of the Messiah, but they were distracted by sin, and they lost the opportunity that was being provided to them by the hidden powers in the astral realm, the kingdom of Heaven. They could have changed the history of their people at that time in the whirling movement, the world.

Ed Knorr is reminded here, of Luke 19:41-44: "As he came near and saw the city, he wept over it, saying, 'If you, even you, had only recognized on this day the things that make for peace! But now they are hidden from your eyes (Your destiny)! Indeed, the days will come upon you when your enemies will set up ramparts around you and surround you and hem you in every side. They will crush you to the ground, you and your children within you, and they will not leave one stone upon another, because you did not recognize the time of your visitation from God." The Romans destroyed Jerusalem and the Second Temple in 70 AD. After they had burnt the temple down, they left not 'one stone on another' because they pried apart the rocks to get at the melted gold, deposited between the rocks.

THE SECOND COMING

Daniel 9:27 "He shall make a strong covenant with many for one week, and for half of the week he shall make sacrifice and offering cease, and in their place shall be a desolating sacrilege until the decreed end is poured out upon the desolator."

Now the prophet is discussing the 70th week that lies in further distant future. Ed Knorr has rewritten D 9:27 to read: "He (Antichrist) will confirm a covenant with many for one week or seven years. In the middle of the seven-year week, he will put an end to sacrifice and offering. And on a wing of the Temple, he will set up a flag or an 'abomination' that causes desolation, until the end that is decreed is poured out on him."

There is no Temple at present. It was destroyed by the Romans in 70 A.D. Probably a new temple may be built in the days to come. The abomination, according to Biblical experts takes place in the middle of the 70th week, when it is commenced. However, now we live in an age of technology, which is also easily accessible to the forces that are disruptive and inimical to human society. It is an age of 'tool kits' that enables even a small resourceful club of like-minded people to execute short term take overs and installation of flags that may cause dismay to the sane and the responsible who have a stake, and who want to partner in building of cities, countries and nations, and not in destroying them. In most recent times, we have seen White House in the US being virtually taken over and a flag of disruption hoisted at the Red Fort in the capital of India.

Daniel 12:5-13 "Then I, Daniel, looked and two others appeared, one standing on this bank of the stream and one on the other. One of them said to the man clothed in linen, who was upstream, 'How long shall it be until the end of these wonders? The man clothed in linen, who was upstream raised his right hand and his left toward heaven. And I heard him swear by the one who lives forever that it would be for a time, two times, and half a time, and when the shattering of the power of the holy people comes to an end all these things will be accomplished.'

"'I heard but could not understand, so I said, 'My lord, what shall be outcome of these things?' He said, 'Go, your way Daniel, for the words are to remain secret and sealed until the time of the End. *Many shall be purified, cleansed, and refined*, but the wicked shall continue to act wickedly. None of the wicked shall understand. From the time that the regular burnt offering is taken away and the desolating sacrilege is set up, there shall be one thousand two hundred ninety days. Happy are those who persevere and attain the thousand three hundred thirty-five days. But you, go your way and rest; you shall rise for your reward at the end of the days.'" The words "*purified, cleansed, and refined*" used by the person standing further up the stream, who said the word would remain secret and sealed until the end, seem to be especially significant. In a way, these show the way the humanity needs to adopt, if it is to survive the onslaught of the blind and arrogant faithful or of the treacherous and exceedingly dangerous ideologies based on atheist way of thinking and acting. The situation may be worsening with every passing day and the point of no return may not be that far away now.

It is for the Jewish and Christine scholars, like Ed Knorr and Rob Lindsted to try to decipher what 'a time and two times, and half a time', could possibly mean. The other pointer, nevertheless, is easy to fathom. The crushing or shattering of the holy people's power coming to an end or being over, could only mean that when the power is restored for the most ancient and surviving culture in the world, the Hindus in India and a human mind is returned to them. Only then, and in dignity, they could have been inspired to reveal the spirit of truth to the world, for the nations to consider and to ponder over. It may be a coincidence that three millenniums and a half, or 3,500 years have elapsed in the meantime, since led by Moses and Aaron, the Jewish people had walked out of Egypt. Also, it is some 3,500 years as well since initially 'some people' and later many others began to hate and despise the idol worshipping people in several parts of the world. The author does not mean to blame any person or persons, but people do need to know what ails, so that a cure can be found.

From the moment that the perpetual sacrifice is abolished *and the appalling abomination set up*: the 3rd World War may start after thousand two hundred and ninety days, and it will last for 45 days, if the prophecy is viewed in this context, and if a war must turn into a world-war, nuclear bombs are sure to be used on both sides now. A very disquieting thought, no doubt! But the people on the right side of the divide can still pray that the homo-sapiens should be able to survive and that it may not be the end.

This postlude ends here. The author bows to the Rishis, the Gurus and to the Great Master, and the god whom the women love. Let the 'Father' bless us all; and in, particular, let him bless the Son of Man!

The rishis inform, *Poornam adah, poornm idam, poornat poornam udachyate; Poorna-asya, poornam-aday, poornam eva avshishyate*; That (Supreme Soul) is complete; This (Human Soul) is complete too; When 'Complete' comes out of 'Complete', What remains, is still 'Complete'.

Let the 'Son of 'Man' move, from what is false towards the Truth, from the darkness of ignorance towards the Light of wisdom, and from the death towards eternal life.

Appendix 1

The Collapse of Wave Unction

In modern physics, the double-slit experiment is a demonstration that light and matter can display characteristics of both classically defined waves and particles; moreover, it displays the fundamentally probabilistic nature of the quantum mechanical phenomena. The experiment was first performed with light by Thomas Yung in 1801. Thomas Young's experiment with light was part of classical physics well before the rise of quantum mechanics or the concept of wave-particle duality.

In 1927, Clinton Davisson and Lester Germer at Bell Laboratories made use of the double-slit experiment to demonstrate that a similar behavior, as the photons of light, was being displayed by the electrons also. The experiment was later extended to atoms and molecules also with the same result.

THE 2-SLIT EXPERIMENT

To understand the significance of this experiment, let us consider a flat partition with a narrow slit around its middle. On one side of the partition, at some distance, we install a little gun that can shoot little balls or marbles, while on the other side of this partition we place a recording screen with good sensitivity. As we begin to shoot little marbles at the partition, some of them go through the slit and form a pattern on the screen behind.

Now suppose we install a partition with two slits on it separated by a small distance, in place of the one with a single slit, and resume our shooting of the little marbles at it. What we expect to see is that some of the marbles will pass through one slit and some through the other, so that we shall now see two bands on the screen behind the partition, where it would be hit by the marbles passing through one slit or the other. The results are, of course, as we expect to find—we see two parallel bands on the screen.

Let us now replace the marble shooting gun with a source of light of a particular colour. Most of the coloured light is likely to hit the partition. However, a small amount of it will go through the slits. Any point on the screen will receive waves from both the slits. However, the distance the light has to travel from the source to the screen via the two slits will be different. This will mean that the waves from the two slits will not be in phase with each other when they arrive at the screen. In some places, the waves will cancel each other out, and in others, they will reinforce each other. The result will be a characteristic pattern of light and dark fringes or parallel bands and it will prove the wave property of light. Please see the diagram.

In the second part of the experiment, which was carried out, a source that could fire electrons with a definite speed was used in place of the light source. When the electrons were fired through a single slit partition, there was a uniform distribution of electrons across the screen. However, when the 2-slit partition was used, similar kinds of fringes appeared on the screen, which would be seen in the case of light waves.

One would have thought that opening another slit would just increase the number of electrons hitting each point of the screen, but an interference pattern was seen instead and the number of hits registered on the screen decreased in some places. It was thought that some of the electrons went through one slit and some through the other and acting like waves, the two sets interfered with each other.

The experimenting physicists now decided to fire the electrons one at a time with a distinct time interval between two successive electrons. At least now, one could reasonably expect that each of the individual electrons should pass through one slit or the other as if the slit it passed through were the only one there—giving a uniform distribution on the screen.

In reality, however, even when the electrons are sent one at a time, the fringes still appear, irrespective of the fact that the experiment has been repeated hundreds of times by different teams. Each electron, therefore, appears to be passing through both slits at the same time and interfere with itself to give rise to the fringed interference pattern on the recording screen!

Greatly intrigued, the physicists decided to go one step further. They decided to create a little peephole to find out what had been going on. The physicists now attached a little sensing device to one of the slits to monitor the movement of the individual electrons. This would have enabled them to find out whether a particular electron passed through the wired slit or the other one. The outcome, however, was an anti-climax. The wave function just disappeared under such scrutiny. Please see the diagram below.

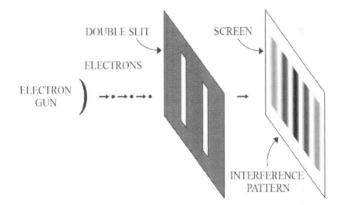

Normal Experiment - Interference pattern is clearly visible

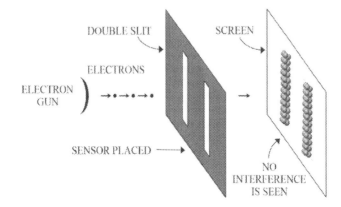

After a sensor was installed - Wave function has collapsed

The electrons began to behave like little marbles, which would go through one slit or the other; the interference pattern was no more to be seen. No matter how small was the measuring device used; it just failed to deliver. The very act of observing the movement of the electron collapsed the wave function! How does this happen? Do the electrons possess some kind of awareness of their own! Do they seem to convey a message to the physicists: "Sorry, here is the line which you must not cross?"

APPENDIX 2

THE AQUARIAN GOSPEL

Before creation was, the Christ walked with the Father God and Mother God in Akasha. The Christ is son the only son begotten by Almighty God, the God of Force and God omniscient, God of thought; and Christ is God, the God of Love.

Without the Christ there was no light. Through Christ all life was manifest; and so, through him all things were done and naught was done in forming worlds or peopling worlds with the Christ (the Son).

Christ is the Logos of Infinities and through the word alone are Thought and Force made manifest. The Son is called the Christ, because the Son, the Love, the universal Love, was set apart, ordained to be creator, Lord, preserver and redeemer of all things of everything that is or evermore will be.

Through Christ, the protoplast, the earth, the plant, the beast, the man, the angel and the cherubim took up their stations on their planes of life. From the great heart of Love unnumbered spirits were sent forth to demonstrate the height, the depth, the width, the boundlessness of Love.

Into the soil of every plane these seeds which were the thoughts of God were cast—the seeds of protoplast, of earth, of plant, of beast, of man, of angel and of cherubim, and they who sowed the seeds, through Christ, ordained that they should grow, and should return at last, by effort of unnumbered years, to the great granary of thought, and each be a perfection of its kind.

And in the boundless blessedness of Love the man was made the Lord of protoplast, of earth, of plant of beast, and Christ proclaimed: Man shall have full dominion over everything that is upon these planes of life; and it was so.

The Christ made manifest Love's power to save; but men forgot so soon, and so Christ must manifest again and then again. And ever since man took his place in form of flesh, the Christ has been manifest, in flesh, at first of every age.

Orthodox Christian ecclesiastics tell us that Jesus of Nazareth and the Christ were one; that the true name of this remarkable person was Jesus Christ. They tell us that this man of Galilee was the very eternal god clothed in flesh of man that men might see his glory. Of course, this doctrine is wholly at variance with the teachings of Jesus himself and of his apostles.

THE SEVEN SAGES OR RISHIS

Chapter 56: In every age since time began have seven sages lived. At first of every age these sages meet to note the course of nations, peoples, tribes and tongues; To note how far toward justice, love and righteousness the race has gone; To formulate the code of laws, religious postulates and plans of rule best suited to the coming age. An age had passed, and lo, another age (Piscean age) had come; the sages must convene. Now, Alexandria was the centre of the world's best thought, and here in Philo's home the sages met. From China came Meng-ste; from India Vidyapati came; from Persia Kaspar came; and from Assyria Ashbina came; from Greece Apollo; Matheno was the Egyptian sage, and Philo was the chief of Hebrew thought.

Chapter 58: The sages opened up the Book of Life and read:

They read the story of life of man; of all his struggles, losses, gains, and in the light of past events and needs, they saw what would be best for him in coming years.

They knew the kind of laws and precepts suited best to his estate; they saw the highest god-ideal that the race could comprehend. Upon the seven postulates these sages were to formulate, the great philosophy of life and worship of the coming age must rest.

Now Meng-ste was the oldest sage; he took the chair of chief and said, "Man is not far enough advanced to live by faith; he cannot comprehend the things his eyes see not. He yet is child, and during all the coming age he must be taught by pictures, symbols, rites and forms. His God must be a human God; he cannot see a god by faith. And then he cannot rule himself; the king must rule; the man must serve. In that blest age the human race will see without the aid of carnal eyes; will hear the soundless sound; will know the Spirit-God. The age we enter is the Preparation age, and all the schools and governments and worship rites must be designed in simple way that men may comprehend. And man cannot originate; he builds by patterns that he sees; so, in this council we must carve out pattern for the coming age. And we must formulate the gnosis of the Empire of the soul, which rests on seven postulates. Each sage in turn shall form a postulate; and these shall be the basis of the creed of men until the perfect age shall come.

Then Meng-ste wrote the first: All things are thought; all life is thought activity. The multitude of beings are but phases of the one great thought made manifest. Lo God is Thought, and Thought is God (The word was with God, the word was God).

Then Vidyapati wrote the second postulate: Eternal Thought is one; in essence it is two—intelligence and force; and when they breathe (causing a vibration to arise), a child is born; this child is Love. And thus, the Triune God stands forth, whom men call Father-Mother-Child. This Triune God is one; but like the one of light, in essence he is seven. And when the Triune God breathes forth, lo seven Spirits stand before his face, these are creative attributes (*Purush, Prakriti and the Five Tattvas or the Elements*—see Jesus Christ and the Spirit of Truth). Men call them lesser gods and, in their image, they made man.

And Kaspar wrote the third: Man was a thought of God, formed in the image of the Septonate, clothed in the substance of soul. And his desires were strong; he sought to manifest on every plane of life, and for himself he made a body of the ethers of the earthly forms, and so descended to the plane of earth. In the descent he lost his birth-right (The *Pati Pramata* or the owner proposer who governed the Nature turned into a *Pashu Pramata*, a beast proposer bound with a rope and governed by Nature—*Jesus Christ and the Spirit of Truth*); lost his harmony with God, and made discordant all the notes of life. Inharmony and the evil are the same; so evil is the handiwork of man.

Asbina wrote the fourth: Seeds do not germinate in light; they do not grow until they find the soil, and hide themselves away from light. Man was evolved as a seed of everlasting life; but in the ethers of the Triune God, the light was far too great for seeds to grow; and so, man sought the soil of carnal life, and in the darksome-ness of earth he found a place where he could germinate and grow. The seed has taken root and grown full well. The tree of human life is rising from the soil of earthy things, and, under natural law, is reaching up to perfect form. There are no supernatural acts of God to lift a man from carnal life to spirit blessedness; he grows as grows the plant and in due time is perfected. The quality of soul that makes it possible for man to rise to spirit life, is purity.

Apollo wrote the fifth: The soul is drawn to perfect light by four white steeds and these are Will, and Faith, and Helpfulness and Love. That which one wills to do, he has the power to do. A knowledge of that power is faith; and when faith moves, the soul begins its flight. A selfish faith leads not to light. There is no lonely pilgrim on the way to light. Men only gain the heights by helping others gain the heights. The steed that leads the way to spirit life is Love; is pure unselfish Love.

Metheno wrote the sixth: The universal Love of which Apollo speaks is child of Wisdom and of Will divine, and God has sent it forth to earth in flesh that man may know. The universal Love of which the sages speak, is Christ. The greatest mystery of all times lies in the way that Christ lives in the heart. Christ cannot live in clammy dens of carnal things. The seven battles must be fought, the seven victories won before the carnal things, like fear and self (ego), emotions and desire, are put away. When this is done the Christ will take possession of the soul; the work is done, and man and God are one.

And Philo wrote the seventh: A perfect man! To bring before the Triune God, a being such as this, was nature made. This consummation is the highest revelation of the mystery of life. When all the essences of carnal things have been transmuted into soul, and all the essences of soul have been returned to Holy Breath, and man is made a perfect God, the drama of creation will conclude. And this is all. And all the sages said, 'Amen'. A selfish faith leads not to light.

The author agrees with everything that has been reproduced here from the Aquarian Gospel of Levi. He would like to draw specific attention to something that Apollo wrote on his turn *"A selfish faith leads not to light"*. It was prudent of him to provide this clear hint, which the humans can use in deciding if a particular faith was on the right path or not, whether it led to light or to darkness and whether it was worth accepting as it was. The need of the new Aquarian Age, is rejection of what is incorrect or a major reform.

About the Author

Vigyan Mitra developed a deep interest in spiritual subjects early in life. His curiosity for understanding life and his personal mystical encounters inspired him to research the field extensively. He retired from the role of CEO fifteen years ago and now prefers to live in prayer and seclusion. Also the author of *Jesus Christ and the Spirit of Truth* and *Matter, Life & Spirit Demystified*, he currently lives in Bhimtal, Nainital, Uttarakhand, India.

Printed in the United States
by Baker & Taylor Publisher Services